SPEAKING EFFECTIVELY IN PUBLIC SETTINGS

A Modern Rhetoric with a Traditional Base

Ray Nadeau
Professor Emeritus, Purdue University

Carol Jablonski
Associate Professor, University of South Florida

Greg Gardner
Professor, Rollins College

UNIVERSITY PRESS OF AMERICA

Lanham • New York • London

University Press of America®, Inc.
4720 Boston Way
Lanham, Maryland 20706

3 Henrietta Street
London WC2E 8LU England

Printed in the United States of America
British Cataloging in Publication Information Available

Library of Congress Cataloging-in-Publication Data

Nadeau, Ray E.
Speaking effectively in public settings : a modern rhetoric with a traditional base / Ray Nadeau, Carol Jablonski, Greg Gardner.
p. cm.
Includes bibliographical references and index.
1. Public speaking. I. Jablonski, Carol. II. Gardner, Greg. III. Title.
PN4121.N243 1993 808.5'1—dc20 93–17032 CIP

ISBN 0–8191–9122–1 (pbk. : alk. paper)

™ The paper used in this publication meets the minimum requirements of American National Standard for Information Sciences—Permanence of Paper for Printed Library Materials, ANSI Z39.48–1984.

Acknowledgments

Like all writers of textbooks on speech communication and especially on speaking in public, we are indebted to those who have gone before us, from Aristotle to Zimbardo and other social scientists of modern times. We are indebted, too, to the many colleagues and critics whose advice and counsel are reflected in this book, and to the students whose continuing comments and suggestions served to keep us "down to earth."

For computer-generated diagrams and graphs, we are grateful to George Stovall, Director of Institutional Studies at the University of Virginia. For similar services plus many other "assists," we owe our thanks to Ty Jones, Tampa area technical writer and consultant. And to John Muchmore, Professor of Speech Communication at Harper College in Illinois, we're thankful for his assent to our use of select materials adapted from a Nadeau/Muchmore text of 1979.

Some instructors may have on their shelves the second edition of an earlier college textbook written by Ray Nadeau. Although a few segments from it have also been adapted for inclusion in the present effort, the new book is very different from either the one mentioned here or in the paragraph above.

Finally, we agree with the German philosopher who said, "All thoughts have been thought." We claim no new thoughts. We do claim some new choices in the selection of ideas to be emphasized and in the interpretations of those ideas. We do believe this text to be markedly different from other books in the field, and we trust that students will find it a useful contribution to their understanding of speech communication and its vital importance in their lives.

R.N.
C.J.
G.G.

Contents

Part III. Interacting with Audiences

To the Instructor

This is a textbook on public speaking. It is *modern*--it reflects the many refinements contributed by the theorists, psychologists, and social scientists of our time. It is *traditional*--it encompasses those early and basic principles of public communication which, knowingly or unknowingly, we continue to follow today. It is *practical*--it is geared to enable the student to assume with confidence the central speaking role that is now so often required in the workplace, in business and professional settings, and in the public forum.

The book is for students taking a basic-level college course on how to interact with listeners in speaking situations ranging from efforts to induce acceptance of information to attempts to bring about changes in attitude. Although the speaking-listening "events" are subject to the usual course and classroom constraints, the student does have the opportunity to prepare and present messages which are of real interest to other students and, at the same time, typical of today's communication world. At the very least, the student becomes more capable and comfortable in meeting every "rhetorical need" from the choosing of a subject and collecting materials to contending with the tensions everyone experiences on "interaction day."

Why Another Book on Speaking in Public?

In this field, only one or two texts make more than passing mention of the contributions of Aristotle and other early writers, and these texts seem to be used mainly in advanced courses at the upper end of the curriculum. In other words, there seems not to be available a basic course textbook which (1) acknowledges and takes advantage of the extent to which early writers "have written" the textbooks of our own day and which (2), at the same time, recognizes the studies and contributions of the moderns. We have undertaken to fulfill that need.

The Instructional Plan

Part I consists of five chapters on concepts and approaches fundamental to all speech communication. In Chapter 1, we describe the complex process of communication as we have come to know it through the social sciences. In Chapter 2, we introduce the student to rhetoric as communication in the classical sense of purposeful speaking in public. The next three chapters treat generally of the important roles played in all communication by reasoning, by language, and by listening.

Part II is designed to help students acquire the basic skills needed to prepare for and take part in whatever presentations are required of them, now and in the future.

Part III enables students to bring what they have learned in theory and skills to the reality of practical speaking-in public situations.

Special Features

This section highlights certain features which we consider essential but which either do not appear in other texts or are not given due emphasis in them.

The holistic approach

In this text, the student comes to understand that no component of the traditional appeals to the listener--ethical, logical, or emotional--exists in isolation and that, in varying degrees, *all appeals play a part in every presentational effort*, including the informational. In other words, the almost universal distinction between "the informative speech" and "the persuasive speech" is meaningless. We do not subscribe to it.

An emphasis on *ethos*

Chapter 10 includes a well deserved focus on the speaker's reputation or *ethos* as perceived by the listeners. The ancients realized that a speaker's public image is vital to the winning of listener assent or action. The moderns agree, and the writers of current texts do encourage the student to be ethical. But there is more to being ethical than meeting standards of "ethics." As early writers pointed out, audiences also expect the speaker to demonstrate good sense along with a real concern for the welfare of the listeners.

And today, of course, we add a good personal "presence" to the traditional list. In the eyes of listeners, then, a speaker's "ethical appeal" or public image depends on the totality of a speaker's perceived (1) expertise, (2) character, (3) concern for others, and (4) personal presence.

Respect for cultural differences

We live in a troubled world. As more and more refugees and immigrants have come and are coming into the country from other lands, the newcomers often bring with them cultures very different from ours. Why do some of them wear such strange garments? Why do they eat those strange foods? Why do they belong to those strange religions? Why do they follow such strange customs? To experience "culture shock," our citizens no longer need to cross a border or travel abroad. All they need do is visit a section of the city or countryside in which "those people" are congregated.

So it is that, in Chapter 7, we include respect for cultural differences as an increasingly important aspect of audience analysis as well as an attitude we should actively promote. Above all, in no public speaking situation should we accept a speaker's making disparaging remarks about the culture (customs, values, attitudes, beliefs) that guides the behavior of another group. Our ways of living, derived over the years from our parents, our associates, and other factors, may be ideal for us, but there are other ways to live productively. We see regard for the cultures of others as essential to audience analysis, to rhetoric, and to learning to live cooperatively in a diversified society.

Sensitivity to sexism

Among the perils of language deserving special mention (Chapter 4) is *sexism*, a word describing the intentional or unintentional use of words to discriminate against those of the opposite sex. An extreme form of it is *sexual harassment*, the effort to solicit favors, sexual or otherwise, through suggestive, embarrassing, or intimidating remarks. Sexism in any form is not a new phenomenon; it is mentioned here to emphasize the importance of a speaker's avoiding it.

In the Tradition of Free Choice

Rhetoric," said Everett Lee Hunt in a 1955 essay, "is the study of people persuading people to make free choices. It may well be regarded as the oldest and most central of humane studies." In the Athens of ancient Greece, citizens took seriously their individual responsibility to become informed and to speak out on public issues. Although freedom of speech has ebbed and flowed over the centuries, that human right and responsibility is now more important than ever, especially in the face of a rapidly changing world. We need look for no better example in modern life that the wide-ranging Congressional and public debates which preceded the Persian Gulf war. We hope that this book will play a part in helping develop individuals who are trained to think for themselves and who are, at the same time, willing to take an active and responsible role in working with others to solve problems or meet the issues of the day.

...and Broader Insights

Why should students be interested in people like Aristotle and his views on speaking in public? Because, in our experience, students find those views to be remarkably like those of the moderns. More remarkably, they find that *studying the old and the new together* offers fresh and important insights into the ways we communicate. They come to realize that we are linked across time by basic principles and practices. They quickly see how we can all benefit from centuries of observation and thinking as we deal with our own speaker-listener situations. And they better understand what Crane Brinton is saying in speaking of Western thought and culture: "We cannot know ourselves well if we know the Greeks not at all."

Finally, as most of us agree, students attending a college or university should be acquiring a general education, encountering new ideas, learning to think for themselves, coming into their own as individuals, assuming full accountability for their own actions, counting some form of community service among their responsibilities, and qualifying themselves for useful careers. A primary road to those goals is efficient and effective communication. To help students travel that road, the writers of this text have drawn upon the best communication theory and practice of the pre-modern and modern worlds.

A Note on Instructional Aids

In the text itself

Many of the instructional aids you would expect to find in an instructor's manual are included in this textbook. For the convenience of both students and instructor, Appendix B contains four day-by-day course outlines. Two are designed to give the student the opportunity for at least two major speaker-with-listeners interactions, and one offers the student participation in three major speaking events. One of the four also includes a unit on speaking-listening in small group discussion, a subject discussed in Appendix A. With or without changes, it is probable that one of the four outlines will meet the instructional needs of a given class--with the added advantage that the student always has that outline at hand as a daily guide and reference.

As for other aid materials, every chapter in the book closes with a series of discussion questions and a number of speaking-and-listening application projects. In addition, ten of the chapters end with a third group of varied student activities. Finally, the Index to the text includes page references to key terms with which the student should become familiar.

In a separate packet

Direct from any one of the authors of this text, a helpful packet of other instructional aids is available at minimal cost plus postage. Planned specifically for distribution or use at the discretion of the instructor, these aids (on thirty-five ready-to-duplicate 8-1/2 x 11 sheets) fall into three categories: (1) detailed assignment sheets and two other handouts, (2) chapter-by-chapter test or exam questions of all types, and (3) a variety of evaluation forms. (For authors' addresses, please see the *Speech Communication Association Directory*.)

To the Student

How an educated person is defined depends on who is doing the defining. Nevertheless, many agree that a person is educated if he or she has developed the ability to study independently, to unify what is learned, to detect problems and collect information about them, to draw reasonable conclusions, and to arrive at sensible choices and sound decisions.

Unfortunately, education alone is seldom the key to success. What you know, think, feel, or believe may be of great value to you personally...but it can't be of value to anyone else unless you're able to communicate effectively. And in our society, a prime way to communicate with others is through appearing before an audience, large or small, to share ideas with it.

Matched with the ability to communicate must be the ability to listen. We do considerably more listening than speaking in our lifetime, so it is clearly important that we know how to listen well, both in our own interest and in that of those trying to communicate with us. Communication between speakers and listeners is a cooperative enterprise; nothing much happens unless those involved work together toward mutual goals.

Examples of the contributions which the ability to communicate can make to your future are all around you. Employees, supervisors, managers, officers, and individuals at all levels of business and industry are often called upon to speak or to be a part of a listening group inside or outside their own organizations. Coaches, doctors, educators, lawyers, accountants, athletes, promoters, professionals, and non-professionals in all fields engage in communication with their associates and with the public.

Moreover, it is a practical "rule of life" that, no matter how talented people may be, they seldom succeed or are promoted unless they have become good speakers and listeners. And in the "major" or field you have chosen, you can be sure (1) that you're going to have to address meetings of one kind or another and (2) that you'll also be expected to be a sensitive listener to the views of others.

In spite of the fact that each of us comes on the scene with some natural talent for speaking and listening, the road to one's full potential in those activities is still formal training. This text and the course you are taking are designed to develop your talents for public speaking and listening, to provide some useful guidelines in those areas, and to offer you opportunities for practical experience.

So whatever your talents and whatever your goals, now is the time to do everything you can to become, as Quintilian (Roman rhetorician of the 1st century A.D.) would put it today, "an ethical person who is skilled in both speaking and listening." That road to success worked in his time and it works in ours.

PART I

Basic Concepts and Approaches

Photo courtesy Rollins College, Winter Park, Florida.

1

COMMUNICATION AS PROCESS

You cannot say nothing. Erving Goffman

When you finish this chapter, you should be aware that...

1. Communication is a continuous, ongoing, two-way process.

2. Meanings given to messages are affected by the perceptions of those receiving those messages.

3. Perception is the process of making sense out of experience. Through it, we attend to, select, and remember elements of the world around us.

4. The sum total of one's selected perceptions constitutes one's "perceptual field."

5. How a listener "translates" word-messages is affected by the verbal, paraverbal, and nonverbal contexts in which words appear.

6. Speakers should be aware of and adapt to feedback.

"So she said.... Then I said...." It is natural to think of communication in terms of a speaker's putting ideas into words and, then, of the listener's reacting--or failing to react--in return. We tend to see the process as depending on words because, after all, those symbols seem to be the idea carriers which a person uses in order to communicate with one or more listeners. In turn, listeners are seen to respond to the words we use in ways that are favorable, neutral, or unfavorable.

Communication Goes Beyond Words

But the communication process goes far beyond words; it is, as the word *process* suggests, a continuing, ongoing, and developing activity on which we depend in order to interact with other individuals or with groups. However, the beginnings and endings of those interactions are difficult, if not impossible, to detect. A person who has given up smoking may fend off the offer of a cigarette with "No, thanks." When did the communication begin and when did it end? Nobody knows. Psychologists agree that individuals adjust to each other's behavior before the words start flowing, while they are flowing, and afterwards as well.

To see an example of varied messages in the process of flowing through the many channels of the communication, watch any two students in conversation. You can draw fairly accurate conclusions about their interpersonal relationship by observing where they are standing or sitting in relation to each other, what changes in facial expressions occur, what tones of voice they use, what kinds of gestures come into play, etc. You also see something of the extent to which messages are modified by "feedback." When one student looks puzzled, does the other do some additional explaining? If one looks up with an expression of boredom, does the other try in some way to recover her or his interest? When one appears to be getting angry, does the other assume a more soothing or moderate tone? Does one party to the conversation seem to be unaware of feedback and of the opportunities it offers for adjusting the message? Without your hearing a single word, you can draw meanings, interpretations, and inferences from pure observation. Add word messages and their modifiers to the mix, and you will agree that one-on-one communication brings you in close face-to-face contact with the many ways in which we communicate, one with another as well as one to several or one to many.

In ordinary conversations, of course, the interaction is primarily social--it consists of "small talk" with a friend, trading comments about a sports event or party, complimenting someone on a success or offering sympathy on a misfortune. There may be elements of purpose in any conversation ("I need to stay on 'the good side' of this person"), but the two doing the communicating are generally talking because one or both find the conversation pleasant and satisfying.

Not only in conversations but in discussions and speaker-audience situations as well, communication is an ongoing series of interactions having no clear-cut beginning and no clear-cut ending. For example, when does a public speaking occasion begin? When the call goes out to a particular speaker because her expertise in a field is well known and in demand? Or does it begin when some of the intended listeners begin reading a speaker's books and articles in anticipation of his coming? With discussion of the coming event among friends, in class, or on a television program? With her introduction to the audience? With his opening remarks? And when does the effort to win a favorable response come to an end? When the audience drifts away after the event? When the speaker finishes speaking and sits down? Does the message have a life of its own through subsequent talks and discussions by other speakers and groups, either in face-to-face situations or on TV? We have to conclude that communication is so complex a process that it is futile to try to find out just exactly when it begins or ends.

The process of communication, then, is not a tennis game in which people hit the ball back and forth. "When we talk about communication," says Birdwhistell, "we are not talking about a situation in which John acts, and Mary reacts to John's action and, in turn, John reacts to Mary's action in some simple, ongoing, one-after-another sequence.... John does not communicate to Mary and Mary does not communicate to John; Mary and John engage in communication."[1] Stated another way, streams of stimuli of all kinds, some of them message related and some of them not, some of them word signals and some of them not, some of them paraverbal and nonverbal (terms explained later in the chapter) and some of them not--all are at one and the same time speeding between speaker and listener. The constant exchange of messages occurs and continues to occur even if Mary and John never begin to talk or if, after doing so, they lapse into silence. As Goffman says, "you cannot say nothing."[2] The individual who seems to be saying nothing is actually sending and receiving messages whenever she or he is in the presence of another human being. Note this short passage in the novel *Billy Bathgate*: "Then he sits and eats my food and drinks my wine and says nothing. Nothing! I remember all right.""Maybe not nothing," Mr. Berman said. "Maybe just the fact of his being there."[3]

Moreover, in spite of what the speaker hopes to achieve, the response from the listener may be quite different. For example, the ideas a speaker offers may be convincing, but whether or not the listener accepts them depends on factors like the listener's attitudes, the listener's feelings, and the listener's trust in the speaker. Thus we have an army of these and other motives and stimuli operating within the listener and affecting the meaning given to the speaker's message.

Perception and Perceptual Fields

To reach the listener, those messages which come from the speaker must penetrate that listener's selective screen. Similarly, any feedback coming from the listener to the speaker must penetrate the speaker's selective screen. Let's examine the part played by perception in setting up those screens.

Perception, as you know, is the process of making sense out of experience, that is, of giving meaning to the objects and ideas we have become aware of through the senses. It is the means by which we pay attention to, filter, and remember elements of the world around us. Throughout your life, you've processed the things you've seen, heard, felt, smelled, and tasted with the idea of using those experiences to your advantage. You learned early in life that touching a hot iron is painful; as a result of that sensory experience, you perceived that it's a good idea to avoid touching hot irons.

Selective perception

However, there are so many sensory stimuli bombarding us all the time that we find it impossible to pay attention to all of them; as a result, we choose to notice certain things and ignore others. Since no one person in this world has the same experiences as any other person, each of us is going to have his or her own set of perceptions. Each of us looks at things through his or her perceptual "screen" and accepts--or fails to accept--incoming impressions into the total network of past experience, one's perceptual field. Stated another way, your perceptual field is the sum total of the ideas, assumptions, experiences, beliefs, and other factors that you have thus far admitted to it and, as such, it has a direct bearing on your present selection of the things you pay attention to, filter, and remember.

That characteristic, *selective perception*, is a part of everyday living. The driver of a moving car does not see, hear, or smell the same things as a friend in the same car. Two people at a sports event do not see or hear the same things. Going down a country road, a fence salesman is inclined to notice fences and their condition, a pilot takes note of planes on the ground or overhead, a developer sees houses or envisions them in open fields, an artist sees landscapes, and an agronomist checks crops--all because of selective perception.

For a final illustration of differences in personal perceptions, note this passage from page 116 of Jeffrey Archer's 1991 novel, *As the Crow Flies*. The character, Charlie, is posing a question to his business partner, Becky: "But what else do you see when you look across the road?" Becky's eyes returned to Chelsea Terrace. "Lots of people walking up and down the pavement, mainly ladies with parasols, nannies pushing prams, and the odd child with a skipping rope or hoop." She paused. "Why, what do you see?" "Two 'For Sale' signs." "I confess, I hadn't noticed them." Once again she looked across the road. "That's because you're looking with a different pair of eyes," Charlie explained.

Stated another way, no one is capable of absorbing and cataloging every sensory impression received, so only those impressions that are of special interest or meaning to us become our "view of the world." We see what we want to see, hear what we want to hear, believe what we want to believe, and discard or ignore everything else. We pay "attention only to what seems in agreement with...[our] existing attitudes, opinions, beliefs, or that which will not cause displeasure...."[4] But whatever the sources of the listener's view of the world (background, home, parental influence, church, economic level, education, independent thinking, etc.), the speaker has to remember that those beliefs make up the personal screen through which the listener admits or declines to admit anything new to his or her total perceptual field or "belief system."

Since we know that no one's perceptual field is the same as ours and that everyone's selective screen differs from that of everyone else, the sensitive speaker recognizes and respects those differences. That speaker has to remember, too, that one's own selective perceptions play a role in the choices made in preparing and presenting a talk as well as in the screening of "feedback" messages from the listeners.

With the understanding that communication is a continuous, messages-streaming-both-ways process, that words are not the sole carriers of those messages, and that both listener and speaker have in place a personal perceptual screen serving to admit incoming messages or to shunt them aside, let's look into how the listener attaches meanings to a speaker's words.

Words and the Meanings of Words

The meanings a listener derives from the words of the speaker are affected, modified, and changed by the contexts in which those words appear.

The verbal context

In Latin, as you may know, *verbum* means *word*, and *contextus* means *joined together*. We use "verbal context" in the sense of a word joined together with other words in a way that affects the meaning of the word in question. The word" fine," for example, depends for its meaning on the words used with it. "That's a mighty fine pig" and "That comb is too fine for my hair" show how context (the words surrounding a word) tells us how to interpret the word "fine." A doctor will report that "The patient's condition is stable," while the horse-owner will say, "I keep my horse at a stable on the edge of town." You decide what "stable" means from the context in which that word is used.

Stated differently, *the meaning of a word is not in the word itself* but in the way it is "translated" by the listener. As I. A. Richards reminds us,

> A chief cause of misunderstanding is the common belief that a word has a meaning of its own.
>
> A word is always a cooperative member of an organism, the utterance, and therefore cannot have a fixed correct usage.
>
> The meaning we find for a word comes to it only with respect to the meanings of the other words we take with it.[5]

In other words, you have to hear or see a word in its setting with other words before you can decide what it means. As we have already noted, the simplest words in our language often have many meanings. Cherry gives examples of 10 different meanings of the word *meaning*! Beardsley notes 55 possible interpretations of *point* and 109 for *run*.[6] What a word means to you is not all that important; what is important is what it means to your listeners.

The paraverbal context

Para is Greek for "going along with and changing in some way." When attached to *verbal*, the resulting word covers the changes in meaning that come from the way a person "sounds" as she or he speaks. In a telephone conversation, for example, your interpretation of meaning depends not only on the words you hear but also on whether or not the person on the other end of the line sounds happy, tired, enthusiastic, disturbed, angry, concerned, sympathetic, interested, smug, joyful, etc. You don't see that other person, but *how the words are said* gives their meaning a special twist.

You do not have to be on the 'phone to understand how the meanings of words can be affected or even changed by variations in a speaker's tone, rate, pitch, and volume. You could be a talking with a group about ways to detect schemes to sell over-priced products to the public. After each description of such a scheme, you could say, "Hurry out and buy that wonderful product!" Everyone listening to you would understand that you meant exactly the opposite of what you were saying. For a second example, "I'm going to Kalamazoo" is a simple sentence which seems to have a simple meaning. However, if you place a certain tone and emphasis on selected words in that series, listeners will take that short sentence to mean that (1) you are *determined* to go to Kalamazoo, or (2) you *prefer to go there* rather than to another city, or (3) *others should follow your lead* in going there, or (4) you are *happy* to be going there, or (5) you are *sad* to be going there, and on and on.

You see another kind of paraverbal context in listener reactions to regional accents. A Boston accent could be a handicap in addressing audiences in certain areas of the South; Southern speech patterns could be an advantage in the same areas. In fact, when you have a telephone conversation with a stranger who has an accent of some kind, you arrive at inferences about the background of that person, and those inferences may favorably or unfavorably affect your response to the verbal message. You can interpret the cordial tone of someone's "I'll think it over" as a friendly sign leading to a future "Yes" or, if the tone is unfriendly, simply as a way of saying "No." And your instructor needs no interpreter to tell him or her the meaning of the class-wide moan which sometimes follows the announcement of an assignment or schedule. Language, then, is definitely more than just the words listeners hear and the context in which they hear them; also surrounding those words is another layer of paraverbal meaning-modifiers: tone, stress, rate, accent, moans, groans, and other voiced sounds.

The nonverbal context

We now add a third meaning-modifying context, that of nonverbal communication. As the prefix *non* suggests, nonverbal is no-sound "speech" which conveys or modifies meanings *without* using words or the paraverbal sounds we associate with words:

> When one presents himself in a communicative situation, he should be aware that he may be saying more nonverbally (through appearance, facial expression, gestures, movements, etc.) than he is saying verbally. Failure to realize the importance of nonverbal cues may very well cause us to fail in our communicative effort.[7]

You are already aware, for example, of the unspoken communication that is going on when you first meet students or members of the teaching staff. You are arriving at some first-impression inferences about them (and they are doing the same about you). Without a word being spoken, you perceive some of these people to be friendly, others to be unfriendly.

In the world of job applications, for instance, it is well known that employers expect an applicant to dress and act in a way appropriate to the post applied for.

If the applicant appears on the scene in sports clothes and does not seem to have acceptable manners, he or she is treated to some routine questions and is then escorted to the door with the familiar, "Don't call me. I'll call you." What is actually said in such an interview has nothing to do with the result. For another example, let's say that every time you encounter a particular student, you get a warm greeting and some friendly conversation. In addition to the words, you get the nonverbal "message" that your company is enjoyed and appreciated. At times, actions do speak louder than words. The same is true of your first "meeting" with a speaker in a public setting or, for that matter, in his or her appearance on TV. There on the platform or screen, you see that individual waiting for the program to begin. From his or her general appearance (e.g., facial expressions, dress, posture, and composure), you arrive at some initial opinions about the speaker and about the extent to which the proceedings are going to be of interest to you. The speaker is at the same time receiving a different set of messages as he or she "looks over" the audience, wonders how accurate and how helpful the audience analysis has been, considers whether or not to make last-minute changes in the presentation, and makes an estimate about the kind of welcome to be anticipated. Whether or not a presentation is televised, this is the age of "visual images" and the influences they exert on listeners. What those listeners see has much to do with that important first impression, with attracting listener attention, and with creating a friendly and supportive atmosphere.[8] In any event, what is taking place at this stage is interactive, nonverbal communication between speaker and audience...and the program has not even begun.

When it does begin, the speaker tries to induce in the listener meanings as close as possible to her or his own. The speaker does so through the use of verbal, paraverbal, and nonverbal forms of "speech," some intentional and some unintentional, some controlled and some beyond control (e.g., height, weight, race, mannerisms). The extent to which the speaker succeeds depends largely on life experiences shared with the listener and on the speaker's ability to "become one with the listener" through an emphasis, stated or unstated, on their common interests and goals. Nevertheless, to the extent that one cannot escape the past, a speaker expresses ideas in ways determined by the point of view from which he or she sees a particular "object, event, or situation" and by his or her "background experiences and attitudes."[9] So it is no wonder that the more speaker and listener have in common (language, culture, education, tastes, beliefs), the better the chance for real communication.

Adjusting to "Feedback"

External-source feedback

Earlier in the chapter, we mentioned the kind of "feedback" in which one party to a conversation adjusts to the behavior of the other. The speaker in a public setting faces the same needs to adjust to the behavior of the audience. (Once again, of course, we remind ourselves that all messages reaching the speaker, including feedback, encounter the speaker's perceptual screen and, as usual, some of those messages get through and some don't.)

The prime source of external feedback is, naturally, the audience. But even before trying to communicate in the presence of listeners, a speaker has some pre-event feedback available in the form of analysis of the audience (as described in Chapter 7). Then, during the actual effort to communicate, the speaker tries to modify the message in the light of on-the-spot interpretations of listener reactions (e.g., frowns, smiles, approving nods, negative shakes of the head, puzzlement, attention, restlessness, applause, heckling, enthusiasm, and resignation.) The sensitive speaker tries to use those interpretations to make continuing adjustments and improvements in the message.

Consider that you're the speaker and your listeners look puzzled at something you've just said. Do you just go sailing along or do you pause long enough to adjust to their puzzlement by using a phrase like "In other words" to introduce further explanation? Or for another example, you present a particular point of view and you see members of the audience shaking their heads in disbelief. Do you ignore those signals or do you go back over that point and either provide some additional evidence or offer to make some available? A listening audience seldom talks back to let you know what it's thinking; that's all the more reason to note its reactions and adjust to them. Certainly, the need to adjust to feedback is no less great for the speaker than it is for the conversationalist. The alert and responsive speaker tries to be ready for any eventuality and does everything possible to use audience feedback to enhance communication with that audience.

A second source of external feedback is the sound of your own voice. As you speak, you use what you hear to rephrase a sentence to achieve more clarity, to increase or soften volume for special effect, to change your rate and pitch for emphasis. And if you still have any reservations about the validity of your message, hearing it again may actually strengthen your confidence in it.

Internal-source feedback

You also feel and "see" yourself in action and, in the light of "inside feedback," you adjust your facial expressions and bodily movements to fit a particular situation. As you speak, in other words, you anticipate "production needs" and make adjustments to meet the needs of the moment. When you are serious, you reinforce what you are saying by looking serious. If the occasion is a happy one, you feel free to look happy. Meanwhile, you hope that the listener is interpreting what you're doing in the way you intend.

Outside Factors Affecting Communication

Finally, the communication process, so very complex in itself, is subject to a variety of "outside factors" which serve to help the speaker get the message across or, on the other hand, serve only to garble it, deflect it, or get in its way.

Occasion and setting

The general atmosphere of the occasion, for example, affects audience response. We have all noted instances in which displaying the flag and patriotic music have established a favorable atmosphere for a speaker's praise of veterans or of a visiting dignitary. Sometimes the presence of reporters and TV crews adds to the perceived importance of an event; at other times, their presence is a distracting "noise" (below). As for a setting, speaking to attentive listeners on a pleasant afternoon in a park would make any speaker happy. The time, place, and circumstances, as well as the occasion itself, have much to do with the success or failure of any speaking-listening event.

"Noises" in general

"Noise" is a term used to describe outside factors which may hinder communication. No matter how much speaker and listeners have in common, the listener translation of the message is likely to be less than accurate if the room is too hot or cold, if the seating is too hard or too comfortable, if the chairperson puts everyone to sleep in advance, if the speaker is hidden behind a too-tall lectern or a maze of microphones, if the sound system squeals, if the listeners are tired or hungry, if the sounds of nearby construction are loud, if music, singing, or other "noise" from a nearby meeting can be heard. None of these factors has anything directly to do with speaker messages or with listener reception of those messages, but they may make communication difficult or even block it out entirely.

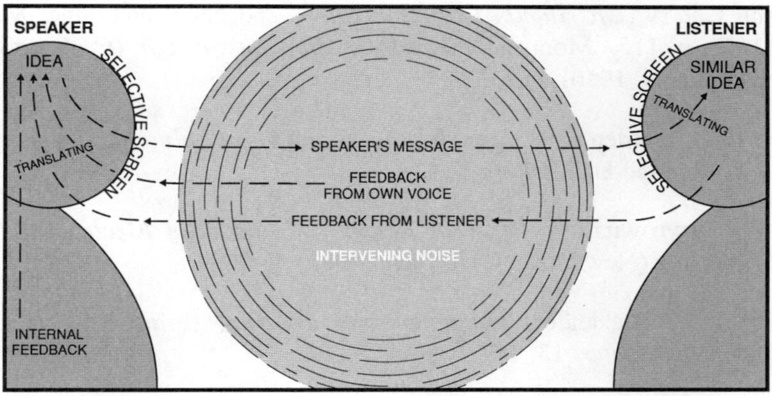

We see, then, that the complex of messages communicated through "speech" is made up of words and non-word signs, that the messages run the gauntlet of the perceptive screens of those communicating, that the meanings of words depend, not on the speaker, but on the people listening to them as well as on the contexts in which the words appear, that the speaker depends (or fails to depend) on feedback to adjust the message to the listener, and that outside "noise" factors having nothing to do with speaker or message may support or hinder communication.

Endnotes

1. Ray L. Birdwhistell, *Kinesics and Context: Essays on Body Motion Communication* (Philadelphia, PA: U. of Pennsylvania Press, 1970), p. 12.

2. Erving Goffman, *Behavior in Public Places* (New York: Free Press, 1963), p. 35.

3. E. L. Doctorow, *Billy Bathgate* (New York: Random House, 1989), p. 288.

4. Frederick Williams, *The New Communications* (Belmont, CA: Wadsworth, 1984), p. 114.

5. I. A. Richards, *The Philosophy of Rhetoric* (New York: Oxford UP, 1936), pages 3, 11, 69-70.

6. Colin Cherry, *On Human Communication*, 2nd ed. (Cambridge, MA: MIT Press, 1966, p. 115. Monroe C. Beardsley, *Thinking Straight* (Englewood Cliffs, NJ: Prentice-Hall, 1956), p. 153.

7. George A. Borden et al., *Speech Behavior and HumanInteraction* (Englewood Cliffs, NJ: Prentice-Hall, 1969), p. 62 f.

8. Joshua Meyrowitz, *No Sense of Place: The Impact of Electronic Media on Social Behavior* (New York: Oxford UP, 1985), p. 94.

9. Hubert G. Alexander, *Language and Thinking* (Princeton, NJ: D. Van Nostrand, 1967), pages 13, 16.

Discussion Questions

1. What do we mean when we say that "perception is the process of making sense out of experience"? Is it possible for each of two individuals to have "the same experience"? Is it possible for two individuals to react in the same way to "the same experience"?

2. Your "speech" (verbal, paraverbal, nonverbal) in conversation with a professor is different from that with a fellow student or with a child. How do you account for the differences? Are you being yourself or are you playing roles?

3. We sometimes say one thing and mean something different or exactly the opposite. Give an example of your affecting meaning through paraverbal emphasis, tone, etc.

4. In interpreting what someone is saying in a telephone conversation, how important is "the paraverbal context"?

5. On occasion, you smile to "take the sting out" or otherwise modify the meaning of something you are saying. Give an example from your own experience or from your observations of the nonverbal behavior of others.

6. What do you think are the advantages of becoming consciously aware of feedback? What kinds of short-notice changes can a speaker make in the process of interaction with the audience?

7. An instructor sometimes has a few more things to say after the end of the class

period. Do you listen very well after that point? Why not?

8. You learn that an expert on foreign policy is scheduled to lecture on campus. Has her communication with you already begun? Does it begin when you see her on stage before the lecture? Does it end with the close of the lecture? Is it possible to say with certainty when communication begins and when it ends?

Application Projects

Speaking options

In these days of many meetings, your chances of being called upon to introduce someone are high. Perhaps you've already had this experience. You have certainly attended meetings in which someone was invited "to stand up and take a bow."

1. ***Introducing a fellow student.*** Pair off with another student and exchange information on special interests, hobbies, majors, goals, etc. The object of the exchange of information is to use it in introducing each other to the class. A typical introduction consists of a few well-chosen, complimentary remarks followed by the student's name. Plan to speak for about two minutes.

2. ***Introducing a fellow student "speaker."*** Pair off and exchange information as above. In this instance, the object of the exchange is extended to find a topic title on which a student is considered to be knowledgeable. Your function and that of the second student is to introduce each other as a "a speaker worth listening to." Plan to speak for about two minutes.With minor modifications, the plan below can be used to introduce a student or a student "speaker":

(a) Begin with a comment or two on why the student's topic or hobby should be of interest to the class. For example, "We're all interested in clean water." Or, "Are you looking for a hobby that's lots of fun but doesn't call for a lot of money?

(b) Call attention to the student's related background, education, training, skills attained, any recognition of those skills, etc.

(c) Start a round of welcoming applause as you say, "Let's welcome Jane [or John] Doe!"

Listening options

1. Write a one-page report on any one student's use of a word or words in a *verbal* context unfamiliar to you.

2. Write a one-page report in which you comment on--and give one or two examples of--a student speaker's use of *paraverbal* modifications to help the audience interpret meaning.

3. Write a one-page report on a student's *intentional nonverbal* emphasis or modifying of meaning in communicating with the audience.

4. Write a one-page report on the *unintentional nonverbal* messages which you "received" from one of the students. Did any nonverbal messages contradict the speaker's intended message in any way?

5. Were you aware of any student speaker's taking advantage of *feedback from the audience*? How would you describe that feedback? What specific adjustment(s) did the student seem to make in the light of it? Write a one-page report.

Additional Activities

1. To demonstrate that the meaning of a word is not in the word itself but in the way in which it is used, find in a dictionary three words (words with more than one meaning, such as *compound, echo, hatch*), each of which can be interpreted or "translated" in at least two different ways. For each word, write or present to the class two sentences in each of which that word has an entirely different meaning.

2. Communication between a speaker and listeners can be affected by the setting, the occasion, and by "intervening noises." Make a list of at least five different ways in which factors having little or nothing to do with the speaker's message can hinder, interrupt, or even block that message. Then, for every item on your list, be ready to suggest ways to solve or compensate for each problem.

2

RHETORIC AS COMMUNICATION

We are all of us preachers in private or public capacities.

Richard Weaver

When I first had to speak before a group, my knees shook.

Robyn Blumner, civil rights attorney

"Know thyself" means this, that you become acquainted with what you know and what you can do.

Menander of Athens

In reading this chapter, you will become aware that...

1. Rhetoric is the art and science of speaking purposefully, responsibly, and effectively to induce a desired response.

2. All speaking of any kind is by nature "persuasive."

3. Speakers should strive to "become one with their listeners" in the effort to reach common goals.

4. Any fears of speaking before a group can be reduced to a constructive minimum.

What Is Rhetoric?

We move from the discussion of the communication process in general to a focus on that form of communication which you know as public speaking but which for centuries has also been known as "rhetoric." (You may even now be taking a writing course by that title in this or another department.) We use the word *rhetoric* with some frequency in this book, not only because the original meaning of the word is coming back into vogue, but because it more accurately reflects the traditional view that all speaking in public is persuasive.

We first recognize rhetoric as a book of principles and guidelines which a speaker (*rhetor* to the early Greeks) tries to follow in interacting with listeners in public settings. Secondly, rhetoric is another word for the activity of public speaking itself. And in that connection, let's agree at the start that it isn't the size of the audience that determines whether or not you are "speaking in public," and it doesn't matter whether you are standing or seated; what matters is *the central role that you assume in trying to communicate with listeners* numbering from as few as three or four to several times that many and more.

So it is that long before the development of behavioral and social sciences, and long before we knew as much as we do now about communication, the writers on public speaking or rhetoric arrived at their "guidelines for speakers" by watching speakers in action and by drawing conclusions from what they saw and heard. In turn, the "students" studied and practiced those guidelines to become the "speakers" of their day.

You may not have thought of English words beginning with *rhetor* as having anything to do with purposeful and responsible speaking. It is more common today to think of *rhetoric* and *rhetorical* in the sense of "mere rhetoric," a phrase we customarily use--with or without the "mere"--to describe emotional, issue-avoiding, or flowery double-talk. The writers below are using *rhetoric* in that sense:

> Charlotte Hinger, author of *Come Spring*: "No writer could possibly devise rhetoric more inflammatory than was actually printed by our pioneer editors."
>
> Kate Callen, Planned Parenthood official: "Planned Parenthood aims at fighting teenage pregnancies with knowledge, not with rhetoric."
>
> Item in *The Washington Post*: "An administration official close to the talks said they were characterized by an absence of rhetoric and posturing."

But if you look up *rhetoric* in a dictionary, the first meanings you see there are "the art or science of speaking and writing effectively" or "a book or textbook on that subject." Only as secondary meanings will you find phrases like "language having no real content" or "language of a showy and meaningless type."

In this textbook, needless to say, we are concerned with the primary meanings.[1] To us, then, *a rhetoric* is a book like this one which is aimed at helping you prepare for and take part in speaker-listener events, and *rhetoric* is the art and science of speaking purposefully, responsibly, and effectively in public settings of all kinds, including the workplace.

The "Rhetorical Appeals"

You've heard of Aristotle (384-322 B.C.), the Greek philosopher, but you probably didn't know that he is the writer of the classic "and still champion" *Art of Rhetoric*.[2] In it, with selection of the best ways to approach a given set of listeners as a goal, he defines rhetoric as that art which enables the speaker "to see in any subject the possible means of persuasion."[3] And to help speakers interact best with listeners, he describes the interrelated appeals (ethical, emotional, and logical) available to influence those listeners:

> The first kind [of appeals] stems from the character [*ethos*] of the speaker; the second kind in inducing a certain [emotional] attitude in the hearer; the third has to do with the logic of the position presented....[4]

That three-avenues-of-appeal approach to audience adaptation is still alive and well--your classmates and others expect you, for example, to be honest with them, to take into account and deal with how they feel about the subject, and to be reasonable.

To Persuade or Not to Persuade

We think of rhetoric, of course, as planned-in-advance persuasive effort but, as we said earlier and as Richard Weaver reminds us, *all speaking of any kind is by nature persuasive:*

> Rhetoric is cognate with language; it is impossible and even ridiculous that the utterances of men could be neutral. We are all of us preachers in private or public capacities. We have no sooner uttered words than we have given impulse to other people to look at the world, or some small part of it, in our way.[5]

It follows that, whenever you appear before others, you are influencing them in one way or another. As for your using rhetoric, you are engaging in it--that is, you are attempting to induce listeners to accept your way of looking at things--whenever you address a group, large or small, which has the free choice of accepting or rejecting your message.

To put it another way, you are intentionally or unintentionally exerting influence when you smilingly greet someone, when you enthusiastically or unhappily describe a vacation trip, when you telephone somebody simply to say "Hello," or when you explain the basics of sailing. As Weaver says, every word you speak is "sermonic"--it conveys an influential message whether you want it to or not.

So even when your purpose on a given occasion is, for example, in the main informational (e.g., "How to invest wisely," "How to handle interpersonal conflicts," "How to go about buying a used car," "How to let out the genius in you"), you are in effect urging your listeners to accept that information. You want them to believe you, to recognize your expertise, to feel that you are looking out for their best interests, and to follow your lead.

> Examples: A *sales manager* who spends an hour informing office personnel about new record-keeping procedures is seldom just explaining the new system--he or she is also trying to gain acceptance of the change in procedures and cooperation in making it work to advantage. A *company representative*, trying to increase sales to a distributor group, depends on information as the primary base for demonstrating that a particular product or service is worth buying. The *manufacturer's representative* who explains to a meeting of purchasing agents the operation of new computer equipment manages to suggest that production will go up if the agents purchase that equipment. The *county agent* describing how crop-rotation can control insects and weeds is at the same time hoping that some in the audience will be induced to try that method.

The foregoing examples happen to have an informational base but, no matter what your goals may be in a public presentation, your broad approach to the listeners will always be a combination of the traditional appeals, ethical, logical, and emotional/motivational.

Identifying with Your Listeners

Your purpose in trying to communicate with any group, small or not so small, will suffer unless you attain some success in "identifying with your listeners." A core concept in public speaking, the need for identification with the audience occurs in many contexts throughout this book. Although that identification is not the specific purpose of any "speech," it has been an objective of sensitive speakers from earliest times...and never more so than today. Kenneth Burke puts it this way: "You persuade a man only insofar as you can talk his language by speech, gesture, tonality, order, image, attitude, idea, identifying your ways with his."[6]

Twenty-three centuries earlier but in similar vein, Aristotle had commented on the willingness of members of an audience to listen to speakers who reflect their way of life and who seem to be one with them.[7] The "oneness" and identification which these and other theorists advocate stems from a speaker's caring about his or her listeners, caring about their collective well-being and welfare, and caring about what they think, feel, and believe.

A vital element in establishing that oneness and identification with listeners is, of course, a speaker's sense of "the occasion," a topic already called to your attention in Chapter 1. As listeners, we have all found ourselves in situations in which, from the start, we felt a genuine kinship with the speaker; his or her interacting with us was clearly intended to serve our best interests, and the entire presentation was fittingly designed to reach that goal. Unfortunately, we have also had the experience of listening to speakers who completely misread the occasion by being too formal on informal occasions or too informal on formal occasions, or by using language above or below the comprehension of their listeners, or by telling offensive jokes, or by "insulting the intelligence" of listeners, or by generally demonstrating little or no understanding, as Meyrowitz puts it, "of what is going on here."[8]

As speaker-listener situations vary, the speaker does find it necessary to play a variety of roles in order to adjust his or her message to a variety of listeners but, as long as those adjustments are in good taste and appropriately directed toward becoming one with the audience, its members in turn give the speaker credit for being aware of what is going on. Moving closer to home, when students in the class listen to you or another student speaker, they should be able to say to themselves, "This student understands us, speaks our language, is concerned about our interests and, instead of trying only to impress the instructor, is doing everything possible to gain a particular response from us."

Easing Your Tensions and Fears

While agreeing that it is useful and necessary for individuals to carry on social, business, or professional conversations, there are still those who contend that the average person is seldom, if ever, expected to speak in a public setting. The problem is that many people think of a public setting and of public speaking as being limited to those occasions when you "wear your best," walk on the stage or platform of an auditorium, step up to a lectern, and then proceed to interact with a hundred or more listeners in the effort to win a favorable response. It is true that you may never face large audiences to discuss major issues. It is equally true that thousands of individuals stand up every day to present explanations or proposals of various kinds to small audiences in occupational and other settings. Unless you plan to become a hermit, you can be sure that you will be doing some public speaking, either because you are invited to make presentations or because you ask for the opportunity to make them. Since escaping "public speaking" is not an option for one who wants to get ahead, you will be glad to know that there are steps you can take to cope with any apprehensions you may have about speaking to this class and to any other group of listeners.

Reviewing your self-concept

Communicating and identifying with others is easier when you can take the stand with a degree of self-confidence and poise. As in other human relationships, one important avenue to self-confidence is *to be yourself.* Your present view of yourself is, of course, based on the process of selective perception we described in Chapter 1. It is made up of "the relatively stable set of perceptions"[9] you have about your identity, your qualities, your abilities, your worth, and your future. As with all perceptions, things aren't always what they seem. In some areas we underestimate ourselves, in others we overestimate ourselves, and in some (not too many) we almost do see ourselves as others see us.

What you think about yourself depends heavily on what you think others think of you. But the opinions others have of you are exactly that--just opinions. Stated another way, you base judgments about yourself and your standing in other people's eyes from what they say or from hearsay--what they are reported to have said. You draw conclusions from the way they look at you and from how they seem to relate to you. You decide, often on very slim or no evidence, that an individual or group likes you or doesn't like you.

So the person you are today is a mix of many influences: your racial and ethnic background, your family situation, your education up to now, the choices you've made and the choices you didn't make, the experiences you've had, and the people you've met. You can waste a lot of time and energy in envy of others, their abilities, their talents, and their possessions. You can gripe about being handicapped in some way and lacking a chance to get ahead. Or you can decide to ignore all that and do the best you can with what you've got. You can resent your religion, or you can decide to disregard it, accept it, or take pride in it. You can drift, kill time, drop out, and blame everything and everybody but yourself, or you can recognize that every individual, including you, possesses a unique set of abilities, talents, and interests on which to build a future. And although prejudice and discrimination still exist, people still succeed no matter what their sex, race, religion, or place of origin.[10] Your future is determined mainly by your deciding to make the best of your own special resources.

What are those special resources? Since everyone is different from everyone else, you may find it useful to ask yourself a few questions:

> Where am I "coming from"? How did I get to be the way I am? Am I sensitive about my background? Why? Does it make any sense to be envious of others? Or to resent things I can't change?
>
> Why do I like some people and don't like others? (Will Rogers once said, "I never met a person I didn't like." Why do you think he was able to say that...and mean it?)
>
> What are my prejudices? Do I think "it's funny" to tell racial or ethnic jokes? Do I try to understand and accept others as individuals rather than as members of a particular group?
>
> What handicaps do I face? Are they real or are they excuses for not trying? If real, what can be done about any of them?
>
> What special abilities, skills, or talents do I have? What evidence do I have that they exist? Am I taking them into account in planning my future?

It's a good idea to check your answers with others. As we noted at the very beginning of this text, communication is the only effective way you have to let people know about you and your capabilities. This, then, is a good time to take a realistic look at yourself as one more step toward improving your ability to communicate. Among other things, you could be selling yourself short or completely overlooking a basic talent you didn't know you had. So, besides doing some thinking about "the real you," do some talking with a counselor or advisor. You can also sign up for whatever aptitude tests are available through the student counseling office.

Finally, remember that getting to know yourself, a worthwhile end in itself, provides a solid base for planning your future. If you're already enrolled in a field which enables you to take advantage of your abilities, your plan for personal growth is largely solved. If you're having second thoughts about your present educational goals, now is the time to consider changing majors or schools. If you haven't yet chosen a vocation or career, getting to know who you are will help you make a later choice with confidence.

In the light of all that, a speech assignment is no cause for alarm. It is instead one more opportunity to add a positive accomplishment to the total of your successful past experiences...and to bolster your view of yourself at the same time.

Competing with yourself only

One of the interpersonal problems in a public speaking class is that some of the students already have some experience in that field and others do not. Of those who do not, some have a tendency to compare themselves unfavorably with those who "shine" and to be nervous about not doing as well as others in the class.

It's true that some students who enroll in a course of this kind already have some experience in communicating publicly. Perhaps they earned high school credit in courses called communication, oral interpretation, debating, or acting. Or maybe they presided as officers of student organizations. With experiences like those behind them, they are likely to be somewhat more self-assured about speaking in a speakerinteracting-with-listeners situation.

For other students, enrollment in a communication course calling for in-class activity is "a first" or close to it. If you are a student in the no experience group, remember that it's a part of being human to feel some apprehension in the face of new situations. It's also a part of being human to worry about fulfilling assignments at levels below those of students with past experience. The answer is to look on the course as a chance to compete with yourself, not with others. You come into this class at a certain level of background and expertise; your only goal should be to leave it with more experience in an activity essential to your future.

Taking direct control

Among other defenses against tension is thorough preparation for your turn "at bat." The student who has gained control over his or her message has already put aside a major source of pressure and stress.

Secondly, remember that you're not alone in the apprehension department; it is felt in varying degrees by everyone else in the class, including those who have had some previous public speaking experience. Knowing what is happening and knowing that everyone shares the problem is another step toward easing tension.

Third, as you sit there waiting your turn to speak, switch your attention to the individual chairing the meeting or to the speaker of the moment. Concentrating your attention on what somebody else is saying will take your mind off your apprehensions and help the speaker of the moment as well. For that speaker, you are a part of the audience and ought to be listening to him or her in any event.

Fourth, make a conscious effort to breathe deeply and regularly. We humans react "as a whole" to conditions of stress, and a faster heartbeat is one of those reactions. It is an accepted physiological fact that, if we can reduce the rate of that beat through controlled breathing, we can to some extent reduce the anxieties which cause the stress in the first place.

Fifth, "think positive"...and the end-result will be positive. Picture yourself as doing a first-rate job of communicating with attentive and appreciative listeners. Adopt the attitude of Valentine Windt, a professor at the University of Michigan, who used to say, "When you walk to the stand, do it with an air of 'zestful aggression.' The way you look should be saying, 'I've got something worthwhile to say! You people are going to be interested in it! And I'm looking forward to talking with you about it!'" That was--and is--very practical advice.

So whenever your name is announced as that of "our next speaker," remember that your investment in preparing for the event gives you every right to "look competent" and self-assured as you take your place on the stand for the cooperative venture we call communication.

In this chapter you have been introduced to basic ideas and principles which you will meet again and again in succeeding chapters. As the art of speaking purposefully in public settings, rhetoric makes use of the social sciences, but it is--and always will be--a creative art, one dependent on the individual speaker's knowledge, talent, and ingenuity in relating to audiences. It enables speakers and listeners alike to communicate in their collective best interests. It is part of the long tradition of the interactive process of presenting ideas to listeners for their free-choice consideration and judgment.

Endnotes

1. For a review of the meanings of *rhetoric* down through the centuries, see James L. Kinneavy, *A Theory of Discourse* (New York: W. W. Norton & Co., 1971), pp. 211-228. For general evidence that we speak and write according to principles first developed by the Greeks and the Romans, see *Readings from Classical Rhetoric*, eds. Patricia P. Matsen, Philip Rollinson, and Marion Sousa (Carbondale, IL: Southern Illinois UP, 1990).

2. According to Cooper, "There is no book on the subject since Aristotle's that is not at least indirectly indebted to his." See *The Rhetoric of Aristotle*, ed. Lane Cooper (New York: Appleton-Century-Crofts, 1960 rpt.), p. xvii.

3. Aristotle, *The "Art" of Rhetoric*, trans. John Henry Freese, Vol. 3 of Aristotle, Loeb Classical Library Series (Cambridge, MA: Harvard UP, 1982 rpt.), 1355b.

4. Aristotle, *Rhetoric* 1356a.

5. Richard M. Weaver, *Language is Sermonic: [Essays of] Richard M. Weaver on the Nature of Rhetoric*, eds. Richard L. Johannesen, Rennard Strickland, and Ralph T. Eubanks (Baton Rouge, LA: Louisiana State UP, 1970), pages 221, 224.

6. Kenneth Burke, *A Rhetoric of Motives* (New York: George Braziller, 1955), p. 55.

7. Aristotle, *Rhetoric* 1390a.

8. Joshua Meyrowitz, *No Sense of Place: The Impact of Electronic Media on Social Behavior* (New York: Oxford UP, 1985), pp. 24-27.

9. Ronald B. Adler and Neil Towne, *Looking out, Looking in*, 5th ed. (New York: Holt, Rinehart and Winston, 1987), p. 31.

10. For a discussion of the extent to which cultural, ethnic, and racial stereotypes have affected choices of occupations, see Margaret Hennig and Ann Jardim, *The Managerial Woman* (Garden City, NY: Anchor Press/Doubleday, 1977).

Discussion Questions

1. Have you heard anyone outside the class use the word *rhetoric* within the last few days? Or read in the papers about somebody's doing so? In what context was the word used?

2. Have you recently heard or read "a message" that you would label "rhetoric"? Why? What were the circumstances?

3. In what way are you "preaching a sermon" whenever you engage in ordinary, everyday conversation? Or in communication which seems to be primarily informational in character?

4. If a presidential candidate has spent most of his or her life in New Orleans, how can that individual "become one" with a small town audience in Iowa?

5. If your self-concept or view of yourself is in part the product of past experiences, what can you do to ensure that your speaking assignments will serve to enhance that selfconcept?

Short Speaking-from-Manuscript Options

In the speaking options below, you have the relatively easy opportunity to become familiar with a short manuscript, to use it as a base for communicating with your listeners, and to take another step toward becoming "at home" on the stand. (If you'd like some help how to read a manuscript, see the short section on that subject in Chapter 10.)

1. Read again the Kenneth Burke quotation (in the middle of the chapter). Then, select a relatively impersonal and formal paragraph or two *from any source* (including an essay or composition you wrote for another class). Identifying the source, "read" your selection to the class; follow it with the "reading" of your own version of the same passage, one which you have written to achieve identification with members of the class. Plan to read for about two minutes.

2. From a speech printed in *Vital Speeches* or any other source, select one or two relatively short passages which seem to you to follow--or not follow--Burke's advice. "Read" your selected passage(s); then, "read" your written comments on how the speaker did or did nt seem to identify himself or herself with the listeners. Plan to read for about two minutes.

Listening Options

1. Write a one-page summary of your reasons for commending one of the student "readers" for bringing to the class the widest distinction between the impersonal prose of a passage and the same passage rewritten to communicate personally and directly.

2. Write a one-page citation of reasons for your commending one of the student "readers" for her or his handling of a page or two of manuscript and for personally establishing a degree of "oneness" with the class at the same time.

Additional Activities

1. Find a current, printed example of (a) rhetoric as an effort to induce acceptance or agreement from readers or listeners and (b) rhetoric in the sense of meaningless and empty talk.

2. There is a "mix" of appeals to the audience in every public speaking event. Read a speech, listen to a speaker in action, or view the videotape of a speaker's interaction with listeners. Be ready to give examples of the way in which the speaker used ethical, logical, and emotional appeals.

3. As a speaker, you will be trying to identify yourself with your listeners. Using one of the same sources as above, report on how well or how ineffectively the same or a different speaker achieved real identification or "oneness" with the listeners.

4. Writing about one's self-concept:

a. Name a particular occupation and list five ways in which you believe choosing it could contribute positively to your self-concept.

b. Write a paragraph of 50 to 75 words explaining how a choice you made in the past had some effect in shaping the person you are now.

c. Write a paragraph of 50 to 75 words explaining how a decision to enter a particular occupation or profession has changed or might change the person you are now.

d. Write a definition of *self-concept* and a short paragraph explaining how your self-concept did or could influence your career choice.

e. "Things aren't always what they seem." Write a definition of *perception* and, then, write a short paragraph on how you see your perceptions favorably or unfavorably affecting your view of yourself at any time in the past.

f. Write a self-appraisal consisting of a list of four or five of your perceived strengths as a public speaker, a similar list of what you see as your weaknesses, and a short paragraph on how you expect this course to affect those strengths and weaknesses.

Photo courtesy Rollins College, Winter Park, Florida.

3

REASONING LOGICALLY

To master [logical appeal], one must be capable of logical reasoning.

Aristotle

When you finish this chapter, you should be aware that...

1. Logical appeal, the appeal to reason, is one of three interrelated components of a speaker's adaptation to listeners.

2. You reason "inductively" by drawing conclusions from separate-unit examples or story-type examples.

3. You reason "deductively" by drawing conclusions from other conclusions.

4. The common premise is a generally accepted conclusion which, stated or unstated, plays an important role in reasoning.

5. We rely on listeners to supply the link between stated and unstated premises and conclusions. This is called "the enthymeme connection."

6. In public speaking, we reason in terms of probability, not certainty.

7. Especially useful to speakers are reasoning from cause and effect, by definition, by classification, and by authority.

When you hear one or more listeners say, "You're not being logical!" you can assume that your way of reasoning, at least by their standards, is falling short of the mark. On the other hand, if you are reasoning logically (i.e., following accepted principles for reaching inferences or coming to conclusions), you have a better chance of convincing listeners that the position you're proposing is the one they should adopt. This chapter is aimed at helping you gain that advantage--it is a review of the part which logical reasoningplays as one of the interrelated appeals (ethical, logical, and emotional/motivational) a speaker uses in inducing a desired response in listeners.

In paraphrase of a passage from Aristotle's *Rhetoric*, "you must yourself be capable of reasoning logically if you want to appeal to listeners through their sense of what is reasonable."[1] *Reasoning logically may be defined as the process of drawing valid inferences or conclusions from items of evidence or from other inferences or conclusions.* If your evidence is adequate and the conclusions, however arrived at, are justified, you have some basis for expecting listeners to respond favorably to your appeals to their good sense. In Aristotle's view, the logical proofs through which you appeal to that good sense and bring about belief consist of "examples [induction] and enthymemes [deduction] and nothing else."[2]

Bringing About Belief Through Examples

Separate-unit examples

We commonly think of an *example* as a separate item or unit that is like all other items or units in its class. An apple is like all other apples in some respects and, if we examine a number of them, we can arrive at some inferences (also called generalizations) about apples in general. We take water samples from a polluted lake and, when we have enough samples to be representative of that water, we draw a conclusion about the amount of pollution in that lake. We conduct a survey to find out how people feel about political candidates and, if the survey is carefully designed and administered, we announce voter preferences which people accept as accurate. Individuals, items, units, facts, statistics, and data of all kinds are typical of this class of examples.

One of the basic ways to reason is to put together a number of related examples and then, by the process of induction (i.e., by "bringing them forward" as evidence), to draw an inference which those examples seem to support.

For an illustration of the drawing of inferences from a set of examples, this time in the form of statistics, consider these figures:

> Voters who go to the polls declined from 62.8% in 1960 to 53.3% in 1984.
>
> In the 1980 election, an estimated 70% of those with incomes over $25,000 voted; only 25% with incomes below $10,000 went to the polls.
>
> 81% of those with college degrees marked the ballot, while 51% with only a grammar school education did the same.[3]

After satisfying ourselves that those statistics come from a reliable and unprejudiced source, we could draw inferences like the following:

> The percentage of eligible voters who vote has been declining.
>
> If those election figures hold for the future, the higher your income, the more likely you are to vote. Again, if those figures hold, the better your education, the more likely you are to vote.

One way to reason, then, is to use a given collection of facts, statistics, data, or single units of any kind in order to arrive inductively at one or more inferences which we hope our listeners will accept.

Extended examples

However useful the above kinds of separate items may be as the raw materials from which to draw conclusions, the unit Aristotle has in mind as basic to induction is the extended story-type example. In trying to predict the future, as he explains, we draw conclusions by comparing *extended examples* either (1) in the form of accounts of actual happenings or (2) in the form of stories that we make up to fit a given situation.[4]

If, for instance, something happened in the past under certain circumstances, we may expect it to happen again under the same or similar circumstances. In our looking at someone nominated for appointment to the Supreme Court, we may scrutinize "the story" of that person's past decisions and use them in trying to predict how she or he may rule on similar cases in the future. Accounts of what political candidates have done in the past are studied for indications of what those candidates might do in the future. Supporters of state lotteries describe the past successes of lotteries in other states. A bill advocating tighter reins on a government agency is debated from the standpoint of past experience with that agency's failure to operate within the law. Concerned citizens oppose a housing development along a river by calling attention to the ecological damage from a similar development in the past. During periods of economic recession over recent decades, the government has helped turn the economy around through spending money on public works and other projects; when the next recession occurs, we may reasonably expect the government to consider intervening again. In other words, we look at something that happened in the past and use it to explain what is happening now or what may happen in the future.

We also reason by showing relationships between or among "happenings" that are occurring now. Community decisions on whether or not to operate hostels for transients hinge on accounts of the experiences other communities are having with such hostels. For another illustration, it could be said that "Our city firemen are underpaid. Neighboring cities having essentially the same populations and resources as ours pay their firemen more. City A pays 10% more, City B 8% more, City C 12% more, City D 11% more. Therefore,...."

For the "made up" or invented type of extended example (as opposed to accounts of actual examples), a speaker could say that electing an inexperienced candidate for president would be like choosing an unskilled sailor to guide an oil tanker through treacherous waters.[5] (The "inexperienced candidate" could, of course, answer that experience doesn't mean much if the captain is asleep at the helm.) Invented examples can be colorful and, if used as a part of a broader argument, are acceptable to most audiences.

We have been discussing extended examples--also known as analogous examples --as being useful in explaining or predicting a happening by comparing it with a like situation which happened in the past or is happening in the present. An extended or analogous example with a special twist is called an analogy: it is an effort to show that, if two extended examples are alike in almost every known detail, they could be alike in still another detail known to be true of one but *not* known to be true of the other. For instance: The U.S. and Great Britain are alike in many ways. Britain has had some success in dealing with the problem of drug abuse. If the British drug-control system works there, perhaps a version of it could work here.

Speakers use extended or analogous examples (and their refined cousins, analogies) with care; the possibility always exists that listeners may see as many differences as likenesses in the situations described. In short, real or invented analogous examples, like their separate single-unit counterparts, lead to inferences. When the same inferences are presented to audiences for their consideration, some or all of the original examples which led *to* them may then be cited as backing *for* them.

One way to reason, then, is to reach conclusions inductively by bringing forward a representative number of separate-unit examples or by comparing extended incident or story-type examples.

Bringing About Belief Through "The Enthymeme Connection"

A second way to reason, commonly called deduction, differs from induction only in that your building blocks are now inferences or conclusions rather than examples of any kind. You put together a couple of related inferences or conclusions (either previously arrived at through induction or generally accepted as true), and you use the relationships between them as your license to arrive at still another conclusion. (In this text, *inference* and *conclusion* are used interchangeably and synonymously.)

For want of a better modern term, we use the classical word *enthymeme* to describe the kind of free-form deduction that all speakers use and all listeners expect. Enthymeme means and even sounds like "in the mind" and, by extension, means "bringing together or connecting in the mind." It's the word Aristotle uses for the *informal deductive* pattern of reasoning through which the speaker introduces--but does not fully state--the related inferences or conclusions which he or she is bringing together in order to arrive at another inference or conclusion. To put it another way, the speaker relies on the listeners to "bring to mind and connect" the related inferences or conclusions which, stated or left unsaid, are required to reach the conclusion proposed. By contrast, nothing is left to the listener's imagination in formal logic. There, you start with an accepted general statement (major premise), add a second statement (minor premise) in order to place what you are talking about within or outside the limits of that first statement, and then draw the unavoidable conclusion. You are familiar with this kind of syllogism:

All human beings are mortal.
Socrates is a human being.
Socrates is mortal.

In the perfect world of the syllogism and true premises (or premises accepted as true), there is no escape from the conclusion and no room for uncertainty. But in the uncertain world of rhetoric and the rhetorical enthymeme, speakers and audiences must work with premises and conclusions which are at best only probably true, and with some which are not even stated.

In support of a political candidate, for example, you could say, "Richards would make a good mayor because he has experience in public office." Your *unstated* first premise is broad and all-inclusive: "People who have experience in public office generally make good mayors." Your secondary or minor premise places Richards within that larger category: "Richards has experience in public office." Your conclusion --stated first instead of last--is "Richards would make a good mayor." To highlight the difference in forms:

Syllogism

People who have experience in public office make good mayors.
Richards has experience in public office.
Richards would make a good mayor.

Enthymeme

Richards would make a good mayor because he has experience in public office.

The enthymeme above telescopes three syllogistic statements, *none of them necessarily true*, into one sentence which, in this instance, begins with the conclusion.

In other words, the enthymeme is the result of doing "what comes naturally" in adapting the process of deduction to interpersonal and public communication. Listeners are expected to see and understand the relationships existing between stated and unstated premises or between premises and an unstated conclusion. Further, the stated elements are phrased informally and appear in no set order. Even when the conclusion in the sequence is stated first (as in the "Richards for mayor" example), listeners have no problem in seeing the relationships between or among the ideas. Very few listeners have ever heard about enthymemes, but they have no difficulty with interpreting the reasoning involved, especially when they hear cues like *because* (in the sentence about Richards), or like *so*, *since*, *consequently*, *in consequence*, *as a consequence*, *for the reason that*, *therefore*, *for*, *owing to*, *it follows*, *as a result*, *leads us to conclude*, *implies*, *indicates*, *shows*, and *strongly suggests*.

In modern times, speakers aren't alone in relying on "the listener" to complete a chain of thought. Advertisers and other promoters have extended the principle of the enthymeme by relying on the interplay of message and "visuals" to encourage readers, listeners, and viewers to reach unstated conclusions. For example, you see an ad featuring an attractive young woman displaying a small bottle of cologne designed for men. If you're a male, you're supposed to conclude that, if you buy and use that brand of cologne, your chances of dating an equally attractive young woman may improve. Or you find a TV commercial singing out that a particular cola is "the choice of the new generation" while at the same time showing celebrities partying with singers and dancers. The ideas brought together through message and lively imagery suggest that, if you want to belong to the "new generation," drinking that brand of soft-drink will help you become a member of (or retain your membership in) that select group. Advertisers know very well that they do not have to "spell out" a line of thinking to lead consumers to conclusions. Instead, they depend on consumers to make the necessary word-image connections and reach conclusions for which the commercials provide scarcely the hints.

In conversations, in discussions, in the public forum, and in the marketplace, then, you never hear the formal syllogism. With or without color, music, and song, what you do hear is the enthymeme, the informal deductive mode through which the speaker not only takes advantage of the listener's knowledge, experience, and beliefs but also enlists that listener as an active party to the communicative act.

In real life, the traditional distinction between induction and deduction tends to blur. In fact, you could say that all reasoning is inductive in the sense that we reason by going (1) from evidence to a conclusion and, at the next higher level, (2) from conclusions (presumably based on evidence and, therefore, themselves a form of evidence) to another conclusion. Be that as it may, we can agree that the materials going into reasoning are examples of all kinds on the one hand and, on the other, conclusions or inferences used as "premises" to reach another conclusion. The basic patterns are easy enough to understand:

example + example(s) = conclusion

and

conclusion + conclusion = conclusion

Recognizing the Strength of Common Premises

As you may have gathered from the earlier discussion of the enthymeme, a rhetorical premise is a belief-statement that you "send forth" to serve as the base for a conclusion. No discussion of rhetorical premises, stated or unstated, is complete without special emphasis on those held in common by the audience. Premises common to any society are, of course, those strong attitudes, values, and beliefs shared by most of the people in it or by specific audiences within that population. As Perelman says, "...all argumentation depends for its premises as indeed for its entire development--on that which is accepted [by the audience], that which is acknowledged as true, as normal and probable, as valid."[6] Whenever possible, therefore, the speaker should try to link reasoning to a common premise or premises (i.e., views, desires, or values) known to be cherished by the audience.[7] This is not to say that you should avoid taking a position contrary to one held by a given audience; it's to say that you must take that audience-held premise into account before and during your communicating with that audience. Instead of opposing that premise directly, it is often possible to move away, at least temporarily, from the contested premise to a higher level of uncontested common premise--like everyone's interest in "justice for all" or "the general welfare."

A list of common premises held by most of our citizens would include statements like these: America is the land of opportunity. Capitalism is superior to other economic systems. We must preserve the family farm. A good education is the key to success. No one can win a nuclear war. Wealth is no guarantee of happiness. We must win the war against drugs.

Other premises are held in common by specific groups. In reporting on Quaker schools in Philadelphia, Sue Chastain says, "Friends schools are known...for the way their lessons incorporate traditional Quaker values of sexual equality, pacifism, and egalitarianism."[8] Asking a Quaker audience to oppose a particular military policy would clearly be easier than making the same request of an American Legion Post.

Special Patterns of Reasoning

The few general headings below, distilled from longer classical lists,[9] are special approaches derived from the basic patterns and designed to give a speaker additional help in adapting logical appeals to a given audience.

Reasoning from cause and effect

The relationships among Aristotle's extended examples are based, as you noted, on comparing actual or invented situations that are close to being alike. In cause-related patterns of reasoning, we are still looking at comparable situations but we try to show a *direct tie* between their causes and effects:

1. Cause to effect (*known cause*, effect predicted).

   We see a cause and, knowing that it produced a certain effect in the past, we predict that it will produce much the same effect in the future.

   "*A country going progressively deeper into debt* is headed for economic collapse."

2. Effect to cause (*known effect*, cause assumed).

   We see an effect and, knowing that essentially the same effect was produced by a certain cause in the past, we infer that this particular effect was produced by essentially the same kind of cause.

   "*The pillars of the new bridge are cracked;* the construction must have been faulty."

3. Effect to effect (*known effect*, same or similar (effect assumed).

   We see an effect of a cause and infer that the same effect is likely to occur again whenever the same cause is again at work.

   "*High posts in government seem to go to Harvard graduates* more often that to the graduates of other institutions. Chances for appointment to a high post in government are enhanced if one has a degree from Harvard."

As with all inferences or conclusions, we have to be on guard against faulty reasoning. Are other causes contributing to the effects we observe? Are the causes observed strong enough to produce the claimed effects? If strong enough,were the circumstances so unusual that they will never occur again? Above all, will the listeners accept our interpretation of the cause-effect relationships and the conclusions we draw from them?

Reasoning by definition

Definitions set up the boundaries for the communication playing field; without them, confusion reigns. Defining may not be reasoning in the strictest sense, but "What are we talking about?" is a question you have to answer before any reasoning is possible. Consider this example of a failure to define:

> A conservative candidate touts the advantages of "liberal democratic capitalism," and his equally conservative audience wonders, "What's all this liberal democratic stuff?" Afterwards the candidate protests, "But I told them, 'liberal democratic--small l, small d!'" His campaign manager replies: "You know what you mean and I know what you mean, but these audiences don't know what you mean."[10]

For another example, you cannot promote "democracy" without letting your listeners in on the meaning of the word as you are using it and as you hope they will interpret it. Are you talking about a government in which the people make the decisions? Or about one in which elected representatives make the decisions? Or about the principle of equality of rights, treatment, and opportunity? Or about the "freedom to hold democratic elections"? It goes without saying that, before you start reasoning with an audience, the members of it must have a clear understanding of what it is you're reasoning about.

Reasoning by classification

Classifying is closely related to defining. It is possible, to define "a liberal" as one "who never met a social reform without liking it" and then, through reciting a politician's voting record, to show that she or he was, according to that definition, "a liberal." We could do the same with "a conservative." What must be remembered is that we are doing the defining and classifying, and that others may not readily accept our definitions and labels. But if you win audience acceptance of classifying something or somebody as belonging to a particular group or class, you have been reasoning by classification.

Reasoning by authority

We "reason by authority" only in the sense that our quoting of an expert in any field is based on the reputation that person has established in it. An authority is often cited as the source of or backing for something we say. More than ever before, we know more and more about less and less and, to a degree unknown in the past, we have to depend on the expertise of others. Individual listeners as well as audiences expect you to know what you are talking about, but it does not surprise them to hear you quote an authority in the field. In fact, quoting an authority can be counted upon to bolster almost any case. All you need do is be sure that the authority quoted, paraphrased, or mentioned...

1. is currently expert in the field.
2. knows the problem at hand.
3. has no vested interest in the solution.
4. has good sense, good reputation, good will.
5. is acceptable to the audience.

Weighing Probabilities

When all is said and done in discussing the principles and patterns of reasoning, we have to remember that the reasoning associated with logical appeals is based only on what is probable. In our past efforts to share information, gain consent to a proposal, or "win an argument," we have surely discovered that certainties are hard to come by. We may be sure about the accuracy of some facts. We can't be certain about our interpretation of those facts, about our analysis of problems, about the accuracy of our conclusions, or about the effectiveness of proposed solutions. We try instead to determine what is plausible or seemingly true, what is possible or capable of being true, what is probable or likely to be true. We resort to past and present knowledge and experiences in the effort to predict future outcomes ranging from what is hardly possible to what is more than likely to happen under a given set of circumstances. So it is that, in the discussion of public affairs, speakers and their listeners consider degrees of "likelihood," not of certainty. The best which speakers can hope for is that the conclusions they reach and the outcomes they predict are highly probable...and will be accepted as such by their listeners.

To illustrate: In early 1990, members of the U.S. Senate and the House of Representatives were debating whether or not to approve the President's request for authorization to use offensive force against Iraq in the Persian Gulf. Some argued that the President should be given that authorization; others argued that the economic sanctions then in place should be given more time to work. All members of Congress were basing their arguments on essentially the same bodies of political, economic, and military evidence, but they were sharply divided on the conclusions to be reached from that evidence and especially on those to be drawn about future probability, that is, about what would happen if the sanctions were continued for a time or what would happen if the President were given the authorization requested. To the listeners was left the problem of deciding which of the two positions made the better sense. Lane Cooper says, "People in actual life make their choices first, and then argue in accordance with those choices."[11] Maybe that was true in this instance. But it is equally true that many speakers make reasoned choices only after a thorough study of all available evidence. Nevertheless, we have to remember that those speakers may still arrive at different conclusions and at very different predictions about what is going to happen.

It follows that the convincing speaker is the one who best "weighs the probabilities"[12] and leads the listeners to believe that his or her vision of the future is more likely to come to pass than the future seen by somebody else. We see audiences weighing the probabilities presented to them every day. Competing engineering companies solicit contracts for construction projects, competing advertising agencies solicit product and service accounts, competing political groups make promises to voters. In every instance, listeners hear the speakers and make their own decisions about whose views on the probabilities make the best sense. Other things being equal, the most reasonable prediction wins the day.

Passing the Toulmin Test[13]

The reasoning processes in this chapter seem simple enough, but "jumping to conclusions" still occurs. Toulmin advises us to check our claims (his word for inferences or conclusions) against related warrants (his term for broad, generally accepted premises) and against possible intervening factors. In other words, as we see in the diagram, it's wise to scout the surroundings before staking your claim.

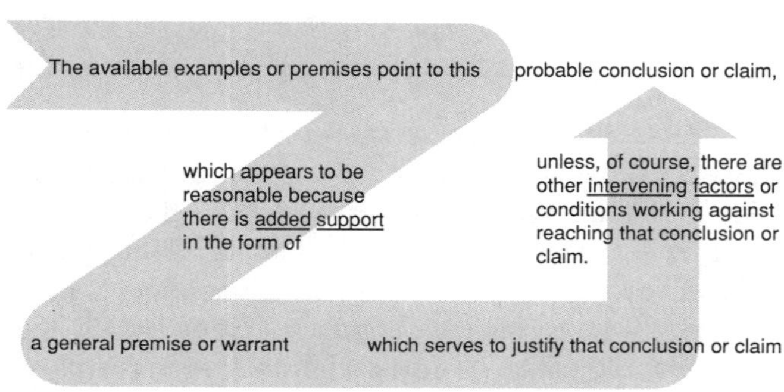

Let's see how this kind of checking works in practice. If the automobile companies have just raised their prices [evidence], the claim or conclusion that "Living costs will go up" makes sense only if you accept the following warrant or major-premise reason to believe it: "Rising prices for big ticket items lead to a rise in living costs." In turn, the broader general reason to believe it (i.e., the warrant) makes sense only if there are no intervening conditions standing in the way. So in spite of higher car prices, for example, the cost of living could go down in the face of significant intervening forces like bumper crops, more imports, a change in customer buying habits, greater competition between car makers, lower steel costs, lower fuel costs, etc., etc. In other words, as we construct arguments or as we listen to them, we should take a good look at the stated or unstated common premise which is supposed to provide the backing or "warrant" for any conclusion advanced. "Rising car prices mean higher living costs" only if you accept the idea that "Higher prices for big-ticket items mean higher living costs," and only if there are no other major factors affecting those costs. As Yogi Berra would say, "A conclusion ain't a conclusion until it concludes."

In summary, we have seen that collecting and interpreting examples of many kinds can lead to conclusions. We have also seen that premises (accepted statements, propositions, inferences, opinions, conclusions, generalizations, etc.), arranged in a variety of informal patterns can lead to conclusions. We have discussed the importance of taking common premises into account when trying to induce listener belief. We have outlined a few special patterns you will find useful in reasoning. We have noted that rhetoric and the forms of reasoning associated with it are concerned not with certainty but only with probability. We closed with the Toulmin test, a valuable check on reasoning.

Endnotes

1. Aristotle, *The "Art" of Rhetoric*, trans. John Henry Freese, Vol. 3 of Aristotle, Loeb Classical Library Series (Cambridge, MA: Harvard UP, 1982 rpt.), 1356a.

2. Aristotle, 1356a.

3. Curtis B. Gans, Committee for the Study of the American Electorate, as reported in *The Washington Spectator*, 13 (May 15, 1987), p. 2.

4. Aristotle, 1393a-94a.

5. Based on Aristotle, 1393b.

6. Chaim Perelman, *The Idea of Justice and the Problem of Argument*, trans. John Petrie (New York: Humanities Press, 1963), p. 156.

7. Values and standards of any culture provide the base for common premises in that culture. For one listing of American values and standards, see Chapter 13 of this text.

8. Sue Chastain, KNT News Service, in *The Orlando Sentinel* (February 28, 1987), p. D-11.

9. Aristotle, 1396b-1400b.

10. Political commentary by William Schneider, *The Atlantic Monthly*, 260 (July, 1987), p. 74.

11. Lane Cooper, [An expanded translation of] *The Rhetoric of Aristotle* (Englewood Cliffs, NJ: Prentice-Hall, 1960 rpt.), p. xxiii.

12. Based on Aristotle, 1355a.

13. Stephen Toulmin, *The Uses of Argument* (Cambridge, UK: Cambridge UP, 1958), Essay III. (Discussion, diagram, and the example of "living costs" are adapted from Toulmin's essay.)

Discussion Questions

1. What is reasoning?

2. We try to induce belief through *examples* and *enthymemes*. What traditional processes of reasoning do those two terms represent?

3. What is the difference between an example as an item of evidence and an extended example?

4. What is an actual or real analogous example as distinguished from one "made up" or invented? Give example.

5. What is the literal meaning of the word *enthymeme*? Is there a better term for describing the informal deductive chain we find in rhetoric?

6. What is a *common premise*? Of what importance is it in winning a favorable response from listeners? Must it be stated?

7. Why do we say that rhetoric is concerned with probabilities and likelihoods rather than with certainties?

8. In what way is defining a kind of reasoning? How do you arrive at a definition? What is one of the "essential properties" of a human being? What is one of the "nonessential properties" of a human being?

4

USING LANGUAGE RESOURCEFULLY

Language which does not convey a clear meaning fails to perform the very function of language.

Aristotle

Learning to use language intelligently begins by learning not to be used by language.

John C. Condon, Jr.

When you finish this chapter, you will be prepared to improve your use of language by...

1. Expressing your ideas clearly, by being direct and to the point, by using action words, and by using precise words.

2. Expressing your ideas appropriately by remembering where you are, by talking about shared experiences, and by using self-qualifiers.

3. Expressing your ideas colorfully by appealing to the senses, by "painting word pictures," by appealing to feeling, and by using repetitive word patterns.

4. Becoming sensitive to the perils and traps of slanting, meaningless generalities, stereotyping, sexism, all-or-none statements, name-dropping, and name-calling.

What do you suppose is the "clear meaning" of this sentence from the speech of a candidate for public office?

> It is absolutely essential to our hope for peace, stability, democracy, and better foreign policy to have a world that is growing and expanding with a tide that is rising, upon which all boats can rise, as opposed to this zero-sum, fiercely divisive Darwinian struggle in which nations are locked into mercantilistic practices and protectionistic policies that drive people apart, as opposed to bringing people together in a liberal democratic fashion as I think America was founded upon two hundred years ago.[1]

Aristotle would say that the candidate is "destroying clarity with a fog of verbiage."[2] He is failing to induce in the listener those clear-cut and concrete experiences which the listener can understand, visualize, and put to use in moving toward--or not moving toward--the goals proposed.

Ensuring Understanding and Interest

We know, of course, that we rely on words as basic conveyors of ideas. We know, too, that the meanings of the words we choose are "in the listeners" and that word meanings are further affected by the verbal, paraverbal, and nonverbal contexts surrounding them. But assuming that we are careful about the meanings listeners attach to words and about the contexts in which they appear, what can we do additionally to increase listener understanding and interest? Among ways to reach that goal is to make sure that our language is clear, appropriate, and colorful.[3]

Expressing ideas clearly

To borrow a phrase from the diplomats, we're talking here about "sending a clear message," one which the listeners will readily understand. Your message may be worthwhile but, if listeners don't understand it, you're wasting your time and that of everyone else in the room. From the standpoint of language only (and not from the clarity that stems from organization and other factors discussed in later chapters), what can you do to avoid "the verbiage fog"?

Be direct and to the point. When someone speaks in long and complicated sentences (like the political candidate quoted at the beginning of the chapter), the listener gets lost. It's good practice not only to speak in "listener language" but also to speak in fairly short sentences. You will find it easier to use shorter sentences and words common to your listeners if you make a habit of using as many personal pronouns as possible. It is difficult to be excessively formal when your messages are sprinkled with "you," "we," "I," "us," etc. Further, the use of personal pronouns automatically emphasizes the oneness with listeners that we all try to achieve.

From a Philadelphia speech by Lee Iacocca, automotive executive, here's an example of direct style:

> Everybody in this room knows all about Ben Franklin--or at least you think you do. Well, I knew there would be a lot of talk about him today [at a meeting of the Poor Richard Club], and I didn't want to get caught short, so I asked our research people to give me a hand. They've got a computer that taps into all kinds of resources, and one of them is the Encyclopaedia Britannica. They came up with an amazing discovery. When you say "Ben Franklin" to the computer, it spits out 73 different citations![4]

In Iacocca's approach, you have no lengthy sentences, no big words, and no formality. He uses the kind of familiar idiom that would fit almost any audience.

On the matter of speaking to the point, you're familiar with Abraham Lincoln's memorable address on the occasion of the dedication of the Gettysburg National Cemetery. Edward Everett, the main speaker of the day (November 19, 1863), held the crowd spellbound for two hours, but in a letter to Lincoln shortly afterwards, he said, "I should be glad to flatter myself that I came as near to the central idea of the occasion in two hours as you did in two minutes."[5]

Use action words. Your past experience as a listener tells you that it is more interesting to hear a speaker say "The governor vetoed the bill" than to hear "The bill was vetoed by the governor." The first sentence leaves no doubt about who did what to what; the listener visualizes a living human being in action. The second version is indirect and less appealing. (As you remember from your grammar, we're suggesting you use "the active voice" as often as possible.)

Use precise words. Words like "walk," " house," " street," "dog," " beautiful," and "good" are a part of everyone's vocabulary. However, commonly overused words like those are of little help in holding the attention of the listener. You increase listener interest by choosing words which indicate more precise shades or degrees of meaning. For instance, these are more descriptive ways to say "walk": saunter, hurry, stride, march, amble, tramp, tread, stroll, strut, swagger, limp, hobble, parade, shuffle, etc. Some alternatives to the other routine words at the beginning of the paragraph: mansion, shaded lane, terrier, striking, and excellent.

In short, it is a part of our nature to listen more attentively to speakers who take the time to phrase what they're saying in accurate and descriptive terms.

Expressing ideas appropriately

Remember where you are. The speaker at a graduation ceremony should not be telling off-color jokes (it happens!); it is just as much out of order for the speaker at a festive dinner to be too serious. Again according to Aristotle, "treat weighty matters weightily, light matters lightly, and be sure that the level of your language is the same as the audience expects from you."[6]

Talk about shared experiences. Business people like to hear illustrations about business activities. Professionals respond more readily to descriptions of happenings in their special fields. General audiences react favorably to the same approach; almost everyone has seen or been in a car accident, has experienced air travel delay or lost-baggage problems, and has had fortunate or vexing experiences with business and professional people. Students prefer "for instances" like the one in this commencement address:

> Zonker and Mark [Doonesbury characters] noticed a despondent student coming out of the library. Zonker asked, "What's the problem?" The student replied, "It's nothing anybody can do anything about. It's just that tomorrow I'm graduating and on Monday I'm assuming a position with the Chase Manhattan Bank." And Zonker says, "Hey man, I'm sorry."[7]

Avoid "the know-it-all syndrome." Listeners not only expect a speaker's language to fit the occasion but they also expect that individual to be appropriately restrained about his or her qualifications. You may know almost everything there is to know about a specific subject. However, no one is right all of the time, and even the experts make their share of mistakes. Listeners appreciate hearing a speaker use self-qualifiers such as *it seems to me*, *in my opinion*, *from where I sit*, *from my point of view*, *in my experience*, *although others think differently*, *the facts seem to indicate*, *apparently*, *it's my impression that*, *the evidence suggests*, *perhaps we can infer*, and so on. Threading a few well-placed self-qualifiers into a speech increases your "ethical appeal" with listeners; it's also fine insurance if your analysis of a situation or your predictions turn out to be wrong.

Expressing ideas colorfully

A third way to increase listener interest is to make a special effort to use vivid language wherever and however you can. Once you have pinned down the broad outline of any presentation, it's not all that difficult to take the time to enliven your remarks along these lines:

Appeal to the senses. Since we depend so heavily on our senses--sight, sound, touch, smell, and taste--to provide us with the experiences we find so valuable in life, it follows that the ability to recreate sensory experiences for listeners is a valuable asset in communicating with them. Mike Sanders, Western Oregon State College, shows he understands appeal to the senses in this short passage:

> Now I'd like to set a small scenario for you. You're driving down the road and freeway in the rain, you're going to make a left hand turn lane, so you turn your signal on and look in the mirror and all you can see is a bunch of water, I mean, there's a car back there, but there's water all over the window, and you're not sure how far back it is, but your turn is coming up, so you got to do it sooner or later. So you do one of two things; either you assume or think that that car is back there far enough to make a safe lane change, or you roll the window down and stick your head out there in all that water and be sure. But you know, if you have a coat of Rain-X [rain repellent] on the outside mirror and on the window, you never have to make that decision again....[8]

The quotation below, from a speech by Brenda Dempsey, Eastern Michigan University, is another which takes advantage of the everyday common ground we share with listeners:

> When Denise Waddle and her family moved to a nice, middle-class section of Jersey City, New Jersey, they had dreams of healthy living, block parties, even a big back yard so their kid could make mud pies. In less than one year in their new home, their two year old son had been poisoned, and their newborn showed high levels of poisoning in his bloodstream. Unknowingly, the Waddles had been poisoned by their own back yard, for high levels of lead contaminated their water...and their lives.[9]

Paint word pictures. You can "see" what Jay Lane of Utah State College is talking about in this excerpt:

> According to Ian Fielding in his book entitled *Dust*, there are about two million of these dust mites in every twin-sized bed. Kind of

> makes you want to wrap your body in Saran Wrap, doesn't it? Well, that was the response of Mrs. Mosier [writer of an article on dust], but don't worry. Even after finding all this out, she, her husband, and their two million tiny pets have learned to share the bed just fine. Of course, that was before she found out her air conditioner had gangrene.[10]

Say it with feeling. Early in Chapter 13, you will find a detailed discussion on "emotional appeal," that component of adaptation to the audience which, with ethical and logical appeal, is a part of every presentation a speaker makes. Here, however, we simply make the point that listeners react with sympathy and understanding when the speaker is saying something with genuine feeling. For example, the short saying-it-with-feeling passage below is from a talk by Shelley Schnathorst, University of Northern Iowa:

> Failure to develop standards, reliance on an equivalent standard instead, and finally incomplete reporting all combine to create inadequate protection [of consumers by the FDA]. It is a protection which Tama and James Jackson wish they had had when their firstborn baby, a baby boy, developed jaundice. The baby was placed in an illuminated hosplital incubator which rid the child's body of the yellow coloration. The next day the incubator was empty. Their baby was found in intensive care with a fever of 106 degrees. The next morning, the Jacksons' firstborn died. The cause of death, the incubator. With a broken thermometer and alarm and a defective on-off switch, the incubator literally became an oven. To prevent such horrors, immediate action needs to be taken."[11]

Use repetitive patterns. At some point in working on a presentation, especially one dealing with a serious subject (e.g., solving a problem, changing an attitude), you may see an opportunity to add emphasis to an important passage by using a repetitive, rhythmic pattern. Inserted sparingly to highlight specific ideas, this pattern can be very effective. Three examples...

> "Golf can be the sport that ruins dreams. *The only bruises* in golf are to the spirit. *The only bones* that break are those in the skeleton of the personality. *The only blood* that flows is from a sort of internal hemorrhaging of self-esteem."[12]

> The employees of the park are chosen with care. They all have to *look the same*, *smile the same*, *dress the same*, and *act the same*.

> "*Let us march* to the realization of the American dream. *Let us march* on segregated housing. *Let us march* on segregated schools. *Let us march* on poverty...."[13]

Similarly, a series of questions beginning with "How long" or "Why" or "When" are used to advantage in many a presentation.

In fact, the better speakers seem to see the need for one or more repetitive series in every speech they give. These series give a special emphasis to particular passages, and they offer another lively path to listener interest.

Identifying Perils of Language

Enhancing listener understanding and interest through choices of language will do us no good if, at the same time, listeners perceive us to be so eager to score that we stoop to some questionable tactics. Times haven't changed; as Aristotle said in his *Rhetoric*, "people become suspicious of anyone who, they believe, is laying a trap for them."[14] So to avoid any hint of conniving or deception, the speaker-in-training is well-advised to be sensitive to hazards like those described below.

Be sensitive to slanting

At some time or other, almost every speaker faces the temptation to slant. Slanting is "stacking the cards" in one's favor by concealing opposing evidence and views. If you are not convinced that slanting is "a part of life," you have only to read the coverage of some controversial issue in any two competing newspapers or news magazines. As you read, underline the adjectives and adverbs and note the choices of words in general. You'll find that descriptions of the same controversy are often slanted to favor the positions held by specific writers, editors, owners, publishers, and other "opinion leaders." The same kind of slanting occurs in conversations, discussions, and speeches. Instead of slanting, our goal as responsible speakers should be straightforward communication; those who discount the intelligence of listeners are asking only for disaster.

You are aware, too, that some of the "factual news" you hear and read consists of releases which contain only what the releasers want you to hear and read. On either the public or private scene, information or disinformation (nice word!) may be selectively leaked, censored, rumored, managed, withheld, exaggerated, simulated, distorted, glossed over, and otherwise "interpreted" for the listeners. As those hired or required to fashion opinion know, it is possible to manipulate the views of listeners by carefully packaging the information offered to them.

When you speak, your listeners should never be given reason to feel that you're doling out only the information you want them to have and withholding the rest. They have the right to expect you and any other speaker to provide them with all the facts bearing on an issue.

Be sensitive to meaningless generalities

When you use an abstract term in a talk, (e.g., honesty, patriotism, peace, prosperity), move down the line to specific examples as quickly as you can. Charley Reese, a syndicated columnist offers this illustration of what happens to communication when a person uses an abstract term with no intention of ever getting down to particulars:

> When a politician tells you that we must do this or that in, for example, the Sudan to "protect American interests," he or she is using a high level of abstraction to avoid real communication.
>
> American interests? What are they? Does the politician mean there are Americans living over there? Does he mean we have a military base over there? Does she mean some corporation has a business there? Just what are "American interests" in the Sudan?
>
> Communication designed to block communication is a disturbing Orwellian trend in our society. One way to fight it is to insist on keeping language as specific as possible.[15]

Be sensitive to stereotyping

Stereotyping is the assumption that all individuals in a particular group fall into a "standard mold" (Greek *stereos* + *typos*). If a speaker says, "People in the inner-city don't want to work," she or he is guilty of stereotyping. The speaker who says politicians are skilled only in winning elections is similarly at fault. Stereotypes are convenient classification baskets--all native Americans are the same, so they go in this basket; all New Yorkers are the same, so they go in that one--and so on for instructors, activists, construction workers, stock brokers, Republicans, Orientals, the clergy, agnostics, fundamentalists, Democrats, farmers, Southerners, cab drivers, *et al.* As we speak or as we listen to speakers, we have to remind ourselves that what many regard as true of a group may not be true of individuals in it...and may not even be true of the group.

Be sensitive to sexism

Sexism is a form of stereotyping that deserves separate mention. "Broadly defined, sexist communication precasts either males or females into roles on the basis of sex alone."[16] For example, some people still use terms like policeman (for police officer), female engineer (for engineer), fireman (for fire fighter), poetess (for poet), postman (for postal worker), male nurse (for nurse), workman (for worker), freshman (for first-year student), and brotherhood of man (for human family). The pronouns are another problem; many speakers continue to use "he" as an impersonal and so-called neutral word, although "she" is entitled to and should get equal billing. One solution is to use the two words alternately; another is to substitute plural subjects (e.g., people, farmers, politicians) and the plural pronouns that go with them (e.g., they) Wherever you see or hear "man" or "woman" or other words in a context which discriminates against the opposite sex, make a mental note to avoid that kind of sexist discrimination in your own usage. "A basic rule for good communication involves analyzing the audience. Therefore, wise communicators understand and apply the knowledge that many people, both females and males, react negatively to sexist communication."[17]

Be sensitive to all-or-none statements

We should try to inoculate ourselves against the all-or-none disease. Any individual who seldom sees the "greys" and the in-betweens is guilty of careless thinking and, for that reason, we certainly expect the responsible speaker to be careful enough to qualify *all* or *none* with words like *ordinarily*, *normally*, *usually*, *sometimes*, *few*, *almost*, *some*, *quite*, and so on. Both as speakers and as listeners, we should also qualify words like *everybody*, *nobody*, *always*, *never*, and *constantly*. There is a time and place for all-or-none words and statements (e.g., "All men and women are created equal"), but the sensitive speaker is cautious in the use of them.

Be sensitive to name-dropping

This "bad habit" involves the naming of respected persons or organizations in such a way as to imply their support or approval. The leader of a government may say that some world figure (e.g., the Pope) supports his or her policy toward another country; a day later, the other figure denies any such support. Closer to home, it is not uncommon to read a letter to the newspaper editor protesting the use without permission of the writer's name in support of someone else's position. Some speakers follow the same practice; without permission of any kind, they cite backing from individuals and organizations. Their deception is exposed only if the "endorsers" protest. In any event, the ethical speaker (you) avoids claiming backing which does not exist.

Be sensitive to name-calling

In any presentation you make, it's unlikely that you'll be calling anybody names. Still, in the heat of the fray, speakers have been known to forget some of the rules. Name-calling is a tactic through which a speaker sometimes tries to side-track the listener's attention by an attack on an opponent's character or motives. For one example, when supporters of a defense appropriations bill resort to calling their opponents "weak on patriotism," you have some reason to think that it's really the argument for the measure that's weak. In other words, to hide a weak case and inflame passions at the same time, some speakers find it easier to call those who oppose them names like agitators, leftists, rightists, activists, do nothings, liberals, conservatives, fanatics, weirdos, extremists, militants, and other terms not fit to print. If your argument is sound, stooping to name-calling can only weaken it...and detract from your own reputation at the same time.

> Urging you to use language interestingly and sensitively places no real burden on your speaking or writing. We know that "watching our language" is one way to sharpen it and, at the same time, avoid our falling into its pitfalls. Still, the suggestions offered here (expressing ideas clearly, appropriately, and colorfully), practical in themselves, will also serve to remind you of other ways to be interesting and pitfall-sensitive too. And when you're preparing a presentation, it does no harm to have an English grammar close by along with a copy of Roget's *Thesaurus* or its computer equivalent.

Endnotes

1. According to William Schneider's political campaign report in *The Atlantic Monthly*, 264 (July, 1987) 7, p. 74.

2. Aristotle, *The "Art" of Rhetoric*, trans. John Henry Freese, Vol. 3 of Aristotle, Loeb Classical Library Series (Cambridge, MA: Harvard UP, 1982 rpt.), 1486a.

3. Aristotle, 1403b-1414a.

4. Lee Iacocca, "We're Taxing Our Own Kids," *Vital Speeches of the Day,* 51 (March 15, 1985) 11, p. 143.

5. From Gary Wills, "Lincoln: The Power of Words in Time of War," *Life Magazine*, 14 (February, 1991) 2, p. 24.

6. Aristotle, 1408a.

7. Win Borden, "Recommendations for Graduates," *Vital Speeches of the Day*, 51 (April 15, 1985) 13, p. 401.

8. Excerpt from *Championship Debates and Speeches* (Normal, IL: Illinois State U Printing Services, 1988), p. 117.

9. Excerpt from same series as above, 1988 edition, p. 144.

10. Excerpt from 1987 edition, p. 119.

11. Excerpt from 1988 edition, p. 113 f.

12. From a Russ White review of Tom Boswell, *Strokes of Genius* (New York: Doubleday, 1987).

13. Excerpt from a speech by Martin Luther King, Jr., as quoted in Edward J. Corbett, *Classical Rhetoric for the Modern Student*, 2nd ed. (New York: Oxford UP, 1971), p. 472.

14, Aristotle, 1404b.

15. Charley Reese, syndicated column on "Give Cold Shoulder to Officials Who Snow You with Abstractions," *The Orlando Sentinel*, August 29, 1986.

16. Bobbye D. Sorrells, *The Nonsexist Communicator* (Englewood Cliffs, NJ: Prentice-Hall, 1983), p. 1. The examples following the quotation are mostly from Sorrells.

17. Sorrells, p. 3.

Discussion Questions

1. Under *Expressing ideas appropriately*, we use a "Zonker and Mark" example because it seems to fit our student readers. Does it? If not, what kind of example would be more appealing to students?

2. In the short excerpt from Mike Zander's presentation, to how many different senses does he appeal? To how many does Brenda Dempsey appeal? Is the language in each instance the sort that would appeal to college and university students?

3. Shelley Schnathorst appeals to feeling in the account of the jaundiced baby. Are there any improvements you would suggest in her word choices? Would these improvements necessarily be better choices for everyone else in the class?

4. What do you think of the practice of "slanting" through withholding evidence that would be damaging to a case? Is it ever justified? Under what circumstances? What happens when people find out that "they have been had"?

5. Is it possible to be guilty of stereotyping without being aware of it? Are you inclined to fit people into broad classifications or groups? What are the dangers in doing so?

6. On the use of self-qualifiers in a presentation, isn't it a weakness to admit that you could be wrong? Or that the evidence you present isn't absolutely leak-proof? Benjamin Franklin used to say that the way to convince others is to state your case accurately and fairly, and then shake your head and say that that is the way it seems to you, but that, of course, you could be mistaken. What do you think of that approach?

7. Can you cite any allness statements which you commonly hear? Will your talking about them help to eliminate them? If you do eliminate them, what benefits do you stand to gain?

Application Projects

1. Find a paragraph or two (like the Lee Iacocca example) which seem to you to be expressed in a clear, direct style. The source may be the report of a speech, a letter to the editor, a selection from a magazine article, etc. Be prepared to read it to the class and point out the characteristics that make it direct and to the point.

2. Or find a paragraph or two which are the opposite of being clear. Read the passage to the class and point out why it is not clear.

3. Or find a similarly short passage which is not clear, read it to the class, and then read the new and direct-style version that you have written to replace of the same passage.

Additional Activities

1. To become more aware of the use by able speakers of repetitive word patterns, check an issue of *Vital Speeches of the Day* (or any other collection of speeches) for the purpose of locating and reading to the class one example of a speaker's using repetitive patterns.

2. To become more aware of sexism in language patterns, read to the class a printed example (e.g., textbook, pamphlet, brochure, news release, company policy statement, company travel rules) in which the pronoun "he" is used exclusively in reference to the individual male or female. Or read to the class an example which features a fine balance between uses of "he" and "she" in reference to individuals.

Photo courtesy Rollins College, Winter Park, Florida.

5

LISTENING RESPONSIBLY

Without an audience composed of effective listeners, no productive communication would exist.[1]

Whatever profession we choose, the most important thing we can develop along the way is listening.

Fred Rogers

When you finish this chapter, you should be aware that...

1. Speakers and listeners share responsibility for the success of communication.

2. We spend more time listening than we do speaking, but we often don't listen very well.

3. Listening *actively* takes effort but benefits both the listener and the speaker.

4. Listening *analytically* enables you to evaluate the speaker's message in terms of its advantages or disadvantages.

5. Listening *defensively* helps you cope with those who would use communication to mislead or deceive.

If your earlier years were anything like those of the average youngster, your parents and teachers spent some of their time asking these questions: "Do you hear me?!!" or "Are you listening?!!" And perhaps, when you were older, you began to wonder if your parents and teachers heard *you*.

Listening is something we tend to wish others would do more of, but the truth is that we all need to improve our listening skills.

The individual who doesn't listen well is at a distinct disadvantage. Take note of these typical answers to the question, "What can I get out of better listening?"[2]

> "A lot of things I'd rather not hear."
>
> "And maybe the knowledge that those things I'd rather not hear aren't so bad after all."
>
> "On the other hand, that maybe they were worse than I thought."
>
> "A more accurate view of myself and the way I affect others."
>
> "A chance to learn more."
>
> "Better communication."
>
> "Speakers who do better because I'm really listening."
>
> "A better understanding of the things I talk about."
>
> "I don't know--I've never listened very carefully."

In classical times, the answers would have been much the same. Aristotle notes the speaker's concern about inducing listeners to be well-disposed, attentive, and receptive.[3] Cicero and Quintilian mention the same problems and goals.[4] Theorists of all periods stress the need to bring listeners "into the proper frame of mind" to heed the speaker's message, and their main concern is to help the speaker adapt that message to the audience. It is only in our own day, however, that we have come to study what listening is, how much listening we do, how poorly or how well we listen, and how important it is to listen actively, analytically and, sometimes, self-defensively.

What Is Listening?

The popular understanding of listening is that it is a conscious effort to pay attention to sounds. However, as we learned in studying the process of communication in Chapter 1, listening is much more than making the effort to pay attention to sounds. To us, listening is a key element in the communication process, one in which messages are continuously passing back and forth between the communicators and, in public speaking, between speakers and their audiences.

We see listening as that part of the process in which the listener receives and assigns meaning to all incoming messages: verbal, paraverbal, nonverbal, and any other meaning-affecting influences. So listening is more than what comes in through the ears; it is also the way through which we also give meaning to what *see* and *sense*. (In the total interaction, as you already know, a listener "speaks" as she or he listens, and a speaker "listens" as he or she speaks.)

How much listening do we do?

Steil, Barker, and Watson cite a study indicating that, as a student, you probably spend more than half of your communication time in listening (about 32% listening to people and about 21% listening to television, radio, and other forms of mass communication). According to the same study, students spend 16% of their communication time in speaking, 14% in writing, and 17% in reading.[5] In other words, you do far more listening than you do speaking or communicating in some other way.

In the business world, Wolvin and Coakley point out that, since people may be engaged in listening up to 63% of their workday, "one can see that they are being paid up to 63% of their salaries for listening."[6] If, for example, you become a manager, supervisor, or salesperson, you will likely be engaged in listening for at least 50% of your working day. The percentage goes higher for doctors, psychiatrists, lawyers, counselors, and other professionals who deal directly with individuals--they often spend as much as 80 to 85% of their working time in listening.[7] Whatever you do in life, chances are you're going to be doing considerably more listening than speaking.

How well do we listen?

Not very well. After noting that, in this country, we teach writing most, reading next, speaking next, and listening least, Steil, Barker, and Watson are critical (1983) of an educational system that places so little emphasis on the kind of communication we engage in most often:

> Our hit-or-miss educational system is not working. Research shows that most of us...need improvement [in listening]. Much of what is heard is not remembered. Over 30 years of research clearly indicates that we listen at approximately 25% effectiveness and efficiency (Dietze and Jones, 1931, Steil, 1975). In other words, on average, we deal productively with about 1/4 of what we listen to!
>
> Think for a moment about the communication breakdowns you have experienced.... Listening mistakes cost time, money, human relationships, psychological and physical pain, lawsuits and more.[8]

Referring to public speaking, Nichols and Stevens comment:

> A person who frequently makes public speeches soon becomes deeply impressed with an important fact: People in general do not know how to listen. They may come to hear you speak, but they are not necessarily good listeners. The burden of making people listen has always been thrown almost entirely upon the speaker. ...the speaker soon learns that he must engage in an everlasting courtship of his listeners if he wants to be heard.[9]

In other words, we don't listen well. For the "good news," however, we have come a long way toward recognizing that speaker and listener share accountability for the success or failure of communication. We know, too, that we can improve our listening through (1) *listening actively*, (2) *listening analytically*, and (3) *listening defensively*. Each of those three aspects of listening is important enough to warrant a separate, mini-chapter treatment in the pages which follow.

Listening Actively

Active listeners

1. Cooperate with the speaker by ignoring distractions and making the conscious decision to listen.

2. Show interest in both the content of the message and in the speaker as a person.

3. Keep an open mind; try to see things from the speaker's perspective.

4. Regard listening as a learning experience, the opportunity to add to one's education.

5. See in the speaker's presentational techniques the occasion for taking stock and improving one's own techniques.

Listening actively is more that just sitting back and waiting for an individual or speaker to make us "well-disposed, attentive, and receptive." After all, if we want others to listen to us, the least we can do is make a real effort to listen to them. More than that, listening is "working actively to solve problems of meaning...by purposefully putting together what we have known or experienced with what we perceive of the message, the speaker, and the occasion."[10]

In later meetings of this class, for instance, students will be asking you to accept or support their ideas on a variety of subjects. As you sit among the listeners, you will have several options: listening to the speakers and cooperating with them in "solving problems of meaning," or looking out the window, or surveying and appraising other members of the class, or giving the appearance of listening while studying for another course, or silently rehearsing in preparation for your turn to speak, or thinking about a party you enjoyed, or planning the next one, or trying to solve a personal problem, etc. The first of those listening options offers you solid advantages over the others. Listening actively to a speaker can make you a more sensitive human being, can contribute to your education, and can make you a better speaker.

Listening actively makes you a better listener

One of the best compliments you can pay a person is to say, "She's a good listener" or "He goes out of his way to hear me out." You appreciate someone's being truly sensitive to your ideas and feelings, someone's saying "I know how you feel." In other words, a good listener is willing to set aside his or her problems in a sincere effort to see and feel from the speaker's perspective. A listener's concern encourages you to speak freely and, if you show some of the same concern in return, communication between you flows easily and naturally.

The same rules hold when you are listening to the public speaker. In Chapter 3, you will recall, "becoming one with the audience" is cited as a general aim for all speakers. In return, as a listener, you should be willing to put yourself "in the speaker's shoes"--that is, to think and "feel with" the speaker in his or her effort to communicate with you. You may have some questions or doubts about the speaker's motives, but that individual deserves your encouragement as long as she or he seems to you to be making an honest attempt to relate to you in a constructive way. Encouraging the speaker requires that, for the time being at least, you suspend your own views and judgments. It requires in the tradition of fair play that you listen to the person who "has the floor." We are all in this daily struggle together and, speaking or listening, we need support. Your listening attentively tells a speaker that you accept him as he is, that you respect her rights to express ideas, and that you are treating either individual as you would want to be treated under similar circumstances. Speakers are like the rest of us--they communicate more comfortably and efficiently with audiences they perceive to be sensitive and cooperative in turn.

Listening actively adds to your education

It stands to reason that speakers, in class sessions or outside them, have things to say that will broaden your education. In the effort to adapt messages to audiences, speakers work hard to include facts, figures, and examples that their audiences will readily understand; it is almost impossible to listen to a speaker without learning something you did not know before. Further, if you have an "open mind," you will leave many a class session with some questioning of your ways of thinking, some changes in your attitudes and beliefs. And no matter how you feel about certain issues, exposure to the views of others cannot but have an effect on your ways of thinking. The grade you earn in the course may be some measure of your speaking/listening effort in the eyes of the instructor; there is no measure of the personal growth and general-education level you can reach by listening actively to a series of speakers.

Listening actively can make you a better speaker

While you're listening to encourage the speaker and to learn as much as you can, you can also find ways to improve your own communicating. You can see, for example, how a speaker adapts to an audience, and thereby add to your own skills in doing so. You can note how a speaker "talks your language," and learn to tailor your choices of words and phrasing to fit a particular audience. You will notice that one student uses gestures that you would feel comfortable with in your own speaking, and that another's visual aids are of a type that you could use--well designed and easy to see. One student's organization is simple and clear, another's seems to be needlessly complex. One quickly establishes contact with the audience, another seems to be in a another world. In the passing parade of approaches and techniques, there will be some which you will recognize as being "yours" and others as being readily adaptable to your own speaking needs.

Listening Analytically

Analytical listeners

1. Recognize when a speaker is trying to win them over to a particular point of view or course of action.

2. Assess the speaker's motives to determine what interest the speaker has in taking up this subject with this audience.

3. Assess the extent to which the speaker shares or respects the basic assumptions and values held by the audience.

4. Assess the speaker's reasoning to determine the strength, accuracy, and fairness of the speaker's case.

5. Assess the extent to which the speaker shows good will and a commitment to the needs and interests of the audience.

6. Consider the total message, including the speaker's expertise and reputation, before accepting it as believable.

When you listen to a speaker who is trying to win you over to a way of thinking or to a proposal for action, you will want to extend your active listening to include analysis of the speaker's case. You don't want to be too skeptical, but you do want to evaluate the information or the position advanced. The headings and questions below[11] offer a basic plan for your listening analytically:

Perceived intent

Why is he talking in this way? What is her purpose? What seem to be his motives? Is she concerned about what happens to us or about what happens to her? Does he understand our needs and goals? To which of our needs or goals is she appealing? Are they within reach? What do we have in common with the speaker or he with us? Is she trying to "become one with us" for our benefit or for hers?

Perceived strength of position

Is there enough evidence for the conclusions reached? If the evidence is weak, does the speaker seem to be aware of that fact? When figures are cited, does he give us the source of those figures? Is there any mention of upward or downward trends? If she says that certain causes led to a present problem, does she really show that those causes are directly related to the problem? And that no other causes had anything to do with it? When comparisons are made, do they deal with similar things? Or with "apples and oranges"? Does the total argument make good sense? Does the speaker feel strongly that the proposal being made is in our common interest?

Perceived credibility

Is the speaker believable? Does she appear to be well informed? Are his facts and figures current? Does she tell us what her sources are? Does his background qualify him as expert in this area? Is she ignoring contrary evidence and argument? Does he admit that he may not know all the answers? Does she have a reputation for "telling it like it is"? Can we trust the speaker's judgment?

A question-and-answer period often gives you the opportunity to ask one or two direct questions about matters of interest to you. With or without questioning, it is reasonable to check the details of a speaker's proposal or argument.

Listening Defensively

> ***Defensive listeners***
>
> l. Scrutinize a speaker's message to detect those forms of demagoguery seen in slanting, sterotyping, and similar traps.
>
> 2. Scrutinize a speaker's message for a lack of information, for misinformation, or for intentional disinformation.
>
> 3. Question a speaker's sales message to separate fact from fiction.
>
> 4. Question a speaker's ideas to determine the extent to which they are actually supported by the evidence.

In Chapter 4, you will recall, we described some of the traps (slanting, stereotyping, etc.) awaiting the unwary speaker. As a listener, you will sometimes find it necessary to add a third listening mode, that of listening defensively, in order to prevent a speaker's leading you into those same traps, either because the speaker is unaware of them or, more likely, because the speaker knows exactly what he or she is doing.

Over and above the more easily defined traps already described, what the irresponsible speaker can do to mislead or deceive the listener takes many forms: flattery, intimidation, insinuation, inaccurate description, omission of negative evidence, distortion of reports, lifting words out of context to make a quotation say something different from the author's intent, suggestions of misconduct without proof, defamation, demagoguery--you name it, the unethical speaker does it.

You can just about sense when you have to "go on the defensive." The first outright misstatement or distortion you hear alerts you to the fact that you had better be on your guard. And one who then begins to listen defensively is better able to screen fact from fiction, appraisal from libel, argument from fallacy, idealism from opportunism; in short, that kind of listener is better able to contend with the unscrupulous speaker (as well as with the rising flood of misinformation we have to contend with from other sources). Listening in self-defense is not a retreat from the active and analytical modes we advocated in the preceding sections of this chapter. Rather, it is recognition that there are times, no matter how cooperatively you're listening, when you will be forced into (1) prudent questioning of "sales messages" and (2) prudent questioning of "idea messages."

Questioning of sales messages

In one of the speech transcripts at the end of Chapter 11, a student is selling the advantages of a personal computer. In another from the same set of speeches (but not included in this text), a student promotes a compact disc interactive system. Both talks are straightforward descriptions of unit characteristics accompanied by honest evaluations of the benefits available to the potential buyer.

At the other end of the continuum, you have the purveyors of "snake oil." You learn to listen with questions when, for example, the sports celebrity is endorsing cereal or any other product. Sales in stores may be legitimate efforts to clear shelves of dated stock, but some "sales" give you the privilege of paying higher rather than lower prices. Some television commercials are done in good taste, but others assume that the watcher-listener has no sense at all. The point to remember is that the seller, speaking through an ad or directly to one or more listeners, has the advantage of "holding the floor." Your responsibility is not to let that speaker keep you from seeing the difference between fact and fiction.

Questioning of idea messages

Listen just as critically when some official is making a public statement or trying to sell you an idea. When a representative of some political persuasion or party appears on or near your campus, he or she may make claims that seem farfetched to you. When that speaker pauses for breath, questions like these are reasonable: "What is your evidence for that statement?" "Can you cite any facts to back up that conclusion?" "Isn't that claim only an opinion?" You'll discover that the right question at the right time will often bring such people up short. If they have little or no basis for what they are saying, you will be doing yourself and other listeners a service by uncovering that fact.

In this chapter, we point out that *listening actively* can make you a more sensitive person, can add to your education, and can make you a better speaker--all advantages you can't afford to pass up if you are serious about your future. We also suggest your *listening analytically* when someone seeks your acceptance of information, agreement on issues, or assent to a change in views. We closed with comments on the occasional need for *listening defensively*. In short, for the benefit of others and of yourself, give more than just a casual hearing to those with whom you are communicating![12] As a listener, you are a party to every step in the communication process and, speaking or listening, you hold responsibility for making your own unique contribution to it.

Endnotes

1. Lyman K. Steil, Larry L. Barker, and Kittie W. Watson, *Effective Listening: Key to Your Success* (Reading, MA: Addison-Wesley, 1983), p. 18.

2. Answers selected and edited from Thomas I. Anastasi, Jr., and Sidney A. Dimond, *Listening on the Job* (Reading, MA: Addison-Wesley, 1972), p. 10.

3. Aristotle, *The "Art" of Rhetoric*, trans. John Henry Freese, Vol. 3 of Aristotle, Loeb Series (Cambridge, MA: Harvard UP, 1982 rpt.), 1415a.

4. Cicero, *De inventione*, trans. H. M. Hubbell, Vol. 2 of Cicero, Loeb Classical Library Series (Cambridge, MA: Harvard UP, 1976 rpt.), i. 14. 20. Quintilian, *Institutio Oratoria*, trans. H. E. Butler, Vol. 2 of Quintilian, Loeb Series (Cambridge, MA: Harvard UP, 1977 rpt.), iv. 1. 51.

5. Steil et al., p. 3.

6. Andrew D. Wolvin and Carolyn Gwynn Coakley, *Listening*, 2nd ed. (Dubuque, IA: Wm. C. Brown, 1985), p. 8.

7. Anastasi and Dimond, p. 8.

8. Steil et al., p. 37.

9. Ralph G. Nichols and Leonard A. Stevens, *Are You Listening?* (New York: McGraw-Hill, 1957), p. 30.

10. A freely edited quotation from Paul D. Holtzman, *The Psychology of Speakers' Audiences* (Glenview, IL: Scott, Foresman, 1970), p. 18.

11. Categories and questions based on or suggested by Holtzman, pp. 43-48.

12. For additional listings of guidelines for and the rewards of listening, see Steil et al. (note 1 above), pp. 72-75; Wolvin and Coakley (note 6), pp. 13-17; and Nichols and Stevens (note 9), pp. 17-32. If you wish to read further about listening, the Wolvin/Coakley book has a very useful bibliography (p. 237 f.).

Discussion Questions

1. Do you know any "good listeners"? Why do you place them in that group?

2. What do you do for someone's self-esteem when you listen carefully to what she or he is saying? What happens if you half-listen or do not listen at all?

3. When members of an audience listen actively, they help the speaker interact with them. Can you recall an instance in which the listeners seemed to help the speaker interact with them? Or one in which a general failure to listen made the occasion an unhappy event for all concerned?

4. Have you ever tried looking upon a dull speaking event as a chance to gain information? Can you give an example of your profiting from that approach?

5. Have you done much analytical listening? Under what circumstances? With what results? Why is the word *perceived* used in a heading like "Perceived intent"?

6. Have you ever noticed a speaker's using one or more "tricks" or propaganda devices. What effect did your having to listen self-defensively have on your opinion of the speaker?

Application Projects

1. Attend a public meeting (on or off campus) at which the speaker presents a lecture or proposal. Prepare a 2-3 minute oral report on your experience in *listening actively*. Did the speaker seem to be encouraged by your interest? By that of others in the audience? What gains did you make in new information? Or in noting ways of doing things which you could use in your own speaking?

2. Attend a public meeting (on or off campus) in which the speaker's aim is to induce support for a point of view or course of action. Prepare a 2-3 minute oral report on your experience in *listening analytically*.

3. Attend a public meeting (on or off campus) in which, regardless of the intent of the speaker to speak responsibly or irresponsibly, your aim is to be *listening defensively*. Prepare a 2-3 minute oral report on the success or failure of your detective work.

Additional Activities

1. Practicing active listening. Other than in a regular class, listen to a speaker on or off campus. Then, in three minutes or less, report on how actively or inactively other members of the audience seemed to be listening to the speaker. If the level of listening was high, what factors in the speaker-listener situation contributed to that state? If low, was the speaker aware of that problem? What adjustments, if any, did the speaker make to increase the level of attention in the audience?

2. Practicing analytical listening. In three minutes or less, evaluate a speaker's printed or taped message in terms of its perceived purpose, the strengths or weaknesses of the case as presented, the advantages or disadvantages to the listeners, and the speaker's overall credibility.

3. Practicing defensive listening. In three minutes or less, analyze the printed or videotaped version of one or more speeches by candidates for or by holders of public office. Do those individuals discuss the issues or do they evade them? If evasion is the tactic, what form or forms does it take? What "perils of language" did you detect?

PART II

Acquiring Effective Speaking Skills

6

CHOOSING SUBJECT AND PURPOSE

When you finish this chapter, you will be familiar with...

1. A list of steps that will assist you in preparing to communicate effectively with listeners.

2. Suggestions for choosing a subject and purpose at the informational level.

3. Suggestions for choosing a subject and purpose at the problem-solution or inspirational-motivational levels.

Steps in Preparing a Presentation

This first section of Chapter 6 is a brief review of the steps which will be the focus of discussion in this and the other chapters of Part II.

As you might expect, a philosopher like Aristotle left it to the practical Romans to be specific about the procedures a speaker should follow in preparing a presentation and then interacting with the audience. Among others, Cicero (Roman senator, speaker, and theorist, 1st century B.C.) and Quintilian (head of a school of rhetoric at Rome, 1st century A.D.) recommended a speaker's completing these steps: (1) finding the materials needed to support a position, (2) organizing those materials, (3) phrasing them appropriately, (4) gaining control over the finished message and, finally, (5) making the presentation in such a way as to induce the audience to go along with the speaker's position.[1]

In this class and in the future, you will find it very useful to follow this slightly extended set of essentially the same steps:

1. You choose a subject that is--or can be demonstrated to be--of interest or concern to the audience.

2. You prepare an analysis of that audience.

3. You adapt the phrasing of your purpose to that audience.

4. You collect materials suited to that audience.

5. You organize the materials to fit that audience.

6. You rehearse "the message" to present it in a way you consider most acceptable to that audience.[2]

The first of those steps is the focus of this chapter.

Choosing a Subject with the Listener in Mind

With the possible exception of your speaking from the stand as a member of this class, you may never again face the need to choose "a speech topic." In school or out, after you become expert in a certain field or become known as knowledgeable and active in others, your finding either a "body of knowledge" or a position in which listeners would be interested will seldom, if ever, again come up. Someone will ask you to speak, or you will ask to speak because you see a need to make your special knowledge or point of view available to a certain group. You won't be looking for a subject or for a purpose in discussing it; subject and purpose will find you.

During this semester or term, however, the course syllabus will call for your making two or more in-class presentations. If you think of these "assignments" in the light of your being required to choose a couple random topics, develop them just enough to get by, and then deliver the packaged products to the members of the class, you won't be learning much about communication, and not much communication is likely to take place. Paul Holtzman offers this advice on the more productive and profitable approach to choosing a topic:

> Topic selection and audience knowledge must interact if the goal is maximum listener contribution. This does not mean that the topic must be something that the listener knows--or that he does not know about. It means that the topic must be appropriate to what he knows, to what he doesn't know, to what he ought to know, and to what he can be motivated to care to know....[3]

In other words, from the initial step in choosing a topic to preparing for and finally interacting with an audience, the path to real progress lies in your making every choice and decision with those listeners in mind. Otherwise, you'll be speaking in a vacuum, and the "listeners" will be bored, daydreaming, or even hostile.

With the listener looking over your shoulder, then, your first assignment will require that you prepare and present a talk which is primarily informational in character. We say *primarily* as a reminder that you'll also be "persuading" your listeners in the sense that information is in itself persuasion and that, additionally, you'll be asking them to accept you as believable, as one presenting ideas in a sensible order, and as one who gives them good reason to listen.

Topic Options at the Informational Level

In this category, the subject on which you will "see a need to speak" should be one which (l) will increase the understanding of your student audience and (2) will be a satisfying experience for you as well.

One way to begin the search for a subject is to review your own experiences. You may, for example, be in this country as a refugee, as an immigrant, as a student, as a visitor, or for some other reason. As a rule, we Americans know very little about life in other countries, so anything you can tell us about your daily life, particularly your education, in Australia or in one of the Asian, African,

European or Latin countries may help us understand you as well as the country from which you came. Or using your earlier life as background, you can tell us about the language, social, economic, and other problems which someone like you faces in adjusting to a new life in the United States or Canada.

You could also look for a topic in the traveling you've done. Have you been to the Orient or the Middle East? Or lived for a time in Argentina or South Africa? You might be able to share information of a kind that would help your classmates understand and evaluate newscasts from and about those regions. If you are an experienced "hostel traveler," you could share some practical tips about low-cost foreign travel.

In looking back on jobs you've held, don't be too ready to dismiss a particular experience as "uninteresting" to classmates. If you worked in a lumberyard, how many of the students know how to buy exactly the grade of lumber that will best fit an intended purpose? If you worked in a meatpacking plant, even fewer would know anything about what happens to the living animal entering through one door and coming out the other in neatly packaged "cuts."

Another possibility is to talk about the experiences of other people. If you take this route, it is far better to consider explaining the duties of a fire fighter you happen to know than to depend entirely on printed sources for information on a subject entirely new to you. Student audiences, like most others, are quick to sense the depth of a speaker's "knowledge" on any subject.

Still another option is to consider talking on a "how to" subject. Here again, you have to be--or have to become--well informed, and the topic must be one in which your listeners will be truly interested. You may be able to find plenty of information on "How to wash a dog" but, unless you have a talent for comedy, that subject is not likely to benefit the students. Similarly, explaining an elementary principle of engineering to engineers is guaranteed to put everyone to sleep.

Among the more satisfying and challenging subjects at the information level are those requiring your answering for the class an interesting question of fact. Examples:

> What student loan funds are not being used by the students of this institution? How do you apply for them?
>
> To what extent is sex education taught in the public schools of this state? What are the courses like?

From what sources does our state government get the money for the annual budget, and where does that money go?

From what general sources does the government collect income taxes and where does that money go?

You will be able to extract similar questions of fact from broad topics like these:

Art and the performing arts, e.g. the art we often overlook, especially here on campus and locally; how to appreciate ballet; kinds of opportunities offered through participation in campus and local theatre productions.

Athletics, e.g., the finer points of the game: what to watch for in football (or any other sport that is popular on campus); how the Athletic Department is administered on this campus (personnel, schedules, scholarships, etc.).

Education, e.g., how to encourage your younger sisters and brothers to read; facts and figures about literacy in this country.

Economics, e.g., how to manage a budget; how to compare life insurance policies; what is the evidence that a college education really pays off.

Employment and careers, e.g. how to prepare a résumé and a short cover letter; how to make a good impression in an interview; charting a career path after landing a position.

The environment, e.g., facts about pollution in the air, ground, and water.

Health care, e.g., facts and figures about exercise and/or nutrition; what everyone needs to know about first aid; what everyone needs to know about AIDS; what are the causes and consequences of stress.

Legal problems, e.g., when do you need a lawyer and how do you choose one; how to prepare your own will; how to cope with landlords, live-in friends, et al.; what to expect if you are arrested while driving "under the influence."

Media, e.g., the impact of TV violence on children; TV portrayal of women and blacks and its impact on social values; media news coverage; state control of the media by authoritarian governments and the effects of that control.

Politics, e.g., how to make your voice heard at different levels of government; how to evaluate the capabilities of rival candidates for office; the significance of the U.S. Census for Congressional Districts in this state.

Psychology, e.g., learning disabilities and what to do about them; what dreams tell us about ourselves; how drugs affect us mentally and physically; mental breakdowns: what they are and how people can cope with them.

Science, e.g., how our lives have been affected by Einstein's contributions; how the discovery of DNA and its properties have affected the study of the human family; what are the issues surrounding creationism/evolutionism.

Social problems, e.g., what are the causes, consequences, and cures for alcoholism; why are children abused and what can we do about it; how many of us are unknowingly guilty of discrimination; the extent to which racism persists in this country; the causes of homelessness.

From the facts you assemble, some conclusions may be drawn, but you are not trying--and shouldn't try--to prove anything. You are simply providing *specific information which the students do not have* and in which you believe they will be or can be interested.

Another first-speech option open to you may be to define and make clear an abstract concept or quality (e.g., morality, patriotism, justice, truth, altruism). How do you choose one that will really interest the class? You've heard many a talk in which the speaker said nothing; that's an ever present danger in working with abstract ideas. One approach to finding a worthwhile concept topic is to open a dictionary at random and list the abstract-idea words which you find in the next four or five pages. Next, check three or four of the concepts that you might like to investigate and run them past two or three classmates to find out which of them might be of interest to those students. (If you're thinking of choosing to define and explain an abstract idea, be sure that you have in mind some interesting examples in the form of incidents or individuals.)

Phrased as "subject sentences," here are some specific examples aimed at creating or increasing understanding through explanation and description:

Process	When you open a can of beans, do you wonder how they got there?
Technique	Do you know how to take a good outdoor photograph?
Product	This camcorder is "user-friendly."
Procedure	You've seen surveyors peering through their instruments. This is what they're doing.
Design	Some pottery designs are marvels of creative art.
Function	An airplane wing does perform some functions of a bird's wing.
Structure	This is how our city government is set up.
Question of fact	What are the hiring policies of our city government?

Plus some examples aimed at clarifying abstract ideas:

Concept	What is altruism? And what or who are some concrete examples of it?
Theory	The theory of evolution is still not too well understood.
Law	You've heard the term "habeas corpus." What does it mean and how does it work?

However you go about finding a subject (through personal experience, somebody else's experience, or digging into a subject to add to your information about it), a little conscientious effort will help you discover one that will appeal to all or most of the students in the class.

Topic Options at the Problem-Solution Level

A second speaking assignment usually requires the student to work on "a persuasive speech," one seeking agreement on a proposition of some kind or one attempting to evoke emotion or changes in attitude. (When there are three speaking opportunities, the second often calls for a speaker's trying to induce listener agreement on a proposition, and the third becomes mainly an effort to enlist changes in feeling or in states of mind.)

If the course syllabus calls for your making a presentation in this area, you will be trying to induce your listeners to agree that the position you take on a problem is important to them and that, if you propose a solution to the problem, there are good reasons why they should support it.

Where do you find subjects calling for support of or opposition to a stand on a particular issue? You may have already run across possible choices in conversations or in discussions. Campus and local newspapers regularly feature editorials and letters on issues of current interest. Another source is TV discussion programs. Libraries, too, maintain "current issue files" of clippings and article reprints.

How to develop the positions you take on problem-solution issues is discussed in detail in Chapter 12.

Topic Options at the Inspirational-Motivational Level

These are projects calling for (1) your inspiring the class to be enthusiastic--or to be unenthusiastic--about some idea or organization, or for (2) your motivating it to strengthenor weaken--an attitude or belief, or for (3) any other subject that is primarily inspirational or motivational in character.

For example, you've heard many a special occasion or inspirational speech in the churches, in the schools, and at political or organizational meetings. In the same category are commencement addresses and some of the better "pep talks" you hear at rallies and dinners of all kinds.

In the area of strongly held attitudes (not excluding prejudices), many people believe that they are powerless to influence what goes on in government. If you do not agree with that view and want to be one of those trying to change it, you have found an attitude-change subject. Other examples: "Elected officials are the prisoners of vested interests." "Every U.S. citizen has the constitutional right to own a handgun." If you choose to attack a racial or religious prejudice, choose one to which a majority of your immediate audience is thought to be addicted.

For more detail on choosing and developing subjects having an inspirational/motivational emphasis, see Chapter 13.

> Whatever the assignment or project at any level, how you go about your initial "reading of the situation" will help you decide what to talk about and what your goals will be in talking about it. Finally, choosing the right subject for any kind of speaking assignment has much to do with the comfort level you'll experience while you're working on it and with the success you'll enjoy in the final interaction with listeners. Make your choices early in the course, check them with other students and/or your instructor, and work on them over time instead of at the last minute. That kind of programming makes for peace of mind and the confidence that leads to success in interacting with audiences.

Endnotes

1. Cicero, *De Oratore*, trans. E. W. Sutton, Books I and II in Vol. 3 of Cicero, Loeb Series (Cambridge, MA: Harvard UP, 1979 rpt.), i, 31-32, 137-147. Quintilian is the source of much of our information on the early history of rhetorical theory and the teaching of it; see his *Institutio Oratoria*, trans. H. E. Butler, Books I, II, and III in Vol. 1 of Quintilian, Loeb Series (Cambridge, MA: Harvard UP, 1980 rpt.).

2. This version of the classical steps is based on Lloyd Bitzer's discussion of the complexities of "The Rhetorical Situation," *Rhetoric: A Tradition in Transition*, ed. Walter R. Fisher (East Lansing, MI: Michigan State UP, 1974), pp. 247-259.

3. Paul Holtzman, *The Psychology of Speakers' Audiences* (Glenview, IL: Scott Foresman, 1970), p. 88.

7

ANALYZING THE AUDIENCE

Students in speech classes are real people who <u>can</u> be enticed into transaction on the basis of valid audience analyses.

Paul Holtzman

Your audience is just as sharp as you are.

Alistaire Cooke

When you finish this chapter, you should be aware that...

1. Your intended listeners play a part in shaping both the content and the form of any well-planned rhetorical effort.

2. Each time you discuss a new topic with a given group of listeners, that group becomes a new audience and requires a fresh audience analysis to meet its needs.

3. Effective audience analysis calls for finding answers to "presentation-shaping" questions like these: What is my perception of the intended audience? What is the audience's perception of me as the speaker? What inter-listener influences may be at work? What environmental influences will be at work?

We begin this chapter with the assumption that a situation has arisen in which you have seen the need to speak or you have been called upon by others to speak.[1] Associated with answering that call has been the initial choice of a speech topic and a tentative purpose for it. We say *initial* and *tentative* because, after you have analyzed the audience, you may decide to modify the purpose of the talk, and you may even decide to abandon your original choice of subject.

On the need for careful audience analysis, Aristotle is only one of the many who have emphasized the need for knowing what the listeners are like in order to adapt what you say to them.[2] Today, however, we not only know more about audience analysis, but we also have a better understanding of the role listeners play in determining both the content and the form of a speech:

> To achieve his [or her] purpose, the communicator must find out all he can about the audience he is to address and then, by picturing himself as one of them, decide how to present his material in the most favorable light. In this sense, even before it ever comes into being, an audience influences a communicator and hence the act of communication....[3]

Under ordinary circumstances, of course, the audience you plan to analyze is self-selective; those who come to hear a speaker are there because they want to be, and others stay away for the same reason. Once in the room, the prospective listeners go through some further self-selecting in the sense that some may choose to listen and some may choose not to. Your speaking in the classroom, however, is not an ordinary circumstance. Once enrolled, you and the other students are there because you have to be. You soon come to know exactly who will be in the audience and, after a couple weeks in class, you may believe that you know your classmates well enough not to be unduly concerned about "audience analysis." Wrong! *The students in a given class become a different audience every time you present a different subject or position for their consideration.*

The way the students feel about one subject or issue (e.g., student rights) will differ from how they feel about another (e.g., required courses); they may be very much divided on the subject of abortion and very much unified in supporting election of a student to the college board; and they may readily accept you as knowledgeable in one subject area and not at all knowledgeable in another. The faces before you may remain the same but, depending on the speaking projects you take on, your audience analysis is going to give you different answers every time. In that sense, you will be dealing with a different audience every time, and each of those audiences will choose to "collaborate" with you--or not to collaborate with you--in a different way. *Each time you speak, you will be trying to meet differing audience needs.*

In effect, then, what you learn through audience analysis is going to affect your selection of opening remarks, the wording of your specific purpose, the reasons you give the audience for listening, the phrasing and order of your main points, your choices of examples and arguments, the motivations you offer for listener thought and action, and the way you bring your speaking to a close. In a very real way, your future listeners work with you to prepare the kind of presentation that they would respond to favorably. You are, in turn, responding to the need to communicate with those listeners, and your best hope for success lies in meeting their expectations. Our focus in this chapter, then, is on analyzing the audience--that is, trying to answer those questions4 which are, at this point (just after initial choices of subject and purpose), so important in shaping the speaker's effort to communicate:

What is my perception of the intended audience?
What is the audience's perception of me as the speaker?
What inter-listener influences may be at work?
What environmental influences will be at work?

What Is My Perception of the Intended Audience?

Your first reaction to that question could be, "As far as my interacting with members of this class is concerned, I think of the audience as a typical cross-section of undergraduates, some in their late 'teens and some older." Fine but, in terms of adaptation to that audience, what you need to know is "What information do I have to have to help me induce them to increase their understanding of a subject or to think, feel, believe, and act in a way that will be helpful to them as well as to me?"

Assessing audience knowledge

A first requirement is that you have some idea of how much your listeners already know about your subject, what they don't know about it, and whether or not they can be induced to care about knowing any more about it. In addition to your trying to assess what the listeners know or don't know, you also have to know something about the experiences they share with you in relation to your topic.

So, on the assumption that very few, if any, of your classmates have vacationed in the Caribbean area, you've decided to tout the advantages of vacationing at a plush resort in the Virgin Islands. Have you yourself had that experience? How many in the class are likely to have had that experience? If no experience, how many could afford that kind of vacation? If not many could afford it, how many would resent your bringing up the subject? In any event, how many would care about knowing more about *your* vacation? Under those circumstances, you might have a real problem trying to interact with your listeners. You could "give a speech" all right, but it could hardly be the cooperative enterprise that makes for real communication.

For another example, let's say the local newspaper has been running an investigative series on corruption among officials in the state capitol. You've been following the series, so you have come to know a lot about the situation. Even better, the materials you would need for a presentation are right there in the series of articles; all you would have to do is to put enough of them together to "look good" and last for the allotted time. Fine again, but the other students in the class have been exposed to the same series; they probably know as much about the situation as you do. Repeating the details will not only bore them, but you'll be insulting their intelligence as well.

On the other hand, maybe you've been a member of a class working to assess environmental problems in the county. You have become aware of facts about the local environment which have not yet attracted public interest, you know also that the problem is worsening, and you feel strongly that it is time to alert others about it. The base or common experience from which you start in this situation is the general public awareness that pollution is a real and growing hazard. You then undertake to induce your listeners to join you in examining the local pollution scene and in understanding its implications for the future. In other words, you take the listeners with you from a *shared take-off point* (general agreement that pollution is hazardous to one's health) to a new awareness of pollution problems as they affect everyone in the county. There are many variations upon a theme, but the essence of adaptation to listeners is a respect for what they know (without repeating it), the offering of good reasons for accepting additions to what they know, and the credible assurance that listening to what you have to say will be well worth their time.

Respecting cultural differences

Up to this point, we have been talking mainly about analyzing an audience by discovering ways to adapt the subject to listener knowledge about it and to listener experiences with it. However, there are times (and the number is increasing) when the speaker must go considerably beyond a determination of audience knowledge levels. One of the myths of our society is that it is a melting pot, that immigrants come to our country and, after a time, lose their cultural identity. Immigrants do become valuable assets to our political and economic life, but great numbers of them also take pride in retaining essential elements of the cultures from which they came.

In the various cities of the country, for example, we have sub-city enclaves consisting almost exclusively of Polish-Americans, or of Iranian-Americans, Lithuanian-Americans, African-Americans, Hispanic-Americans, Japanese-Americans, Irish-Americans, native Americans, Vietnamese-Americans--the list could go on and on. The point we make: if you are invited to speak to a group tracing its culture from another land and sharing a common heritage in language, religion, political sympathies, and social customs, you will have to make a special effort to find the common ground that all speakers seek and, above all, you will want to study that culture to avoid offending the sensibilities of your listeners. U.S. citizens have a reputation, often but not always warranted, for not understanding the cultures of other countries and for not making the effort to find out about them. After all, we think, everyone should conform to our patterns of life and living. Whether we like it or not, however, cultural diversity is with us to stay. The sensitive speaker will extend the process of audience analysis to include finding out as much as possible about any audience coming from a culture unlike her or his own.

As you move beyond presentations that are primarily informational to more complex subjects like those requiring your taking positions on issues or trying to change attitudes, you will again be expanding your analysis. In addition to investigating what your listeners know or don't know, you'll also want to discover what they believe, how strongly they believe it, and their reasons for believing it. (Details on how to meet those "added needs" are included in Chapter 12, dealing with speaking on problem-solution issues, and in the Chapter 13 discussion on evoking emotion and motivating change.)

What Is The Audience's Perception of Me as the Speaker?

Theorists have long emphasized the reputation of the speaker as a primary (if not *the* primary) influence in the minds of listeners.[5] If your audience trusts and accepts you as one qualified to speak on a subject, half the battle is over. If the audience doesn't know your qualifications or, knowing them, doesn't trust you to look out for their interests, the battle is going to be hard to win. In any event, answers to questions like those below will help you check on the state of your "public image" in the minds of the intended listeners.

What attitude can be anticipated toward me as the speaker? Very favorable? Favorable? Neutral? Opposed? Hostile?

If opposed or hostile, what seems to be the reason for that feeling? What can I do to overcome that opposition or hostility?

What can I do to convince these listeners that I am a person of good sense? What is their attitude toward my knowledge of the subject? Will I have to make a special point of my background in this area?

What can I do to convince them that I am a person of good character, that I'm being honest and fair in my presentation?

Are the listeners likely to have confidence that I am a person of good will, one really concerned about their interests? What can I do to convince them that their concern is my concern, that the thinking or action I propose will benefit all of us?

I can't do anything about my stature or general appearance, but what steps can reasonably be taken to make the most of my "presence"?

What Inter-Listener Influences May Be at Work?

At the same time that listeners are responding to a speaker and the speaker's message, they are also interacting with their fellow listeners and responding to the "messages" passing between and among them before, during, and after the communication event. Let's review some of the forces which you will want to take into account in the course of your preparing for that main event.

The "attendance-required" atmosphere

You and the other students in the class are members of a captive audience and, when the audience is captive, the active listening so vital to true communication sometimes suffers--it may be listless, lackadaisical, resentful, or even antagonistic. To overcome the captive-audience problem, your instructor works hard to create a supportive atmosphere in which the students regard themselves as real people discussing subjects that really matter with the other students in the class.[6] You are not "delivering speeches." You are trying to do everything possible to get the desired response from active listeners.

Because a goodly share of other audiences are also "captive" (e.g., in business, industry, and the workplace generally), your speaking and listening in an attendance required class is actually good basic training. The sales force of a company may, for example, be required to attend a series of after-hours sales seminars on the latest in motivational methods. Or professionals in a particular field may be required to attend conventions at their own expense. Inside or outside the class, captive or free, it is in the speaker's best interests to try to anticipate what the general audience atmosphere is going to be--and to take steps to cope with it.

The "go-with-the-flow" atmosphere

Whether or not your listeners will respond as you would like them to also depends in part on the approval or disapproval of their friends or associates--and especially of those with whom they're sitting in the audience. In your own experience as a listener, if everyone in a your immediate group stands up to applaud, you are likely to join them whether you want to or not. If they "sit on their hands," you are likely to do the same. If they laugh, you laugh. If they cheer, you cheer. We have minds of our own but, in group situations, we all tend to be influenced by the groups to which we belong or want to belong.[7]

The "follow-the-leader" atmosphere

Present in almost every audience are one or more individuals on whose judgment others rely. If one or more "leaders" can be won over to the position advocated by a speaker, it is likely that others will fall in line. Identifying leaders is not always possible; when it is, the speaker, by paying some special attention to them, is sometimes able to take advantage of the "trickle down" theory: influence flows from leaders to followers. If a leader seems to approve, other listeners will probably follow suit and, if a leader seems to disapprove, other listeners may do the same.[8]

The "chance-to-question" atmosphere

In the speaker-audience situation, there is no faster way to enliven the party than to announce that a question and answer session or public dialogue will follow the speaker's remarks. Another audience involvement technique is to have the listeners move into a number of small discussion groups. In any event, "audience participation...helps overcome resistance" to a persuasive effort[9] and contributes to the reaching of the speaker's goal in almost any communication situation.

We move now to a listing of typical questions you can use to discover how you can counter or take advantage of the various listener atmospheres at work within a given audience:

> Will the audience be captive or free? Is it likely that the listeners will be interested in what I have to say? Or will they be sitting there passively and even reluctantly because their attendance is required? If the answer is "Yes," what can I do to overcome possible apathy or resistance?
>
> Knowing what we do about the tendency of listeners to be influenced by other listeners, will it be possible to unify this audience into acting together for the common good?
>
> Are known "opinion leaders" likely to be in the audience? Can some special effort be directed toward them or would that approach run the danger of alienating them as well as the audience in general?
>
> If a speaker takes positions on a controversial issue, listeners like an opportunity to reply. Will there be time for a question-and-answer session after I finish speaking? Or some other kind of audience participation activity?

What Environmental Influences Will Be at Work?

Under that final question, you will be considering what message adjustments should be made to best fit the occasion for which your presentation is being planned and for the physical setting in which it will take place.

We have already noted the fact that the speaker must keep the speech-occasion in mind throughout all stages of preparation. Both your message and your general behavior, for example, should fall into one pattern if you are praising a football coach at the festive dinner following a championship season. Your message and your behavior would be quite different on the occasion of your presenting a eulogy of the same coach after his untimely death. Few speakers have a problem adapting to the demands of the occasion. Most of them remember that there is a time and a place for everything; what is accepted as good, clean fun in one instance is, under different circumstances, rejected and resented as unacceptable behavior. We repeat: remember the occasion, and speaking appropriately is likely to take care of itself.

As for the physical setting, there are enough problems in sharing ideas with an audience; interference from unforeseen physical obstacles should not be one of them. Unless you are familiar with the indoor or outdoor setting scheduled for the event, you will want to check it out in advance.

> The size of the assigned room or area is a first concern for any speaker. Is it too large for the size of the audience expected? If so, the audience will be "lost" in it. Too small? If the need should arise, will it be possible to move the meeting to a larger or smaller room?
>
> Is a lectern available? Will the speaker be at floor level? Or on a raised platform or stage? Or seated at a desk or conference table? If there is a sound system, has someone been assigned to see that it is in operating condition and to control volume during the meeting? If a question-and-answer session has been scheduled, are additional microphones necessary and available?
>
> Will you have to contend with "noise" from adjacent rooms or corridors? From the clatter of dishes and the distraction of waiters moving through the room? From street traffic? From nearby construction? Is the sound system capable of surmounting "noises"? Or do you have to do it "by voice" and by repeating everything twice?
>
> You may want to use a few visual aids.[10] What types are suited to the room scheduled for the event? How large will posters have to be to be seen and understood? How can you make sure that projection equipment, if required, will be on hand? If you bring your own equipment, will you need extension cords to reach electrical outlets?

Audience Analysis in Action

No sets of analytical questions will fit all audiences, but the four broad questions we list (and the suggestions offered under each heading) will help any speaker improve her or his communication. In this section of the chapter, the focus is on the first of those broad questions in order to demonstrate how answers to it (and related questions) could shape a student's message. Let us suppose, for example, that you are a criminology major (your claim to some expertise on crime and criminals) and that you strongly oppose a long-accepted policy of simply "warehousing" the prisoners in your state. Statewide polls show that the public is not only satisfied with that policy, but it is also *opposed to raising taxes* for any purpose, including improving the prisons. Nevertheless, you decide to do what you can to promote the idea of better prisons[11] in one of your class presentations. The first question in audience analysis (and the one we are using here for demonstration purposes) is "What is my perception of the audience's attitude toward what to do about the prisons?"

Through a quick and informal conversational poll of a few students, you discover that their attitude is essentially the same as that of the majority of the people of state. Why do they feel that way? The main reasons seem to be that criminals are all alike, they ought to be punished, and they deserve no special treatment or consideration at the taxpayers' expense. To counter that attitude and the beliefs supporting it, you decide initially to consider developing your arguments along these lines:

We need better prisons...

I. To protect new prisoners from hardened criminals.

II. To prepare all criminals for jobs on the outside.

III. To restore prisoner self-respect by more humane treatment.

That approach, a straightforward citation of reasons for improving the prisons, would be appropriate for some audiences, but you know that most of your listeners feel strongly that *the prisons are good enough as they are*. Can a way be found to phrase your arguments in way that is less blunt, *in a way shaped by your listeners?* Remembering that a speaker must always aim at "becoming one with the audience," one way to "listen" to listener concerns is to use *their* "main points" (the beliefs supporting their attitude) as the base for *your* ideas and arguments. Your revised listing could then look something like this:

We need better prisons in spite of the fact that...

I. First, as you say, criminals are all alike.

(Not quite. Prisons today are schools for criminals. We need to protect new prisoners from getting graduate degrees in criminality. Their continuing to be criminals will cost you more money in the long run.)

II. Again, as you say, criminals deserve to be punished.

(True, but if they are not prepared for jobs, they will definitely go back to crime...and cost you more money in the long run.)

III. Finally, as you say, criminals should be treated like criminals.

(True again. Prisons should not be country clubs. However, human beings have to be treated decently if you want any improvement in behavior. Otherwise, they will be criminals forever...and cost you more money in the long run.)

Stated or unstated, the common premise or view[12] on which everyone would agree is that the people of the state do not want to spend more money on the prisons than necessary. That is why it would be important to make the point that not doing anything about the prisons "will cost you more in the long run." Or stated another way, "in the long run, improving the prisons would cost you less than not improving them." However you say it, you will be stressing the point that "The choice is to pay somewhat more now or to pay considerably more later."

> In this chapter, we have emphasized four central questions for analyzing the audience. The first provides a key to exploring your perception of the audience in relation to the topic you have under consideration: what do the listeners know about your subject or position, what do they not know, how can they be induced to want to know, what are their views on controversial questions, what are their attitudes, how strong are they, and how can they be changed or modified. The second major question reminds you of the speaker's responsibility to present a credible image, one based on the audience's perception of that speaker's good sense, good character, good will, and good presence. The third question leads the speaker to look into the inter-listener influences which may be operating at the time of interaction with the audience. The fourth and last deals with influences exerted on the event by the occasion and by the physical setting.

Endnotes

1. For a thorough analysis of the situational aspects of rhetoric, see Lloyd Bitzer, "The Rhetorical Situation" in *The Rhetoric of Western Thought*, eds. James L. Golden, Goodwin F. Berquist, and William E. Coleman, 3rd ed. (Dubuque, IA:

Kendall/Hunt, 1983), pp. 17-24.

2. Aristotle, *The "Art" of Rhetoric*, trans. John Henry Freese, Vol. 3 of Aristotle, Loeb Classical Library Series (Cambridge, MA: Harvard UP, 1982 rpt.), 1388b-89b. In a modern study demonstrating that the ancient rhetorical theorists were among the earliest social psychologists, we read, "The experts [early rhetorical theorists] might have disagreed among themselves about the other skills..., but they all stressed the need to study the thoughts and feelings of audiences." See Michael Billig, *Arguing and Thinking: A Rhetorical Approach to Social Psychology* (New York: Cambridge UP, 1987), p. 53.

3. George A. Borden, Richard B. Gregg, and Theodore G. Grove, *Speech Behavior and Human Interaction* (Englewood Cliffs, NJ: Prentice-Hall, 1969), p. 213.

4. Holtzman identifies and discusses 44 "listener factors" to be considered in analyzing the listener and the audience. See Paul D. Holtzman, *The Psychology of Speakers' Audiences* (Glenview, IL: Scott, Foresman, 1970), pp.41-80. The analytical plan in the present text is, in part, a synthesis of patterns appearing in Holtzman.

5. Chapter 10 of the present text includes a discussion of the ethos or image of the speaker and its impact on audience acceptance of her or his views.

6. Holtzman, p. 116 f.

7. Marvin Karlins and Herbert I. Abelson, *Persuasion: How Opinions and Attitudes Are Changed* (New York: Springer, 1970), p. 49

8. See Elihu Katz, "The Diffusion of New Ideas and Practices," in *The Science of Human Communication*, ed. Wilbur Schramm (New York: Basic Books, 1963), pp. 77-91.

9. Karlins and Abelson, p. 62.

10. Visual aids are discussed in Chapter 8.

11. The prison example and the outlines accompanying it are based on a student's experience as recounted in Lynn Quitman's essay on "The Basic Writer," *Essays on Classical Rhetoric and Modern Discourse*, eds. Robert J. Connors, Lisa S. Ede, and Andrea A. Lunsford (Carbondale, IL: Southern Illinois UP, 1984), p. 201.

12. Chapter 3 of this text deals with the theory and forms of reasoning. There is

some additional detail, especially on the location of issues, in Chapter 12. For a detailed discussion of the psychology of emotion and emotional appeal, motives and motivation, attitudes and beliefs, see Chapter 13.

Discussion Questions

1. We speak of the part listeners play in shaping the content and form of the attempt to win a desired response from them. Can you give an example of that kind of shaping of the speaker's effort? In asking a favor from an individual or group, do you sometimes phrase the question in a way that highlights advantage to the listener(s)?

2. This text lists four broad questions to aid the speaker in his or her audience analysis. Can any one of the four be safely omitted? Under what conditions?

3. If an audience is already in agreement with the speaker's position, what is the need for speaking? Cite a recent instance in which the speaker faced no challenge whatever from the audience. What was the audience reaction?

4. If analysis of the audience indicates that the speaker is unknown to it, what measures can that speaker take to establish a favorable image?

5. In association with others in an audience, each of us has at one time reacted in exactly the same way as everyone else in the room. From your experience, can you give a specific example of this influence of listeners on listeners?

6. Cite an instance in which the speaker did not understand the restraints imposed by "the occasion." In what ways did the speaker fail to fit his or her remarks to that occasion? What was the reaction of the listeners?

7. Cite an instance in which the physical facilities were not suited to the requirements for the speaker-listener event. Could that situation have been avoided? How were the speaker or speakers affected? Were they able to overcome the difficulties? How?

Application Projects

1. Attend an open-to-the-public lecture or other publicspeaking event on or off campus. Prepare a 3-minute report on what seemed to you to be the speaker's success or failure in analyzing the audience. Would your own analysis have been

different? How would your analysis have affected the content, form, or presentation of the message?

2. For the same kind of event as described above, prepare a three-minute report on what seemed to you to be the speaker's success or failure in audience analysis from the standpoint of any one of the four major questions cited in this chapter. Would your analysis have been different? In what ways?

Note: Begin your report with a brief description of the event: the topic and the speaker's purpose, the speaker's name with a comment or two on his or her reputation, time and place of the meeting, etc. Once you have set the scene, your listeners will be ready for your "analysis of the speaker's analysis."

Additional Activities

1. Designing a survey to determine student views on a campus issue or proposition.

Your instructor may assign to small groups of students the task of devising a one-page questionnaire aimed at determining (1) a student's position on a current campus issue or proposition and (2) the reason or reasons for the position held.

Then, each student in your class (or volunteers from it) could individually poll 10 students outside the class in an informal effort to determine campus feeling on the issue or proposition under study.

2. Preparing a composite report.

Your instructor may then have a small group or committee of interested students prepare for distribution to members of the class a summary of student views as determined above.

3. Designing a one-page demographic survey as a general aid to or background for analysis.

Small groups of students may be asked to plan a series of questions aimed at soliciting from members of the class general demographic information on age, sex, marital status, race, year in college, major course of study, organizational memberships, job experience, and career interests.

One of the question-forms so created or one already available could then be used to solicit that information from members of the class.

4. Preparing a composite demographic report.

Another small group of interested students could then prepare for distribution to members of the class a statistical summary of the composition of that class.

Photo courtesy Rollins College, Winter Park, Florida.

8

PLANNING THE MESSAGE

Your choice of purpose should reflect the prior experiences of your audience and should be attuned to the events taking place in your environment.

George Campbell (1776)

> In this chapter, you follow through on two more steps in the process of message preparation by...
>
> 1. Adapting your purpose to the intended audience.
>
> 2. Collecting materials in accord with that purpose...
>   a. by recalling your own experiences
>   b. by calling upon the experiences of others
>   c. by using library resources
>   d. by considering the available visual aids

By the time you get to this stage of message preparation, you have already (1) recognized the need to interact with your listeners on a subject of common interest or concern, and you've (2) learned what you can about the listeners and related factors through audience analysis. Further, if you haven't already settled upon a specific purpose designed to fit those listeners, you are now ready to do so. You're also ready to collect materials (e.g., facts, statistics, ideas, quotations) adapted to what you now know about those listeners.

Adapting Your Purpose to the Intended Audience

Even without analysis of the audience, it's hard to choose the subject for a talk without at the same time having in mind the general purpose which you want to accomplish. Now, with your analysis of the audience as a guide, you are in position for a final (or close to final) check on both your original choice of subject and its purpose. In the previous chapter, we noted how that analysis could result in abandoning both subject and purpose because neither was well suited to audience interests and concerns. The same analysis could suggest modifying a subject and/or purpose to better accommodate the needs and expectations of that audience. For example, the members of the class may know little or nothing about the problems of the hearing-impaired, so a student with that difficulty could conceivably talk with real authority about it. But from the vantage point of knowing the interests and concerns of a student audience, which purpose do you think would have more appeal, one aimed at increasing audience understanding about the problems encountered by the hearing-impaired student or one about some of the high decibel noises many of *us* encounter every day and which can lead to *our* hearing loss?

In any event, following your analysis of the audience, ask yourself these questions as a final check on how well you are adapting your subject or position to the intending listeners:

(1) Is my subject/position *worth discussing* in the sense that doing so will benefit the listeners in some way?

(2) Is my subject/position one of *present interest and concern* to the listeners? Or can I show that the listeners *ought to be interested and concerned* about it?

(3) Is my subject/position one for which there is *enough material or evidence* to justify its consideration by the listeners?

(4) Is my subject/position one on which a majority of the listeners are *not already in agreement with me*? ("Not already in agreement" doesn't mean they must be opposed to the position you're taking; they may not know much about the subject, may be confused by opposing claims, or may not have made up their minds about it.)

In other words, no matter what choice of subject or purpose you make initially, take another good look at both in the light of your audience analysis.

Collecting Materials Adapted to the Audience

Once you have pinned down the subject and adapted your specific purpose to the specific audience, you have established the guidelines for bringing materials together at a fairly rapid pace. Over and above whatever direct experience you may have in the subject area, any necessary collecting can be done from "print" or from talking with those having some knowledge about the subject or, when necessary, with known experts in the field. Print sources like newspaper files, magazines, periodicals, and books are available to you through the libraries (more about this later in the chapter). As for the experts, they are usually happy to discuss their specialties.

Informal conversations with knowledgeable people

For instance, it may seem unreasonable that you had to pay a $50 speeding fine plus $30 in "court costs" for a "trial" which never took place because you chose to mail the full amount to the appropriate traffic court. Your preparation for a talk opposing payment for such "trials" could take the form of (1) conversations with the city attorney, chief of police, and the traffic judge, (2) attendance at a couple sessions of the traffic court, and (3) checking the public records to determine the number of tickets issued, the number ignored, the number paid out of court, the number "fixed," the number contested and won, and the number contested and lost.

Planned interviews with experts

An information-seeking interview, on the other hand, brings two people together by appointment to discuss a selected subject.[1] Further, most interviews are initiated by an interviewer who has both a specific purpose and a plan for reaching his or her objective through talking with the expert involved.

As a student looking for information, your planning and taking part in one or more information-seeking interviews can ensure that you will get up to-date and useful information. Whether or not taking part in an interview is a part of the course, think of it as an easy way to gain experience in *communicating purposefully*--easy because, if your questions are well planned, the answers from your "audience of one" will leave you free to take notes or record the responses on tape.

Experts are busy people. It goes without saying that you should 'phone for the appointment two or three days in advance of the proposed meeting. (It is easier to get an expert's consent to an interview if you make clear at the outset that you are a *student looking only for information*, not one looking for a job or for a chance to sell subscriptions to magazines.) Take care to get the details straight; if you are uncertain about how to pronounce your expert's name, either the receptionist or the expert will be glad to enlighten you on that often sensitive point. Make a note of the *exact* time and place agreed upon for the interview. And plan your arrival well in advance of the time scheduled for the meeting. Claiming a misunderstanding about time or place is unlikely to get the interview off to a good start.

Planning your questions. Since you are in the process of looking for materials to be used in a later presentation, you already have a possible plan in mind for the rough order of ideas in that talk. It makes sense, then, to arrange your questions in the order in which you intend to make use of the answers. It is also simple courtesy to write out your questions in advance so that, during the interview, you won't be fumbling for what to ask next.

Assume, for example, that you know something about photography, or something about flying in light planes, or something about both activities, and assume also that you believe the other students in the class could be interested in becoming better informed on the subject of aerial photography. With those or similar assumptions in place, the list of the questions you would put to your expert respondent might read like this:

> [On photographic equipment] I read in a *Flying Magazine* article that a standard 35mm camera is okay for taking photos from the air. Is that true? For what kinds of shots? How many lenses do you need? Under what conditions would you use each one? Are 35mm negatives or standard prints suitable for enlargement? To what sizes? Do you use lens filters? What kinds? Do professionals prefer the larger so-called square-format cameras? What are the advantages of that type of camera? Any disadvantages? How much larger is the negative? Is that negative size a more practical base for enlargements? Is the larger camera harder to hold and handle than a 35mm model?
>
> [On flying equipment] According to your ad in the Yellow Pages, you have your own plane. Is it a high- or low-wing model? What are the advantages of the model you have? What are its disadvantages? Does it permit you to shoot through an open window? Assuming that your plane is two-way radio equipped, does it have a transponder? A DME [distance measuring equipment]? An autopilot? Which of those pieces of equipment

do you actually use on a photo assignment? How stable is your plane in "slow flight"? Once you have it trimmed up, can you control the plane with rudder alone?

[On taking aerial shots] How far from your home airport do you accept assignments? How do you find your "targets" from the air? Do you select camera shutter speed on the ground before take-off or do you do that in the air over the "target"? Flying a plane is a demanding skill and so is shooting photographs--how do you manage to do both at the same time? How do you keep the normal vibration of the plane from being transferred to the camera? How do you keep a lookout for other air traffic? Assuming that you use both hands to hold and aim the camera, do you have any trouble controlling the plane? At what altitudes do you normally fly for routine land-area or industrial-installation photography? How do you decide at what altitude to fly? How do you get permission to fly at that altitude?

Other questions within the classifications above would occur to you during the pre-interview writing stage and during the interview itself. Any list of prepared questions should be regarded as an orderly and time-saving guide, not as a straightjacket from which no departure is possible.

Managing the interview. Bear in mind that a good interview has features in common with the presentation for which you are collecting information: an opening or introduction, a body consisting of planned clusters of questions in a logical order, and a conclusion.

So with questions in hand, you arrive "on time" and open the interview by introducing yourself to the interviewee, by thanking her or him for taking the time to see you, and by restating your reason for the call. Some further getacquainted "small talk" may be in order, but move into your planned series of questions as soon as the interviewee seems ready for them.

As you move from question to question, be ready to jot notes on the answers or, if you have a tape recorder and the respondent is willing, record the answers in that way. Keep moving along with an eye on the time; if the interview is scheduled for a half-hour, you don't want to spend that entire period on the first group of questions, nor do you want to let the expert go on endlessly in response to any one question.

When your questions have been answered or the time is up (whichever comes first), bring the interview in for a smooth landing by thanking the interviewee for his or her cooperation. And if everything has gone well and the interpersonal vibrations are right, this is also the time to ask for the loan of items you could use as visual aids: a camera appropriate for aerial photography, a special lens or two, a proof-sheet of shots shown to a client for approval, and a couple finished enlargements in different sizes. (If your library has a book or books on aerial photography, one or more may have line drawings which you could enlarge to show aircraft conformations and the angles at which photos can be taken from them.)

In the event that the subject you'd like to speak on is one on which you are not yet too well informed (and for which you can't get all the materials you need from the knowledgeable and the experts), you'll be going to the libraries to add to your personal competence and, more importantly, to better serve the interests of your listeners.

Using the library

Knowing how to use library resources is an indispensable skill. College and university libraries normally offer students a free booklet describing the location and use of reference works, periodicals, and general collections. With or without such a booklet, librarians are ever willing to help students find the answers to their research problems.

The general reference desk is an excellent place to start the search. There you will find standard sources of facts and statistics, biographical summaries, indexes to specific fields in the arts and sciences, the *Readers' Guide to Periodical Literature*, encyclopedias of all kinds, current periodicals, popular magazines, and newspapers.

Then, you can check the card or computer catalog for authors, titles, or topics related to the subject you're investigating. If you know, for example, that an author named Walter Gorman has written a book on the strategies of selling, you can locate the book and any others he may have written by calling up or looking under "G." If you know only the title of the book, *Selling*, you check the file under "S." If you want to find out what books are available on the subject of advertising, you check the appropriate section of file "A."

Keeping an accurate record of your reading is a problem which can be solved by you alone. However, many students like to use standard 3x5 cards for note-taking. The fact that cards can be arranged, rearranged, shuffled, or discarded also simplifies the later process of organizing the materials you finally select as being "audience-friendly."

For each book, article, or other source from which you take information, use a separate card to record the name of the author, title of the book, article, or report, etc. (If you are uncertain about how to record that data, ask the librarian to refer you to a manual of style.) Here are two examples of so-called bibliographical cards:

> Gorman, Walter. *Selling: Personality, Persuasion, Strategy.* 2nd ed., revised by Richard F. Wendel. New York: Random House, 1983.

> Rosteck, Thomas. "Irony, Argument, and Reportage in Television Documentary: *See It Now* versus Senator McCarthy," *Quarterly Journal of Speech*, 75 (November, 1989) 3, pp. 277-298.

Then, as you take notes from a particular source, keep them short and write on only one side of a card. At the top left, put the last name of the author or use any other code system you like. When copying a direct quotation, put it within quotation marks. When using a card to record your comment on some part or section of a book or article, the absence of quotation marks will indicate that the observation is yours, not that of the author. Examples of note cards...

Gorman

"'Communications' comes from the Latin word *communis*, meaning common. The more a communicator has in common with other people, the better he or she can communicate with them." page 129

Gorman

Excellent diagram of "Career Options in Sales" on page 28. Possible blow up for use as a visual aid?

Rosteck

"Practicing journalists appear to use 'rituals of objectivity' as formal strategies to avoid charges of bias and unfairness." page 283

A card can carry any kind of information, of course, but only related items should appear on any one card. Long quotations can be shortened by using the familiar device of three dots (...) to indicate omission of a nonessential word or words. As your note-taking proceeds, you will want to file the bibliographical cards in alphabetical order by author. The note cards can be filed under any topical headings that make sense to you. Chosen with care, some of those headings often end up as main or sub-points in a final outline.

Considering the available visual aids

Visual aids are discussed here because, as you collect materials for a presentation, you will come across "visual aid possibilities" in one form or another (described below). Knowing what kinds of aids are available puts you in a position, as your preparation proceeds, to consider whether or not the interaction with your intended listeners would be helped or hindered by their use.

In other words, properly selected, a visual aid can help you express your ideas. If it's not properly selected, it can get in the way and interfere with communication. The existence of a visual aid is not a valid reason to use it; the only useful aid is one that helps you make a point.

A basic requirement, of course, is that a visual aid should be large enough for everyone in the room to see. Only when your listeners can see the aid do you have a chance of meeting the second requirement, namely, that your listeners feel it makes your ideas easier for them to understand.

Your instructors and others may sometimes use "visual aids" in the form of slides, computer-screen-images, over-head screen-projection, sound-films, closed-circuit-television, audio-casette tapes, video tapes, etc. All the foregoing aids call for electric power, extension cords, and special equipment of the kinds seldom available to students in the classroom. They also take away from the student the central role so crucial to his or her early training and experience in speaking from the stand. So for any speaker, student or professional, who wants to stay in the driver's seat, who wants to interact continuously with listeners, and who wants to avoid the hazards of equipment breakdown, the visual aids most readily available or most easily prepared are (1) actual objects, (2) photos of objects, (3) mock-ups, (4) models, (5) drawings, charts, and maps, (6) diagrams, and (7) graphs of the common or computer varieties.

Actual objects. Again, these must be large enough for your listeners to see, and they should be light enough to pick up and display (e.g., an antique camera, a lap-top or a hand-held computer, a modem for telephone-line transmission of computer generated copy or graphs, a hand-held copier, a fax machine, an alarm system for cars).

Figure 8.1 Student describing functions of the parts of a camera.

Photos of objects. It is easy for a speaker to display one or more large photos, either by hand or from a tripod. For example, an enlarged photo of Hereford beef cattle could serve as part of the introduction to a sharing-information talk on "how to shop for good cuts of beef," the "cuts" being outlined in a line drawing or diagram of one of those animals. Or if you believe your listeners would like to know more about the different breeds of horses, enlarged photos of those breeds would certainly give your descriptions "audience appeal."

Mock-ups. Mock-ups of objects are light-weight copies especially designed for demonstration and discussion purposes. As you know, they are made of heavy paper, cardboard, plastic, very light metal, and other materials. In a physiology class, for example, a plastic head or other part of the body may be assembled or disassembled to fit a given lecture. In mechanical engineering, the principle of the differential gear is often demonstrated with a mock-up cut-away assembly made of light metals and easily held in the hands. As always, be sure that the details of any mock-up can be seen by every member of your audience.

Models. If your hobby is to build or work with model ships, planes, trains, prairie schooners, vintage cars, or rockets, you have one or more on hand which could be used to discuss modeling or to explain the motive forces involved. For example, you could explain the construction of a Ford Trimotor model, or you could use a model of that antique plane to describe the forces which keep a plane in the air.

Figure 8.2 Student describing forces that affect rocket in flight.

Drawings, charts, and maps. A drawing is the representing of something by lines made with a pen, pencil, crayon, or marker on a paper or paperboard surface. Examples: a flip-chart series on the influences of Greek architecture on American building design; a map of your state featuring the locations of major historic sites and their special attractions; a drawing of a driveway warning system (Figure 8.3) to show how an approaching vehicle triggers the alarm.

Basic drawings, preferably in simple but heavy lines, appear in textbooks, dictionaries, and other printed materials. If you have no way to have them copied in a size large enough for easy display, make your own rough copies freehand. A printed map or your drawing of it can be mounted on any stiff backing and displayed from an easel. Visual aids of these kinds do not have to be professional in appearance; the only requirement is that they be large enough to be seen and clear enough to be understood.

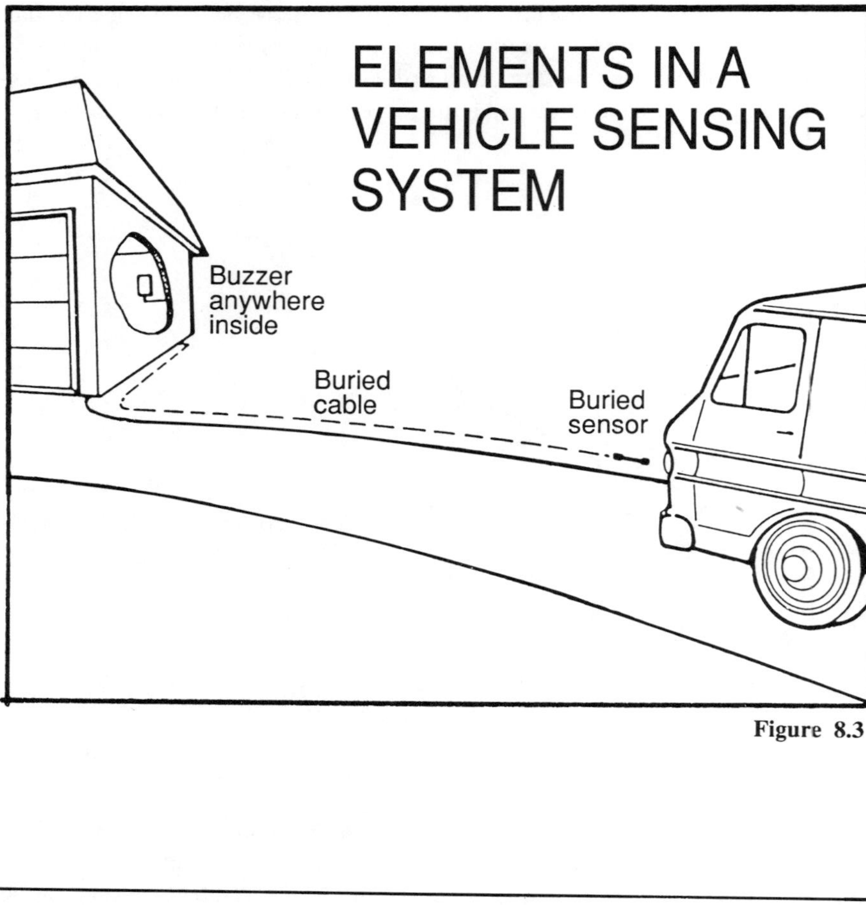

Figure 8.3

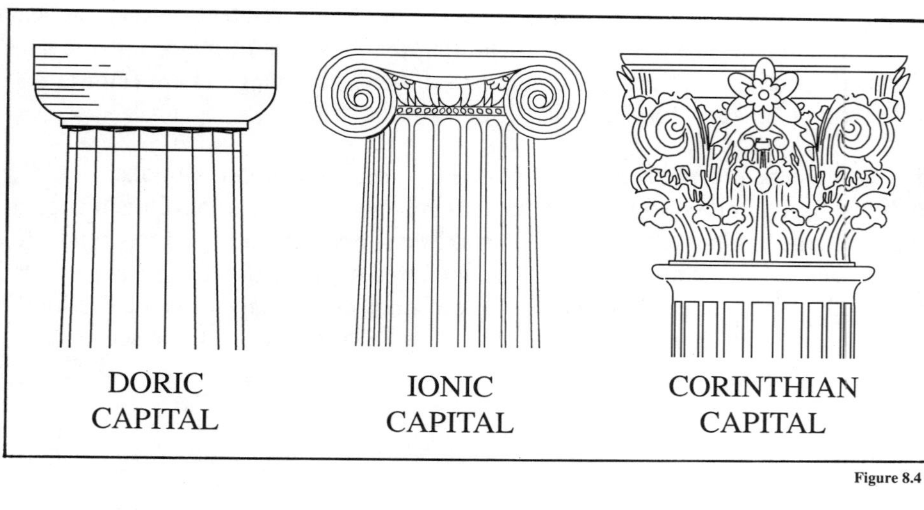

Figure 8.4

Diagrams are drawings which show little or no details of physical appearance; instead, they indicate units and their functions. You have seen many examples of "pieces of pie" diagrams. They are frequently used in pairs to help an audience visualize budgets, one "pie" showing percentages of income and the other percentages of outgo. Pies are also used to show percentages of any commodity, force, or social trend; the two below show how, in the United States, "First births and mothers' ages" varied from 1970 to 1987.

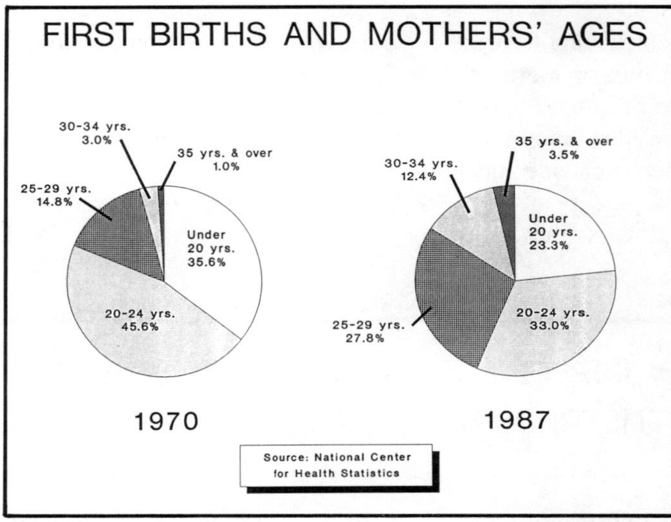

Figure 8.5

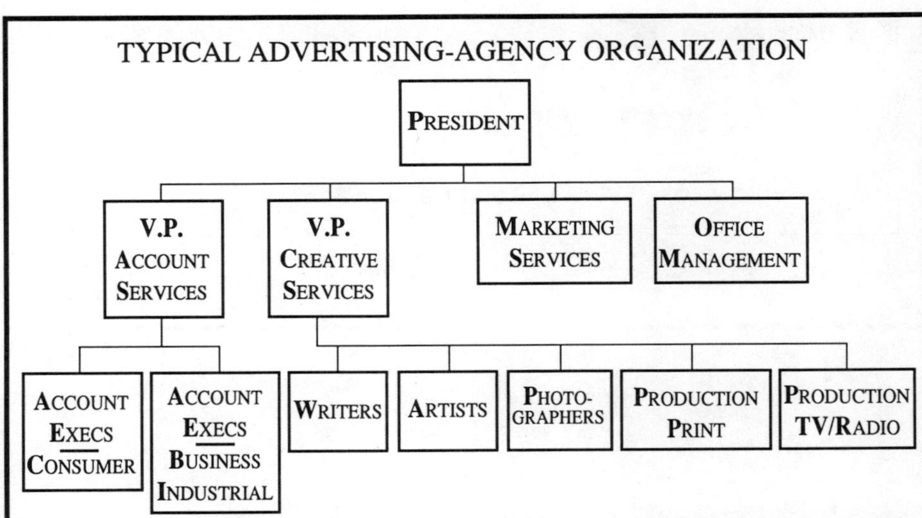

Figure 8.6

Graphs. The more common graphs fall into *bar* and *line* categories. If you know something about statistics and how to present them graphically, you can draw your own graphs. If you have access to a computer, the necessary graphics software (e.g., Freelance, Harvard Graphics), and a plotter or laser printer, "drawing" graphs becomes easy. In whatever way you produce a graph, you can enlarge it yourself or, again, one of your local quick-printing outlets can enlarge it for you. With the final product in hand, it is always good practice to "heavy up" important hard-to-see lines with pencil, ink, or crayon.

Instead of your having to produce your own graphs, it is more likely that you will come across one or more of them in the course of your "collecting materials." One example of a *horizontal bar graph* is that showing what percents of buyers/specifiers consider the reputation of a brand-name product to be as important to them as its technical specifications. A typical *vertical bar graph* is that showing smokers as a percent of the U.S. population. The *line graph* below shows in billions of dollars the growth of the federal deficit from 1974 to 1985.

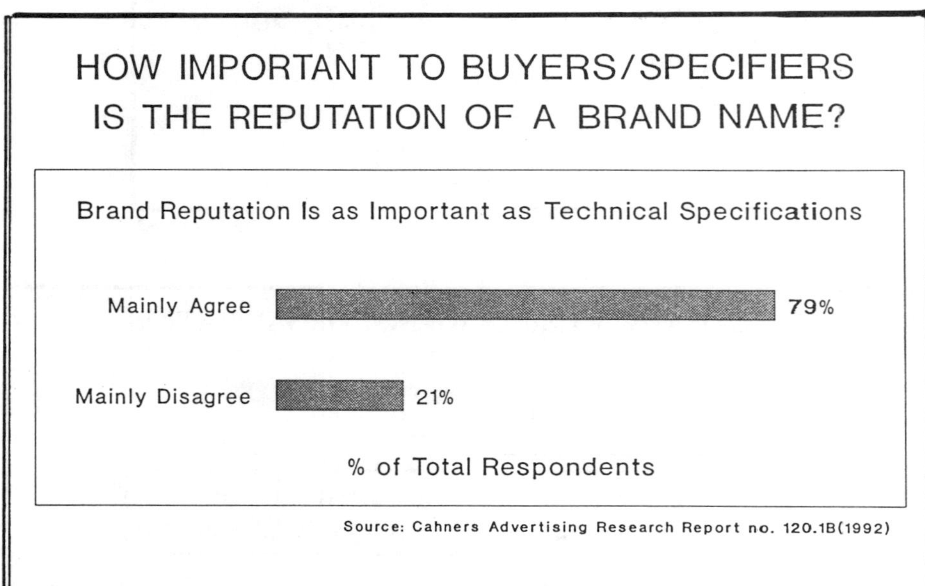

Figure 8.7

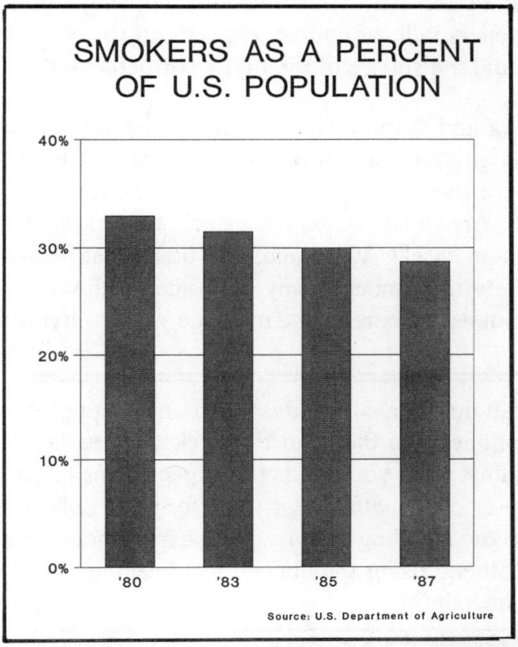

Figure 8.8

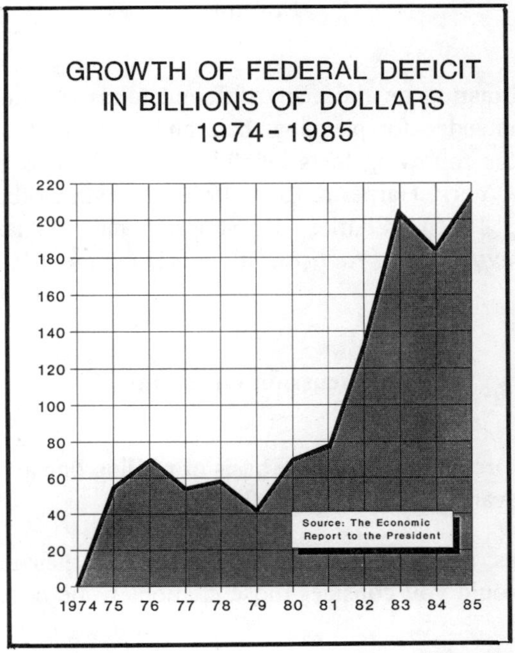

Figure 8.9

No audience will find fault with your tracing or copying a graph in a size suitable for display; the listeners will, of course, expect you to tell them where you found the original graph and the source of the figures or percentages appearing in it.

Finally, in preparing and displaying visual aids, planning in advance solves most problems. Are you going to hold it or them in hand? Will you have to pick them up from a desk? Are they to be suspended from clamps or hooks in back of the speaker's position? Are those hangers in place? Or are the aids to be mounted in order of display on an easel? Visual aids can be a great help--but only if they are simple in design, few in number, easily seen and readily understood. Above all, use them as *aids*, not as the core of the message you are trying to convey.

> Based on the audience analysis described in Chapter 7, we opened this chapter with comment on the need to check your earlier choice of subject and purpose against what you see as the expectations of your listeners. The rest of the chapter dealt with suggestions for your collecting the necessary materials through recalling your own experiences, calling upon the experiences of others, using the library, and keeping an eye open for visual aids that might be helpful.

Endnote

1. For more information on the many different kinds of interviews and on the procedures recommended for planning them and arriving at their objectives, the student will find the following texts helpful: Cal W. Downs et al., *Professional Interviewing* (New York: Harper & Row, 1980); Marvin Gotlieb, *Interview* (New York: Longman, 1986); Charles J. Stewart and William B. Cash, Jr., *Interviewing: Principles and Practices*, 5th ed. (Dubuque, IA: William C. Brown, 1988).

Discussion Questions

1. Is it possible to prepare a talk on the basis of reading one article or publication? What are the disadvantages of doing that?

2. In their speeches, some speakers cite the sources of their information. Under what conditions would you consider those citations to be necessary? Desirable? Unnecessary?

3. Have you ever been "all primed" to listen to an illustrated lecture only to have a power failure before it could begin? Or an equipment failure? Or the equipment operator failed to show up? Or the images on the screen were poorly focused? How did the lecturer handle the situation?

Application Projects

1. If you have had some experience in searching for materials in the library, explain how you went about it and how you did the necessary note-taking. Pass around a few samples of your notes.

2. Be prepared to demonstrate how to use *The Readers' Guide to Periodical Literature*. Discuss the use of that work in tracking down recent articles on a subject of general interest.

3. Bring to class your very rough pencil, ink, or crayon enlargement of a diagram or graph you have seen in a magazine or newspaper. Comment on whether or not it contributed to understanding. Could it just as well have been omitted?

4. Bring to class a full-page ad from one of the popular or trade magazines. Comment on whether or not the illustration contributes to or detracts from the effectiveness of the ad headline.

Additional Activities

1. Reporting on information secured through an information-seeking interview.

Although the interview is a valuable tool for the collection of information, a student often hesitates to request one with an acknowledged expert in a particular field. To overcome that reluctance as well as to give everyone this experience in information-gathering, each student in your class may be asked to present a 3-minute account of an information seeking interview with a local expert. A class discussion about these interviewing experiences could follow.

2. Previewing visual aids.

Whether or not to use visual aids depends on the subject and on the speaker's purpose in taking it up with listeners. However, for the benefit of the experience, you should try to use at least one visual aid in at least one presentation during the course. The "presentation with an informational-emphasis" frequently offers an ideal opportunity for the use of such aids. A class day or two before the speaking series is to begin, there could be a "showing" of the aids students were planning to use. Class discussion would be limited to comment on physical and mechanical detail--how the aids are going to be handled (hand held, easels, etc.) and on whether or not they are large enough to see and, if print is involved, to read.

Your brain, Peekay, has two functions; it is a place for original thought, but also it is a reference library. Use it to tell you where to look, and then you will have for yourself all the brains that have ever been.

From Bryce Courtenay, *The Power of One* (Random House: New York, 1989), p. 157.

9

ORGANIZING THE MESSAGE

When you finish this chapter, you will have gained experience in organizing the materials you have collected...

1. By laying out your notes in a possible order of use.

2. By using a skeleton outline to experiment with the organization and phrasing of key elements.

3. By "fleshing out" the skeleton into complete outline form.

"Inconclusive" is the best way to describe studies of whether or not organization materially helps the listeners. From the standpoint of the speaker, however, an organized structure provides a sequence which helps that individual decide whether or not there is enough material available in a given area to make a point, helps him or her remember key ideas, and generally makes a good impression on listeners ("This speaker is organized and must be a competent person"). We may reasonably assume that an organized structure, at least in some instances, may be useful to the listener, and that it is a substantial aid to the speaker.

Organizing the materials you have selected is not too difficult. You already have some idea of the sequence in which you may be using them, so lay your notes on the table in that general order. Your laying out of materials in a preliminary order (subject to shifting from one position to another) provides a base for your construction of one or more trial outlines and, then, the complete outline.

Before discussing the more common organizational patterns, let's first go over essential outline elements as they would appear in the *trial outline*, that skeleton version which, on a single sheet of paper, gives you a chance to do initial checking and experimenting before you proceed to work on a final full-blown version.

Elements in a Trial Outline

Statement of your specific purpose:________________________________

INTRODUCTION

Attention-getting opening sentence(s):______________________________

Statement of "subject sentence" (thesis): ____________________________

Review of reason(s) for audience to listen:___________________________

Statement of personal competence (if necessary):______________________

MAIN POINTS

I. ____

(Make an estimate of whether or not you have the materials necessary to make that point. If not, either change the wording of the point or find additional materials to back it up.)

Transition from I to II:

II. ____

(Again, estimate the materials required to make the point.)

Transition from II to III:

III. [if needed] ____

(Again make an estimate of....)

Transition from III to IV:

IV. [if needed] ____

(Again....)

CONCLUSION

Summary (if necessary or desirable):

Concluding sentence(s):____

Working with one or more trial versions of an outline enables you to check your plans in advance before you are too far into a final outline to make changes easy. With the audience always in mind, this is your opportunity to try out different ways to phrase key elements, especially your subject sentence and main points. On the phrasing of those main points, it's a good idea to make them as short, simple, and similar as possible. As for transitions, they're the signposts that tell the listeners you are moving from one point to another.

Basic Outlining Patterns

The discussion of the different outlining patterns below is largely centered on the initial trial or skeleton outlines; in every instance, a student following one of these patterns would, of course, extend it to the complete outline stage. As examples of finished products, there are two complete student outlines at the close this section. (Word-for-word transcripts of student presentations appear at the ends of Chapters 11 and 12.)

The step-by-step pattern

You will find this plan especially useful for describing a process or a procedure. The steps involved become your main ideas, and an explanation of what goes on in each one becomes your development. If there are more than four or five steps, look for a way to discuss them under two or three broader headings. It's easier for listeners to follow and remember two or three main points instead of six, seven, or more.

From what you've been able to discover about your intended listeners, let's assume (1) that they know little or nothing about how a magazine advertisement is produced, (2) that they would be interested in an explanation of the process, and (3) that you know something about the subject. At the left below is a listing of fourteen procedural steps. At the right are two broader headings, both of which you could arrive at by looking at the original fourteen steps for a short while.

Steps in Producing an Ad

[I.] Creating the ad

1. Creative conference on theme, illustrations, size of ad, etc.
2. Writing the ad copy
3. If photos are to be included, shooting and/or assembling them
4. Preparing the layout
5. Submitting copy/layout/photos to client
6. Revising copy/layout
7. Retouching/cropping photos
8. Submitting revised materials to client

[II.] Finishing the ad

9. Ordering type specified
10. Executing finished art
11. Checking finish against approved copy/layout
12. Ordering offset negatives and proofs
13. Final checking of negatives
14. Mailing insertion orders and negatives to publications

You have now selected a subject and specific purpose which you believe to be well adapted to your listeners, you have selected the materials suited to them, and you have chosen a basic structure, the step pattern. In this instance, that means you will have two major points with eight subpoints under the first and six under the second.

Planning the introduction. When you begin to speak in a public setting, the goal of your "introduction" is fourfold: (1) to get the attention of your listeners, (2) to let them know what you are trying to accomplish, (3) to point out what they have to gain through listening to you, and (4) to give them reason to believe that you are well informed.

Getting attention comes first. The order in which you accomplish the other goals of the introduction may vary and, if everyone in the room already knows you are a well-informed expert on the subject, you can skip mention of your special expertise. Whatever you decide to say, a good "rule of thumb" in your relatively short class presentations is to limit the introduction to no more than a fifth of the total time available to you. That kind of limitation will ensure that you have enough time to deal properly with your main purpose in speaking.

Here are a few ways--more will occur to you--to make your listeners "sit up and take notice" at the beginning of your introduction:

> Start with a brief example, illustration, incident, or human-interest story related to your topic.
>
> State a startling or shocking fact. ("If depletion of the ozone layer continues, land-based life will end.")
>
> Comment on the occasion which brings the listeners and you together.
>
> Quote an authority on the subject to be discussed.
>
> Ask a question pointing up the need for the information you are going to provide.
>
> Tell a joke only if it bears *directly* on the subject, only if it is new, and only if you tell jokes well.

Incorporating the four goals of an introduction in the ad production outline could look something like this:

INTRODUCTION

[Attention-getter]: This ad [holding it up] appeared recently in several magazines. You can't read it from where you're sitting, but you can see that it features a bold headline, a subhead, some copy, a company signature, a color photograph, and some background art. But how was it put together? How did it reach this completed stage?

[Personal competence]: I know at least a part of the answer to those questions. Last summer, I worked as an "intern" in the print-ad production department of a local advertising agency.

[Subject sentence]: My intention today is to retrace with you the steps taken to produce the ad I just showed you.

[Reason to listen]: Knowing how an ad is prepared is fascinating in itself and, who knows, some of you may even decide to look into advertising as a career.

MAIN POINTS

I. First, how does an agency go about creating an ad?

[Here, you would discuss steps 1 through 8 in your original list. As visual aids, you could have on hand manuscripts of two or more copy versions, prints of any photos involved, and one or two early layouts of the ad.]

[Transition]: Now we have client approval for the ad, and we are ready to answer a second question...

II. How does an agency finish the ad for publication?

[Steps 9 through 14 now provide the base for continuing your discussion. Visual aids could be photostats of the type set for the ad, retouched and cropped versions of the original photo or photos, finished art with type pasted in and with a "window" for the photo, proofs of the ad, and a copy of one or two magazines with the ad as printed.]

CONCLUSION

[Summary]: I hope that I have succeeded in giving you a good picture of the process of creating and finishing an ad.

[Closing remarks]: Of course, you couldn't get a really close look at the exhibits I held up as examples. When this class ends, you are welcome to inspect those items, and I will also be glad to answer any questions you may have. Thank you.

Planning the transitions. In the skeleton outline above, note the transition between the first main point and the second. As we noted earlier, a transition is a signal telling the listeners that you have finished talking about one point or subtopic and that you are now going on to another. You would often use a similar signal in moving from subtopic to subtopic. For instance, "When the copywriter has finished writing the ad, that 'copy' is ready to be turned over to the artist for an initial layout." Transitions take many forms. Without them, your "train of thought" will seem to the listeners to be moving in a jerky if not annoying fashion. With transitions, your audience always knows exactly where you are in the course of the presentation.

Planning the conclusion. From the wording of the conclusion in the skeleton outline above, you see that closing remarks almost plan themselves. The speaker sometimes includes a summary of the main points and a restatement of the purpose of the talk. At other times, the conclusion is just a series of remarks aimed at bringing the interaction with listeners to an appropriate end. With or without a formal summary, the conclusion should be short.

The place-to-place pattern

Everything said about the step pattern of outlining (and about introductions, transitions, and conclusions) applies to this spatial approach except that the body of the talk can be likened to taking the listeners from place to place on a guided tour. The danger in "conducting a tour" is that, unless you find ways to make it lively, it can be as deadly as having to watch someone's vacation slides.

For an example of spatial outlining, let's look to the Midwest. New Harmony, Indiana, was the scene of an early commune experiment; George Rapp and his German immigrant "Rappites" founded the town in 1814 as a cooperative, joint-property colony. The main-points-only outline below is spatial, but *the focus is on the daily life of the people.*

I. The progressive Rappite School is in the center of the town.

> [Description of a *typical school day*--subjects taught and books used in the early 1800s]

II. A cluster of Rappite homes is only a quarter-mile to the north.

> [Description of *family life* in one of the Rappite homes.]

III. The Rappite granary is a short walk to the west.

> [Description of the Rappite communal grain production and storing system.]

The time-to-time pattern

Without going into details with a specific example, this approach to organization is based on following a series of events in the time or chronological order in which they happened, are happening, or may happen in the future. For example, a speaker tells a group about his or her company's plans for constructing a new office center and does so by discussing the several phases of that expansion as they would occur *month by month*. Or a public official uses a time framework to describe how a new educational program is going to be phased into operation *year by year* over the next few years.

The topical pattern

Sometimes the order of topics is "speaker's choice," that is, the sequence of ideas is determined by the speaker's view of audience needs and expectations and not by the process or progression (as it is in the step-by-step, place-to-place, and time-to-time patterns). The speaker takes into consideration his or her understanding of listener preferences and, with that analysis in mind, (1) chooses the topics to be discussed and (2) the order in which to discuss them. In the slightly expanded skeleton outline below, the speaker deals first with "academic opportunities" (instead of the "nonacademic") because that is the topic of first concern to most students.

INTRODUCTION

[Attention-getter:] We are attending a fine community college. Nevertheless, many of us would like the chance to finish our programs at a major university.

[Subject sentence *and* reason to listen:] For those of you who haven't fully explored that possibility, I'm going to review with you the special opportunities open to students attending a large and nationally-known school.

[Personal competence:] Before my family moved here, I spent one semester at the University of Iowa. That short experience didn't make me an expert on higher education, but I did learn something about a typical state university.

MAIN POINTS

As you would expect,

I. Academic opportunities are greater at a university.
  A. A university offers more programs.
  B. A university has better-known professors.

[Transition]: In addition to your having access to greater academic opportunities, you would also find that...

II. Nonacademic opportunities are greater at a university.
  A. You meet students from a wider range of backgrounds.
  B. You hear lecturers who have international reputations.

CONCLUSION

[Summary and closing remarks]: In other words, a university education provides more opportunities in your chosen field. It also give you wider contacts with students and with outstanding persons in the university community as well as outside of it. Not everyone wants to attend a university but, if you haven't yet considered the advantages of doing so, I hope my remarks have been helpful. Thank you.

A topical pattern is like all other outlines in that you "flesh it out" with supporting materials in the form of examples, illustrations, statistics, quotations, etc. Its major difference from other outlines is that there is no easy and automatic sequence for the speaker to follow. Instead, you have to try out different orders of ideas until you find one that you believe will make sense to your listeners.

For another example of a topical outline in skeleton form, let's suppose that you wanted to discuss with your listeners the public confidence enjoyed by someone like Barbara Jordan, former member of Congress and currently Professor of Public Service at the University of Texas. Something like this could be your thesis or subject sentence:

> When Barbara Jordan talks about expecting public figures to obey the laws, people listen. Why is that? My purpose today is to describe the personal qualities which lead people to believe this fine American.

Then, you might choose to set up the main and immediate subpoints in this way:

I. Jordan has a strong *sense of justice.*

- A. What does that term mean to us?
- B. How does she demonstrate that quality?

II. Jordan has the *courage of her convictions.*

- A. What does that term mean to us?
- B. How does she demonstrate that quality?

Or if you wanted to increase your audience's appreciation of the concept of leadership, you could define the term and then plan the body of the talk in this form:

You show leadership when...

I. You surround yourself with able people.

II. You allow room for individual initiative.

III. You maintain contact with what is going on.

...or on another abstract term:

Concern for others means...

I. Taking action to meet the physical needs of others.

II. Taking action to meet the psychological needs of others.

Your support for the main points in the outline on leadership would be examples of ways in which people demonstrate or have demonstrated that quality; in the second outline above, you would cite examples of ways in which individuals show or have shown concern for others.

Typical Complete Outlines

When you are working with step, place, or time patterns of outlining, there is little or no problem in placing the topics in proper order. Your main concern is not order of ideas but how to adapt them in phrasing and handling to the concerns of the listeners. Topical patterns are more difficult; the speaker has to do all the planning but, at the same time, the speaker has more freedom in trying to meet audience needs. For those reasons, the two complete student outlines which follow are of the topical variety. The first was planned by Julie Smith, a student at Rollins College in Winter Park, Florida.

Specific purpose: To induce in my audience an understanding of extended-wear contact lenses and of their advantages and disadvantages.

Introduction

If you're having a hard time seeing this picture clearly [holding up hazy picture of outdoor scene], don't worry, you're not alone. According to an article published last April in MONEY MAGAZINE, this is what 21 million people see when they open their eyes and look outside very morning. Think about it. 21 million people.

Those of you who are dependent on glasses or wear contact lenses know exactly what I'm talking about. But what about those of you who were blessed with perfect vision. You're probably asking yourself, "What does this have to do with me?" Well, very little right now but what about in the future? I also don't think there's anyone in this room who doesn't have a family member or close friend who doesn't wear glasses or contacts. Have you ever thought about what they experience every day because of this handicap? Yes, I said handicap.

Imagine waking up in the morning, looking over at the clock on your dresser and not being able to see the numbers until you get up and go over there to see if you've over-slept, again! Or imagine sitting down to eat at your kitchen table, looking out the window and only being able to see a blur.

Those are only two specific situations which glass and contact wearers deal with daily and which impact on their lives. I know because I'm one of them. At the ago of 10 my vision went without warning from perfect to legally blind in my left eye. In the last 18 years I've had numerous glasses which I would never wear and every type of contact lens available at the time: hard, soft, gas-permeable, and even experimental. But none of them ever allowed me to function in a completely normal way like my family or friends who had perfect vision. Or should I say, none until now. Five weeks ago my optometrist introduced me to extended-wear contact lenses, and they have changed my life. Five weeks ago I woke up, looked outside, and [holding up clear picture of outside scene] saw this.

Not being able to see five feet in front of you no longer has to be the end of the world. Thanks to recent improvements in contact lenses and to the introduction of extended-wear contacts, you or someone you know can have perfect vision again. In this talk, I intend, first, to present basic facts about vision problems, secondly, to discuss the advantages of wearing extended-wear contact lenses and, third, to point out some of the drawbacks that come with those extended-wear contacts. You can help yourself and those you love by finding out if extended-wear contact lenses are best for you and best for them.

Body

I. These are the basic facts associated with the development of contact lenses.

  A. There are approximately 21 million people with various vision problems.

    1. 90% of these 21 million people are able to wear contact lenses.

    2. Each year Americans spend approximately 10% more a year on this $2 billion industry.

  B. Soft contacts were introduced in 1971 as another option to wearing glasses.

    1. Soft contacts now make up about 55% of all lenses in use.

    2. The cost of soft contact lenses usually ranges from $100 to $300.

    3. Made of an absorbent oxygen-permeable plastic, soft contacts require daily cleaning and can be worn only for a limited time.

  C. Extended-wear contact lenses were introduced in 1981 due to customer demand for better lenses.

    1. 3.5 million extended-wear contacts are already in use.

    2. Their use is expanding so rapidly that they are expected soon to command a major share of the market.

  Transition:
  Soft contacts have helped a great many people. However, as good as they are, extended-wear contacts are better.

II. Extended-wear contact lenses offer definite advantages.

  A. Extended-wear contacts are more comfortable than all other types of contacts.

    1. They are thinner than soft contacts.

    2. They are always more oxygen-permeable.

  B. Extended-wear contacts are more convenient.

    1. They can be worn 24 hours a day.

    2. They only have to be cleaned four times a month.

  C. Extended-wear contacts save you money in the long run.

1. Having to remove them so seldom greatly reduces the chances of your tearing a lens.
2. Cleaning them only four times a month saves you money on cleaning supplies.

Transition:

It wouldn't be fair of me to tell you only about the advantages of wearing extended-wear contacts. You should also be aware of their disadvantages.

III. Extended-wear contact lenses do suffer some disadvantages.

A. They require more time up front.

1. They require several appointments for fitting and checking.
2. They take more time in getting used to them.

B. They call for more money up front.

1. Starting over with a new plan means losing the money invested in other types in the past.
2. The thinner extended-wear contacts wear out more quickly and have to be replaced.

C. Their need to be cleaned is often overlooked.

1. They feel so good that people forget to clean them.
2. Infections sometimes result from lack of proper cleaning.

Conclusion

Well, in this brief time, we've been looking at the basic facts associated with extended-wear contact lenses, and we've learned about some of the advantages in wearing them and about some of the disadvantages as well. You now have the information you need to help yourself or to help a loved one to determine if these lenses are a good choice. For me, the decision was simple. I knew immediately that extended-wear contact lenses were best for me. Now when I wake up in the morning, I see this [holding up clear picture of outside scene again] instead of a blur. Now or in the future, the same good fortune could happen to you.

Bibliography

Hennison, Doris, Optician's Assistant. Personal information seeking interview, April 17, 1989.

Heyman, Harriet. "A Clear-Sighted Look at the New Contacts," *Money*, April 1988, pp. 162-68.

Lippman, Richard E. and Margaret Tolbert. "Are Your Contact Lenses as Safe as You Think?" *FDA Consumer*, April 1987, pp. 16-19.

"What's New in Contact Lenses," unsigned commentary in *Good Housekeeping*, March 1987, p. 201.

You will see details in Julie's presentation which you would have planned and phrased differently; no outline is perfect. Nevertheless, we can all agree that the outline does demonstrate thorough planning. The finishing touch is her bibliography, a listing of the sources on which her presentation was based.

The second complete outline was prepared by Bonnie Richardson, a student at Wake Forest University, Winston-Salem, North Carolina.

Specific purpose: To induce in the listeners the desire to help eliminate illiteracy by becoming tutors in one of the literacy programs.

Introduction

You undoubtedly know that a good many Americans are illiterate, that is, they can't read at all or they can't read well enough to "function" in our society. To put it another way, a functional illiterate is one who lacks the reading and writing skills necessary to cope with the reading problems common to everyday life. It's a person who cannot read--or has trouble reading--things we take for granted like road signs, the daily papers, labels in the grocery store, and the monthly bills.

While all of you are aware that illiteracy is a problem, you are not exposed to it on campus. Well, when you graduate and return to the real world, chances are you *will* be exposed to it.

Today, I would first like to discuss the extent of the problem from the standpoints of who the illiterates are, where they are, and what their typical characteristics are. Then, I'd like to touch upon some of the measures being taken to deal with that problem. You'll be glad to know that you can be a part of the rewarding solution!

Body

I. Let's first identify the problem by answering the three questions I brought up.

A. Who are these illiterate adults?

1. The U.S. Department of Education reports that 23 million adults, or 11% of the U.S. population is functionally illiterate. That means that *almost one-fourth of our adult population is illiterate*!

2. The USDA also reports that illiteracy is especially high among those on public assistance or welfare programs, in criminal institutions like jails and prisons, and to some extent in the military.

3. Illiterates are often the product of illiteracy. The value that family members place on literacy may influence the level that other members seek to attain, regardless of their ability or the availability of a good education.

(Transition) Now that we have some idea who the illiterates are, let's look into a second part of the problem.

B. Where are these illiterates to be found?

1. They are found wherever there are concentrations of poor people and clusters of racial and ethnic minorities. In other words, they're found mostly in the ghettos, among non-mechanical and migrant farm workers, and in the urban slums.

2. Geographically, there are more illiterates in the south and east than in the north and west.

(Transition) A final question in identifying the problem of illiterates is this:

C. What are their typical characteristics?

1. Illiterates are people with more or less severe psychological problems, my own student being a good example. He and most other illiterates suffer from...

    a. a lack of self-confidence and self-esteem
    b. a feeling of helplessness
    c. a lack of motivation
    d. a hostility toward authority of any kind

2. Other likely candidates for illiteracy are people whose native language is not English, high school dropouts, and many of the elderly.

(Transition) So we now know more about who the illiterates are, where they are found, and what their typical characteristics are. With some appreciation of the how serious the problem is...

II. Let's now look at measures aimed at its solution.

A. Volunteers are increasingly important in adult literacy programs.

1. Active in this field are church groups, public libraries, and corporations. R. J. Reynolds, for example, has contributed $300,000 to this cause.
2. The primary national organizations are the Literary Volunteers of America and Laubach Literacy Action.

B. The Laubach program is the most popular tutoring program in this area of the state.

1. It involves associating pictures with letters of the alphabet, and then letters with sounds.
2. On a tutoring schedule of about an hour per week, the student moves at his or her own pace through a well-planned series of skill manuals like this one [holding it up].
3. Before long, the student is reading simple sentences and making steady progress toward becoming literate.
4. With that improvement in literacy comes the pride the student takes in overcoming a real handicap in life. For the tutor comes the satisfaction from being helpful to another human being.

Conclusion

Well, I hope that you are by now more aware of the extent of the illiteracy problem and more sensitive to it. In our society, people who can't read have a severe handicap, one that keeps these people poor and can lead to unemployment, welfare, and even crime.

And where do you and I fit into the picture? We can work with one of the organizations trying to eliminate illiteracy. Tutoring takes only a couple hours of your time per week...and helping a person learn to read is more rewarding than you can imagine. Really, doing some tutoring will help educate you, too. You'll realize how fortunate you are, and you'll want to pass on some of that good fortune to somebody who desperately needs it.

And to make joining the effort easy for you, there's a Laubach tutoring group right here on campus [holding up poster]. They show you how to use the tutoring manuals and arrange your working with someone who has asked for help.

I've been trying to show you how illiteracy affects the lives of millions of adults, and I hope I've made the case strongly enough to affect your lives as well. Do yourself a favor. Volunteer today and begin enjoying the experience of helping someone escape from the prison of not being able to read!

Bibliography

Pilot Mountain Baptist Association (Laubach materials).

"Adult Literacy in the U. S. Today," Institute for the Study of Adult Literacy, 1989.

"Adult Literacy Issues, Programs and Options," U.S. Department of Education, bulletin of October 19, 1988.

> As we've been saying in this chapter, the trial or skeleton stage of your planning offers the chance to *experiment with several different versions* of the key elements that will provide the framework for the finished outline. Avoid moving to the finished outline stage until you are completely satisfied that you have settled upon the broad plan that will best ensure your inducing the audience to go along with your purpose.

Discussion Questions

1. Why do we have all those Roman numerals, capital letters, Arabic numbers, and small letters in an outline? Wouldn't it be far easier and just as efficient simply to line up the ideas, facts, and figures for presentation in any reasonable order?

2. Do we use transitions in everyday conversations? What forms do those transitions take? When someone says, "I didn't notice, but you seem to have changed the subject," is that person saying, "If you had given me warning of a change in subject, I'd be better able to understand you"? Does the same thing happen in speaker-audience interactions?

3. If the introduction comes first in a talk, why not prepare it first?

4. Under what circumstances do you think the summary should be left out of the conclusion?

Application Projects

1. You are a communications instructor. Study the two complete outlines at the end of the chapter, and then write a page of constructive comment addressed to either Julie Smith or Bonnie Richardson. On that page, suggest to the student *how a specific feature of content or form could be improved* to make it more adaptable to a student audience. After reading your suggestion to the class, be prepared to defend it.

2. Bring to class the introduction to a speech or to an article from any source. Considering the "audience" for which the exhibit was intended, point out the good and bad qualities of that introduction.

Additional Activities

1. Simplifying the organization of a multi-step procedure for presentational purposes.

Bring to class a list of steps in some process or procedure. The list should have in it at least five steps in one column with the your reduction to two or three steps in a second column. During a class session on organization, you should be able to defend your restructuring of the process or procedure.

2. Focusing attention on transitions.

Bring to class at least five transitions found in a newspaper editorial or in a magazine article. During a class session, be prepared to explain the presence of the transition in one of those five instances. The explanation should cover the need for the transition, the wording of it, and the service it performs in leading the reader from one aspect or point of a subject to another.

10

MASTERING THE MESSAGE

All young men and women owe it to themselves to be able to deliver an idea orally.

Louis L'Amour, novelist

The character of the speaker determines whether real communication happens or not.

Rex Kelly, Mississippi Power Company

When you finish this chapter, you should be aware that...

1. The success of a presentation, assuming that you have prepared it well, depends heavily on whether or not you have practiced enough to gain control over your message.

2. Memorization is for actors, not for speakers.

3. Notes or manuscripts, unless used only as "prompters," get in the way of communication.

4. Practice sessions give you the opportunity to check, change, or add to your choices of verbal, paraverbal, and nonverbal language.

5. Practice sessions give you the opportunity to check on whether or not you have done everything possible to establish or enhance listener perceptions of you as a speaker.

Demosthenes (4th century B.C.) was a famed speaker and statesman in ancient Athens. Someone once asked him, so the story goes, to name the three most important abilities contributing to a speaker's success. His answer: "Delivery! Delivery! Delivery!" His meaning? The time and effort you spend on planning is wasted unless you can finally present the message in such a way as to induce listeners to go along with your purpose in speaking in the first place. To achieve the purpose of any presentation, you have to be able "to put it across" to and for the listeners. So the purpose of this chapter is to help you, as the speaker, to get ready for participating in speaker-listener events. And a primary way to get ready, to borrow from Demosthenes' wisdom, is practice, practice, practice.

Focusing on Communication

You will know you're close to being ready to interact directly with any audience and specifically with the members of the class when you are able, in your rehearsal "dry runs," to present a planned message without omitting anything of consequence. "Without omitting anything of consequence" does not suggest memorization. Even if you write a word-for-word version and succeed in the unlikely feat of total recall, the audience will quickly sense that it is listening to a robotlike recitation. Accept the fact that *you will never give the talk twice in the same words and in the same way*, either in practicing or in the final interaction with listeners. In the course of your establishing control over the message, you will forget an item or two at one time and forget a few different items the next time. But if you leave out an idea here or an example there, who's to know? When you lose your train of thought and can't seem to find a way to finish a sentence, just break it off and begin another with "What I meant to say was...." Speaking without hesitating or forgetting something is a myth--it doesn't happen. *Aim only at communicating.* If you prepare carefully (with or without memory-aiding cards or manuscript), you'll find it impossible to forget your main theme, your main ideas, and most of the support for those ideas. If you still want to do some memorizing, focus that effort on your opening and closing sentences; it is always comforting to know exactly how you are going to open and close a talk.

Handling notes and manuscripts

The purpose, then, of your going through what you plan to say a few times is not to memorize your message; it is simply to establish "a train of thought." From rehearsing at first with your complete outline as a guide, you'll soon be able to shrink that document to small note cards. In fact, one side of two or three standard index cards (3" x 5") can carry the key wording of almost any outline. Cards are easy to hold in one hand and, unless you're constantly glancing at them, listeners will scarcely be aware of their existence, even if you gesture with them.

On the other hand, when a presentation calls for a complete manuscript, use it too *as a prompter only*. No audience listens for very long to a speaker whose eyes are glued to an outline, notes, or manuscript. Perfection should not be your goal. Listeners don't count on your being glib, and they don't want to hear a line of memorized machine-gun chatter. They only expect you to be yourself and to demonstrate a desire to communicate with them in a mutually helpful way.

Whether or not you use a complete manuscript for a presentation, there will nevertheless be times when you will have to read in public. For example, you may find yourself in the position of having to read "the minutes" of a previous meeting, or read a proposal to the town council, or read a part of the service in a church, or read a long quotation as a part of a talk, or read a paper at a convention, or read a statement to the press. In other words, reading to listeners, though not generally recommended for the body of a speaker's presentation, is still a form of communication that is required often enough so that you should know how to do it well.

Here is a five-step set of suggestions to help you escape from "the prison of the manuscript" and maintain close contact with your listeners:

1. Write the manuscript in the same direct style that you would be using if you were speaking without a manuscript. Number the pages; it's surprisingly easy to get a sheaf of papers in the wrong order.

2. Typed or word processed, the manuscript should be double or triple spaced, not only to make it easier to read but also to provide plenty of room for underlining those words or phrases you want to emphasize.

3. Add any other markings or symbols that will help you make the talk "come alive" as you read it. For example, underline those words or phrases you want to stress. As for timing, in addition to the pauses already suggested by commas, you can use a single slash-bar here and there to indicate a very brief hesitancy and a double slash-bar to indicate a more significant pause. The excerpt below, from an address by Rex Kelly of the Mississippi Power Company, has been used to show that particular approach to marking up a manuscript. (The full text of the Kelly speech is well worth reading and appears at the end of Chapter 11.)

> The point is that the speaker must understand the process of communication // and be eager to make the effort / that makes communication happen.

> This type of speaker understands / that everything communicates. It may be convenient / for those who spend many hours on the content of a speech / to go on pretending that the content // is what will get results. But that just is not the way things work out. Repeated studies suggest / that well over half / of what the audience remembers is [paraverbal and] nonverbal.
>
> People respond / to the quality of a voice. Is it easy to hear, comfortable, and confident? Does it convey / just the right level of energy and conviction?
>
> People respond / to how the speaker looks. Are the clothes appropriate, not flashy and not too casual? Is the hair neat and clean? (That may sound petty, but I've seen speakers / whose hair looked like / a cat had been sucking on it for a week.) In short, a speaker owes it to his audience / to look his or her best, and the audience expects / this show of respect.
>
> These elements, no matter how shallow they may seem, are the first / and often strongest indication to an audience of a speaker's credibility. If you want people to respond, you not only have to know / what you are talking about, you have to look like you know / what you are talking about.[1]

4. After you have attached whatever notations, signs, or symbols you prefer as cues, practice reading the manuscript aloud until you feel you are presenting it in a way that does the ideas justice and that the audience will understand and appreciate. Be careful to check the overall timing of your talk. If it is too long, do some editing; if too short, amplify some of the ideas or look for additional materials.

5. Plan to handle the actual presentation in much the same way as the extemporaneous (i.e., not memorized) approach recommended for other speaker-listener events. If your manuscript has become dogeared in the course of practice sessions, see that it is "reprinted" and re-symboled. Above all, remember to use the manuscript only as a cue-sheet; the reader who concentrates on reading instead of on the audience is likely to lose that audience. Although it's easy to gesture with small cards in hand, a bundle of notes or a complete manuscript calls for speaking from a lectern. Unless a microphone is involved, a lectern also has the advantage of allowing the speaker the freedom to move from behind it from time to time. If no lectern or table-top reading stand is available, normal practice is to hold the notes or manuscript in one or both hands. Even in this situation, it's still possible to free a hand for gesture.

Checking Your Language

Reviewing your verbal language

In Chapter 1, we learned that the meanings which listeners attach to "our" words depend on the contexts (verbal, paraverbal, and nonverbal) in which those words appear. Listener experiences and perceptions never coincide exactly with ours, but we can still take steps to assure something close to a match between their interpretations and ours.

That is why, in practicing to make the most of your chance to interact with the members of the class, you will find it useful to double-check your approach to contexts through which the listeners are going to screen your attempt to communicate with them.

Beginning with a review of the verbal language you plan to use, the right words, of course, are those which, in the light of your analysis of the listeners, will stimulate in them the meanings you intend. Further, your concern for becoming one with the listeners will require your using words, word groups, and word patterns that identify you as one of them. From your experience in everyday one-to-one communication with others, you know that the wording of ordinary conversation is straightforward--it consists primarily of short sentences, few if any "big" words, and little or no formality. It's true that some of that conversational language, "street" or otherwise, that you and your friends use would not be suitable for a public presentation. Nevertheless, in sharpening your phrasing to make it appropriate for a given audience, try not to lose the direct style outlined previously in Chapter 4.

Reviewing your paraverbal language

Without repeating the definition and examples of the paraverbal context which appeared in that first chapter, let's say again that we include under that term all the ways in which vocal intonations, timing, volume, and pitch affect the basic meanings which listeners give to a speaker's words and sentences. While we earlier used "I'm going to Kalamazoo" to show how a speaker's tone can affect, change, or contradict meaning, vocal factors other than tone also affect listener interpretations. We can, for example, achieve added changes of meaning in listener minds by the special emphasis we give to words and ideas through slowing or increasing our rate of speaking, through increasing volume at one point and lowering it at another, and through changes in pitch.

So when you are practicing for "the main event," do some experimenting to see how you can best use variations in tone, rate, pitch, and volume to affect meaning in the minds of your listeners. You could, for example, try highlighting your "subject sentence" and main points by stating them more carefully and deliberately. An idea of minor consequence could be speeded along. In other words, try varying your speaking rate and other paraverbal word-modifiers to fit the importance of a point as you make it. Experimenting with these elements will enable you to "get more mileage" out of the words you do use...and more confidence that listeners will really understand what you say.

Reviewing your nonverbal language

The third major class of word-modifiers, as you know by now, consists of gestures and body language generally. If you are already accustomed to using gestures in communicating informally with your friends and others, those mannerisms will be a natural part of your speaking in public. Even those of us who use gestures less freely find it worth the effort to use them...and listeners welcome the additional cues which gestures supply for interpreting the speaker's message. Whatever your past experience with gestures, you will find it relatively easy and profitable to work one or more of the types below into a presentation.

Gestures to direct attention. When you use a visual aid (the different types are discussed in Chapter 8), gesturing "comes naturally" as you show that aid to your listeners and direct their attention to details of it, in it, or on it. If your visual aid, for example, is a large chart or map, you can't avoid pointing to specific locations. If you do use one or more visual aids, keep in mind the need to maintain direct contact with the audience while you do the necessary attention directing to the poster, chart, object, or other visual aid.

There are other kinds of pointing, of course. You can direct attention by pointing to any thing in the room or person in the audience. You can point to indicate directions of the compass. You can point to a letter in your hand, to a flag on the stand, out the window to a plane, and "through" the floor to the earth. It is easy to point to something or somebody that members of the audience can see. Unless there is good reason not to point, directing attention in that way is an easy and effective gesture.

Gestures to describe. Another simple form of gesturing occurs in our describing something square, triangular, circular, etc. As we outline size and shape with hands and arms, "It's about this size," we say. A student pilot describes a part of his or her training program by sweeping the hands through some aerial maneuvers. Another speaker uses one or both hands to demonstrate the tumbling of a car in an accident. Next to gestures for pointing, descriptive gestures practically force themselves upon us.

Gestures to emphasize ideas. You have certainly seen speakers use hands and arms to add emphasis to statements. One will wag a forefinger at you in warning to avoid a particular course of action. In declaring ignorance of what to do about a problem, another will raise hands and arms in a gesture of helplessness. A third will thump the lectern or table to emphasize an idea. All three may use one, two, or three fingers on an upheld hand to give listeners an added signal that a new main point is in the offing. A key to the development of gestures for emphasis is to observe other speakers and adopt those patterns with which you are comfortable.

Finally, it goes without saying that gestures of all three types are very helpful message-supporters and modifiers. In the course of your rehearsing sessions, you will discover that you are easily--if not automatically--gesturing in support of parts of your message. Again, *do some experimenting* and, in each instance, use your own comfort index in making the final to-use-or-not-to-use decision.

Body language. We believe we invented the concept of body language, but many Greek writers discussed the subject, and the Romans called it *sermo corporis*, "language of the body."[2] Intentionally or not, we do accompany gestures with nonverbal word-modifying in the form of body language: smiling, frowning, nodding or shaking the head, bending forward to stress an idea, moving to one side of the lectern to signal a transition or to help maintain listener interest, and engaging in other forms of bodily action to support the message. To a large extent, body language takes care of itself as an extension of the speaker's attention to gesture and of his or her concern about communicating with listeners in a meaningful way.

When you seem to have rehearsed your presentation to the point of having it under reasonable control, you may want to have two or three friends sit in on "a final dress rehearsal." They can constitute a small audience with which to interact and, afterwards, they can provide a few suggestions for improvement in your "performance." If a camcorder is available to you, another approach to pre-performance evaluation is to have someone tape one of your later practice sessions. Some students like the prospect of seeing and hearing themselves in action; others get the same results through having a couple students provide helpful comment.

Checking the Physical Setting

The physical setting for your speaking in the classroom will bring with it no surprises. Nevertheless, your analysis of the physical setting for this or any other event should alert you to any special problems affecting your interaction with the listeners. For instance, if you discover that the available lectern is so high that you're going to be hidden behind it, have you arranged to have a lower one substituted? If substitution is not an option, can a low step or stand be in place when it's your turn to use the lectern? Then, too, if in later life you become a person of some prominence, there's the possibility that a presentation of yours is also to be televised. Prominent or not, when you are "on camera," you will want to be careful to adapt your communicating style to the special requirements of that more intimate medium (e.g., smaller gestures, less movement of head and shoulders, and a more conversational tone). Audiences are forgiving, but they do expect a speaker to "look alive" in a way that is appropriate for the occasion, be that in the classroom or anywhere else.

Again, be ready for the unexpected. If you haven't had a chance to "case the situation" in advance, you may find that the platform from which you're expected to speak is farther than you like to be from the audience. Or you walk into a room in which 25 listeners are more or less scattered through a room designed to seat 150. Or the previous meeting featured videos of award-winning television ads, and the window shades are still drawn. These situations do occur...and more often than you would expect. When they do, improvise. Step off that stand and move down close to the audience. Ask those widely separated members of the audience to "come down front and center to join the party." Get someone, building staff or members of the audience, to open those shades and let in the light. In other words, if you see anything about the physical setting which can be improved quickly without holding up the meeting, no one will object to your taking whatever action is required to set the stage for better communication.

Checking the Timing

The train of thought you have established should be "on time" when it arrives at the terminal. A 7-minute presentation, for example, should end just short of the 7-minute limit or just over it. If the time allowed is 6-8 minutes, that leeway of two minutes is wide enough so that you shouldn't have any trouble coming to a close within that period.

A student sometimes comments that not enough material could be found to cover speaking for the specified time; another may say that the subject chosen was too complex to discuss within the time allowed. In such instances, the fault is not with the amounts of material available or with the complexity of the subject. It is the speaker's responsibility to narrow a theme that is too broad or to broaden one that is too narrow.

If, as you practice, you find that your subject is too broad, keep cutting it down until it is manageable within the time available. Let's assume, for instance, that you're a student in civil engineering who believes that the listeners would be interested in "highway construction methods." You quickly discover that you can't discuss that subject in seven minutes, so you then move down progressively to "streetpaving in cities" to "asphalt street-paving" to "emulsifiedasphalt street-paving" to "emulsified-asphalt hot-mixture street-paving" to "patching pavements with emulsified-asphalt hot mixtures." As you move down the ladder of steadily narrowing topics, you will come to one which can be discussed within the time limitation.

On the other hand, when the subject you have in mind is too narrow, you will be moving up the ladder to wider topics. Just as almost any subject can be limited (as in the paving example), so it can also be extended. However, before you move to extend a seemingly too narrow topic, check first on whether or not additional materials are available. If they are, you won't have to abandon what may be an excellent choice of subject.

A final note on timing--there is a natural tendency toward a slight increase in the speaking rate as you interact directly with an audience. If you see that you are just over the time limit in a near-final or final rehearsal, no further cuts are necessary.

Ensuring Your Credibility

You've heard the expression "Consider the source!" Why is the ethical component of your speaking so important? Because rarely can you induce listeners to accept your way of thinking without it. That's why, when Aristotle cites the credibility of the speaker (*ethos* or "ethical appeal") as close to being the most effective way to enlist audience support for what one has to say, he is thinking of a speaker's keeping that goal in mind, both while preparing for a presentation and in making it.[3] The moderns agree that one's ethical appeal is of crucial importance. According to Cohen, for example, "Who says something is as important as what is said...."[4] And James Golden adds this assessment:

> More than one hundred scientific studies in the past two decades support [Roger] Nebergall's thesis that a speaker's ethos or image has an enormous effect in a rhetorical situation.[5]

To put it another way, a speaker's general reputation has much to do with an audience's acceptance of him or her as "a reliable source." If you are already known to an audience, your reputation as an individual and as a speaker will certainly have preceeded your appearance and, before you say a word, will have a bearing on the audience's attitude toward you. Then, in the course of your on-the-scene interaction with that audience, you will be living up to your reputation...or damaging it.

On the other hand, if you are unknown to your listeners, they will be deciding whether or not to believe you before you stand up to speak, as you speak, and after you speak. Again, their opinion of you is subject to continuing change during the speaking event. The speaker's level of credibility at its end may be quite different from that which she or he enjoyed at its beginning.[6]

How do you make yourself credible in the eyes of an audience? Aristotle says you have to show *good sense*, *good character*, and *good will*.[7] In his view, a person having those qualities thinks correctly and clearly, considers it a duty to "tell it like it is," and feels that the audience is entitled to the best possible advice. Modern theorists and researchers add a fourth element which, in the context of public speaking, we call *good presence*.

Credibility through good sense

Good sense is the decision to use your native intelligence in ways which the audience will consider reasonable. When a speaker clearly knows what she or he is talking about, credibility follows, often in spite of other difficulties standing in the way.

In James Michener's novel, *Texas*, that writer describes a scene in which a "cityfied" architect meets with a group of rough-and-ready ranchers to discuss plans for a library. Had a vote of confidence been taken before he stepped forward to speak, "Gordon would have been shipped back to San Antonio...."

> But when he began to speak, the tremendous authority he had acquired through travel, study,contemplation and actual building manifested itself, and his audience sat in rapt attention.[8]

Similarly, if a professor of communication speaks on her specialty at a convention, her listeners are inclined to listen to her as "an expert." Common sense tells us that the same professor could have problems in addressing a community group on the politics of a Middle East, Baltic, or Central American country she knows little about, has never seen, whose culture she does not understand, and whose language she does not speak. To nobody's surprise, "Research shows that people are most apt to be convinced by an argument from an expert than by the same argument from a non-expert source."[9]

As we have been saying all along, you must know what you're talking about and use good sense in discussing it. Uncritical or emotional listeners may accept your ideas because they're friends of yours, but not too many presentday audiences are made up of those gullible enough to accept without question someone else's statements on a subject.

Credibility through good character

We also expect a speaker to be thorough in research and to be fair in telling us how and why he or she reached certain conclusions. We are inclined to believe speakers who have well earned reputations for saying and doing what we consider to be right.

We quickly lose confidence, on the other hand, in the speaker who tells us one thing and is discovered to be secretly saying and doing something else. In the last two years of Ronald Reagan's presidency, for example, his credibility was severely damaged by the secret sale of arms to Iran, an act contrary to the publicly stated policy of his administration. So your listeners must feel that you are a person of character. If you are not honestly convinced that your subject is worthwhile, your listeners will quickly sense your lack of sincerity...and they will lose interest. Or if they begin to suspect that your primary concern is personal gain or some other strictly personal goal, you will end up as an audience of one listening to yourself.

Credibility through good will

Speakers demonstrate their good will--and gain ours--through convincing us that they are trying to identify with us in the effort to reach a worthwhile goal.

When a star of the entertainment world asks us to help feed starving children in Africa, we assume that her primary motive is to enlist us in a worthy humanitarian effort. Her good will and concern make us want to cooperate. When other stars try to sell us insurance, physical fitness equipment, cosmetics, beer, and other products, we know they're being highly paid for their services. Individuals involved in that kind of promotion show no real good will, and they often lose credibility as a result.

On the other hand, many well-known individuals repeatedly show their concern for others. Paul Newman is in his 60s, married to Joanne Woodward for over 30 years, successful in film, business, and car-racing, a contributor of millions of dollars to a variety of charities, and a life-long campaigner for civil and human rights. In short, he has a public image that is as impressive as it is unselfish.

Another ambassador of good will is Barbara Jordan. A Texan by birth, she won election to Congress in 1973 and served in the House of Representatives through 1978. As a lawyer-member of the Judiciary Committee, she established a national reputation for her insights into presidential powers--and unconstitutional abuses of those powers. In 1979, Jordan was appointed to the prestigious post of LBJ (President Johnson) Professor of Public Service at the University of Texas. Happily for us, she continues to watch the political scene and does not hesitate to speak out against those who exceed their authority. When Barbara Jordan talks, people listen.

In other words, listeners will sense that you are concerned about their welfare, about information that will help them in some way or about proposals that will benefit everyone, including the speaker. Audiences may disagree with a speaker, but they respect one whose goal is clearly "the common good."

Credibility through good presence

By good presence we mean those aspects of an individual's appearance and personality which give the audience the impression of poise and confidence. In your own experience, you have met individuals and speakers whom you immediately trusted for some reason. "She looks so honest." "I'd trust him; he's not afraid to look you in the eye." You may have been seeing those persons through your stereotypes of the qualities you hope to find in new friends. However, the point is that most of us are impressed favorably or unfavorably by the "picture," that is, by the physical appearance, dress, lifestyles, mannerisms, and other outward qualities of the people we meet.

As for ourselves, we can't all have dynamic personalities, be physically impressive, possess a high degree of personal charm, and be "great story-tellers." But we can all emphasize those personal characteristics which do lend themselves to making a favorable impression. No one has a monopoly on good manners, appropriate dress, and the air of competence that a well-prepared speaker radiates.

In summary, mastering the message is simply a matter of practicing a time or two beyond what you think necessary. It is one thing to succeed in running through the talk by yourself or in the presence of a couple friends; to communicate in the presence of an audience is another. The "safety margin" of practice beyond the bare minimum also serves mightily to keep any final tensions at bay. Secondly, as you practice, use the same kinds of gestures that you expect to use in the actual event. Adding gestures at the last minute doesn't work for most people. And if you plan to use visual aids, make sure you become thoroughly familiar with them in the practice sessions.

As for your credibility, if a check of the four necessary qualities finds you short somewhere, it is not too late to do some further planning to bring your "ethical appeal" up to par. Student listeners and audiences everywhere expect speakers to have good sense, to be frank with them, to show good will, and "to make the most of what they have" in establishing a good presence. The speaker's "ethical appeal" is a truly priceless part of the message.[10]

Endnotes

1. Excerpt from Rex Kelly, "Speakers and the Bottom Line: The Character of the Speaker," *Vital Speeches of the Day*, 54 (November 1, 1987) 2, p. 48.

2. For the fullest treatment of gestures and body language in ancient literature, see Quintilian, *Institutio Oratoria*, trans. H. E. Butler, Book XI, Chapter 3, in Vol. 4 of Quintilian, Loeb Series (Cambridge, MA: Harvard UP, 1980 rept). For other references, see Ray Nadeau, "Delivery in Ancient Times: Homer to Quintilian," *The Quarterly Journal of Speech*, 50 (February, 1964), pp. 53-60.

3. Aristotle, *The "Art" of Rhetoric*, trans. John Henry Freese, Vol. 3 of Aristotle, Loeb Series (Cambridge, MA: Harvard UP, 1982), 1356a.

4. Arthur R. Cohen, *Attitude Change and Social Influence* (New York: Basic Books, 1964), p. 23.

5. "Rhetoric as Value: Ethos and Image," in *The Rhetoric of Western Thought*, eds. James L. Golden, Goodwin F. Berquist, and William E. Coleman, 3rd ed. (Dubuque, IA: Kendall/Hunt, 1983), p. 294.

6. George A. Borden et al., *Speech Behavior and Human Interaction* (Englewood Cliffs, NJ: Prentice-Hall, 1969), p. 220.

7. Aristotle 1378a.

8. James A. Michener, *Texas*, 2 vols. (New York: Random House, 1986), 2:878.

9. Camille B. Wortman et al., *Psychology*, 2nd ed. (New York: Alfred A. Knopf, 1985), p. 498.

10. "Rhetoric as Value: Ethos and Image," in *The Rhetoric of Western Thought*, page 300.

Discussion Questions

1. If you have little experience in using gestures and are somewhat wary of using them to help you in communicating, should you avoid them altogether? Or should you recognize that some gesture and body language is better than none? And since it's not possible to stand before a group without a degree of gesture and body language, you may as well work at doing it well?

2. Name a public figure whose statements you generally believe. Why do you feel that person has credibility?

3. Name a public figure whose statements you do not believe. Why do you have no confidence in that person?

4. Cite a situation in which you concluded that a speaker did not have command of the subject. To what extent was your confidence in the speaker shaken?

5. Many politicians hire pollsters to tell them what the voters are thinking. Then, they take stands which fit the views of the voters. What do you think of that practice?

Additional Activities

1. Analyzing the personal credibility of a speaker in his or her presentation on any subject. (*Vital Speeches of the Day* is one source of current presentations.)

Look for evidence of the speaker's credibility as demonstrated in the speech through his or her good sense, good reputation, and concern for the well-being of the listeners.

2. Analyzing the personal credibility of a speaker as demonstrated in the viewing of the videotape or video/audio cassette of an address by that speaker.

Procedure same as for #1 above except that, in this instance, you would be in a position to include observations about the "presence" of the speaker.

PART III

Interacting with Audiences

Photo courtesy Rollins College, Winter Park, Florida.

11

GAINING ACCEPTANCE OF INFORMATION

Always bear in mind that your own resolution to succeed is more important than anything.

Abraham Lincoln

On the day you are scheduled to speak, your goals will be to...

1. Adapt to any unexpected "environmental influences" you may encounter.

2. Persuade the members of the class to accept "the body of knowledge" you have prepared in their interests.

Information Is Persuasion

We begin this chapter with reinforcement of a theme threaded through this book: call them what you like, all talks, presentations, speeches, addresses, discourses, lectures, sermons, or reports are fundamentally persuasive. The persuasive component of the speaker's *ethos* (i.e., reputation for good sense, good character, good will, and good presence) is ever present, even in a mathematics class. Secondly, in every public or workplace appearance, we expect the speaker to be persuasively logical, that is, to present ideas in an order that seems reasonable to us and with some reasonable support. And in all situations, we expect the speaker to demonstrate commitment to our interests, our welfare, and our concerns.

It's not too far out to think of public speaking in terms of ingredients going into a "swirl cake." One event-piece of it may have more of the chocolate swirl (logical appeal), another may have more of the golden swirl (emotional appeal), and a third may have more of the white swirl (ethical appeal). All other pieces of that cake are going to have different proportions of the same "audience appeals." Similarly, the extent to which a specific appeal is embedded in any one event-piece is largely a function of the speaker's skills in analyzing and adapting to a particular audience's tastes, needs, and desires. So it is that every speaker-interacting-with-listeners event is unique; it has never occurred before and will never occur again.

On the other hand, some say it's possible for a speaker to present a totally dispassionate and exclusively informational report on a subject like, say, street congestion in downtown Cleveland. Dispassionate or not, the report cannot be divorced from reliance on its source (ethical appeal), confidence in the evidence quoted to back up the report (logical appeal), and listener reaction to the speaker's implied or stated request that the report be accepted (emotional appeal). True, one of the traditional appeals may be so woefully lacking as to weaken a given presentation, but that is a deficiency in the speaker's analysis and skills, not in the rhetorical certainty that every such presentation is a mix of degrees of all three appeals, ethical, logical, and emotional/motivational.

Why does this information-is-persuasion subject come up again? To point up the view that the credibility of the speaker, the logic of sound order, and the "selling of the information" are essential elements in the so-called informative speech. You don't want to be the student who looks upon this assignment as one in which she or he placidly dishes up any kind of information for listeners who, in turn, placidly sit there and think of something else. Your goal is to communicate information that will be of value to the listeners, and you want that intensity of concern to be clearly apparent; without it, there will be no interaction and no communication.

So for a speaking option related to this chapter, you were "invited" to induce in the class an understanding of a particular body of knowledge. If you've been wondering if you'll ever again be expected to "increase the understanding" of a group of listeners, it may happen sooner than you think. Each of the following situations, for example, calls for an emphasis on information: a corrections officer explaining cell block duties to new officers; a supervisor explaining work rules to a group of new employees; a lawyer describing details of a new retirement plan to other members of the firm; a credit manager outlining the details of a new credit-application form to members of her or his staff; a consumer goods expert telling a consumer group how to get the most for a dollar; a senior security officer explaining a football game traffic-control plan to officers assigned to the game; a factory representative giving newspaper pressmen instructions on operating and maintaining a new press; a safety specialist reporting the latest accident-prevention methods to a group of mining superintendents; a Parks Service guide describing rock formations to a group of tourists. Whatever jobs or posts you hold in the future, it is almost certain that you will find it necessary to increase the understanding of listeners in your occupational or professional life--and you will want to do it well.

That brings us closer to the happy day. By the time you read this, you will have (1) recognized the need to speak on a subject having an informational emphasis, (2) analyzed the listeners, (3) settled upon a specific purpose adapted to them, (4) collected materials suited to them, (5) organized those materials in a way that will appeal to them, and (6) rehearsed your message to present it in a way designed to gain acceptance from them. Although you are now ready or close to being ready to participate in the main event, let's take the time for a final check on a few environmental details.

Adapting to Unexpected Environmental Influences

In Chapter 7, a part of the process of analyzing the audience calls for your determining "what environmental influences may be at work." Insofar as your being one of the speakers on a classroom program is concerned, there is no problem because you are by now familiar with both the occasion and the setting. You can't do much about the classroom setting, but sometimes the occasion (e.g., a day allocated to student speeches) provides an impromptu opportunity to make on-the-spot changes in what you planned to say.

Adapting to the unanticipated incident

Audiences expect a speaker to be aware of what's going on around them and in the world at large. In the classroom or out of it, if you follow one or more speakers on a program, one of them may say something which offers a better leading line for your talk than the one you had originally chosen. Don't hesitate to change the opening to your presentation by referring to an earlier speaker's comment on a related subject, or by calling attention to a remark or two from a speaker preceding you. In fact, there is no faster way to get the attention of an audience than by giving an earlier speaker the compliment of seriously or humorously quoting that individual at the beginning or at any other appropriate point in your own presentation.

The "world at large" is that wide expanse outside whatever room or hall is the site of a particular program. On the day after the last San Francisco earthquake, anyone speaking on a program or reading a convention paper in the Bay area could hardly overlook mention of the disaster that had just taken place. For another example, hotel luncheons are seldom gourmet delights. However, when you stand up to speak after a luncheon that everyone did seem to enjoy, you have a chance to establish almost instant rapport with the audience by complimenting those responsible for handling arrangements for the affair. Yes, you already have an attention-getting opening planned for your presentation, but it's never too late to begin with a sentence or two that the audience might like even better.

Adapting to the unfamiliar physical setting

At those times when you're scheduled to speak in that outside world, you do know the occasion in advance and can adapt to it, but you aren't always able to check the physical setting until you show up to speak. As you look about you in that unfamiliar room, hall, or auditorium, you still have time to plan some last-minute adjustments to that setting.

Make sure you can be heard. Nothing is more irritating to listeners than not to be able to hear the speaker. If the audience and room are both larger than you anticipated, you will want to remember to turn up the vocal volume without losing the variety in tone and rate which help hold audience interest and attention. Regardless of size, two meeting rooms in the same restaurant, hotel, or convention center may be very different in acoustics; something just over conversational volume will carry nicely in one, but you'll almost have to "holler" to be heard in the other. When in doubt, this question is in order: "Can you hear me?"

Make sure you can be seen. Listeners are also irritated if they can't see the speaker too well. If the lectern is too high for you, ask for a small platform to stand on. When no small platform is available, step out from behind the lectern as much as possible. Unless you're a microphone prisoner, standing in front of or to one side of the lectern will enable you to maintain the personal contact you must have with the audience.

If you're not too tall and you find yourself speaking from the floor of a flat-floor room, the audience may again have the problem of not being able to see you. One way or another, try to solve that problem before you begin to speak. More than one speaker has created his or her own platform by asking for and standing on a sturdy chair. In any event, if you can't see the listeners, they can't see you--and that's a terrific handicap to communication.

Match the action to the scene. The eye is drawn to moving persons or things. Assuming that you can be easily heard and seen, you will want to match the "size" of your gestures and bodily movement to the size of the audience. A limited gesture of the hand or nod of the head, however well suited to the smaller room, is unsuited to the larger hall and audience. The audience-oriented speaker moves, gestures, points, and provides enough action to reinforce the ideas he or she has selected for special emphasis. To fully accomplish that purpose, your bodily action must be "large enough" to fit the room and the audience in it.

Whatever the occasion or setting, when you do arrive at the platform or lectern, give yourself a chance to get settled.

Wait until any bustle or conversation has subsided. Then, since our culture calls for "look 'em in the eye," find three or four friendly faces in different areas of the room, and begin communicating with your select few. Shortly thereafter, you'll find yourself communicating with everyone. Make up your mind to enjoy the experience...and you will!

Typical Informational-Emphasis Presentations

In promotional talks by sales representatives, the emphasis on information is often dominant; the salesperson *concentrates on describing features* of a product or service and, in effect, lets the description do the promoting. Kelly Zmak, a student at San Jose State University, made the award winning presentation below. It is heavily informational and, at the same time, a striking demonstration of the fact that information is persuasion.

Capitalize on Your Potential with a Personal Computer[1]

by Kelly Zmak, San Jose State University

Hello. My name is Kelly Zmak. I'm a student at San Jose State, but I'm also a part-time representative of the Computer Circuit Company of Clayton, California.

You know, as college people we all have something in common. We want to be successful. The levels of our success vary, but to be successful is something that we all strive for. Having an advantage in today's world is something none of us would mind. But having a disadvantage is something that none of us can afford. I would say that there are many of you here today that are not capitalizing on your potential, because you do not own a personal computer. And for those of you who do, listen up. Your computer may not have the power, the capabilities, and the features needed to give the home user, the student, and the business person an advantage in today's world.

[Directing attention to the personal computer being exhibited] Introducing the affordable and incredible Apple II GS! The II GS name itself gives a hint to its capabilities. The II come from a long line of Apple II family computers, including the original Apple which was released back in the 1970's and which set the standard for the industry. Since then, there have been the II E, the II C, and now the II GS. The G stands for graphics. Graphics are information represented by pictures or images. And with the GS, these graphics can include some 4,000 hues of color and with the clarity that has rarely been available on a personal computer before. The S stands for sound. The GS is capable of generating up to 15 simultaneous sounds including voice using a special digital oscillator chip designed by the Ansona Corporation, the maker of the Mirage Music Synthesizers, among others. Well, now that you have been introduced to the computer, it is important in thinking about buying a personal computer to ask yourself three questions: (1) What can a computer do for me? (2) Can the computer's capabilities grow as my needs grow? (3) Is it affordable? Let's take a look at each of these questions and how they apply to you as a buyer.

What can a computer do for me? As college people, one of the most common things we need to do is type papers. This includes all aspects of the writing, rewriting, and trying in the end to get it all double-spaced typed and in on time. But with an Apple II GS and a word processing program, many of the tedious, time-consuming aspects of typed papers can be greatly reduced or eliminated completely. Imagine a spelling-checker and correction program that corrects your spelling, makes you aware of the mistakes you have made, and helps you reduce the number of mistakes you will make in the future. The GS can be applied to specific majors as well. Engineers and drafting majors will save hours using a computer assisted drafting program. Interior designers can put architectural structure in two and three dimensional on the new GS. Graphic artists can do what is referred to as cut and paste. This is what used to be done on paper where they actually take the letters and lay them out. This can now be done on the computer, saving hours. Music majors can be incredibly artistic. With the GS sound capabilities then can create, compose, and play music in true tones on the GS. Art majors can be incredibly artistic with The GS color palette of over 4,000 variations in color.

Allow me to demonstrate. The device I am using here is called a mouse. It is one of the features of the GS that makes it easy to use. I think they call it a mouse because in a way it looks like a mouse. The picture you are about to see on the monitor is not a digitized picture. This one was drawn by an artist for the company and, as you can see, the resolution of the computer for clarity is one of its most distinguishing features. That's me you see there. And through the use of digitized feeding, the GS is capable of speaking in eight different languages. You see, the GS was released in eight countries around the world, including the United

Kingdom, France, Italy, and others. Yes, the GS has the power to take you through college and into the business world. With the help of the GS, you might even be graduated at the top of your class!

But what about after you graduate? Thus, we come to my second question: Can the computer's capabilities grow as your needs grow? The GS was designed to grow as the needs of the user grow and, after you are graduated, your needs will probably grow. The design of the computer allows the user-in this case, you--to add additional hardware to allow you to do just about anything you want to do with the computer today and in the future, whether it is expanding the internal numbering of 256K to the capability of 8meg, or whether it's adding additional software. Hardware is merely additional equipment that you add to the inside or outside of your computer. Whenever I talk about capabilities, IBM seems to pop into the minds of my audience. So to quell these thoughts, I'll say this: The II GS is easier to use. It has the largest software base in the world, over 10,000 programs available today. And if that's not enough, you can buy a card that you put into your GS that will allow you to run IBM software, giving you the advantages of both worlds.

Probably the third and most important question when talking to college people is that of affordability. But before you can buy it, you have to know what you're going to get. The GS system includes an RGB analog monitor. For those of you who are not technically inclined, that just means it's a good monitor. Then there's the CPU itself, the keyboard which has an expanded numerical key pad, the mouse, and the 3-1/2 inch high density speed drive. All this for $1,699 which sounds like an awful lot of money to a college student. But with your good credit and no money down, you could qualify for as much as $2,500 the same day you come in and take your GS home with you. With the usual two years to pay off the loan, that is less than $75 a month or $3 a day. According to a recent article in the A+ magazine, a student could save as much as an hour a day using a computer. Now think of it, if you are working in a local campus bookstore for a minimum wage if you are lucky, just in the time you save using your new computer, you could make your monthly payments plus.

This talk began with three questions about what the computer can do for you as a student, whether or not the computer's capabilities can grow with your needs, and whether or not it is affordable. You have one set of answers to those questions, but before I conclude, I'd like to accept any other questions you may have about me, my company, or my computer. It is said that a good salesman generates questions and, on the assumption that I generated some, please feel to ask them now.

Question: Why do you need the 8meg memory when most of the time a user, especially a student, would need just the 256K memory?

Answer: Well, as you know, the computer comes with an internal memory of 256K or, in other words, with 256,000 bytes of memory. I bought an applied engineering card for $169 and inserted it into the cart. That card adds a capability of 1-1/2meg. For an additional $129, I can expand the computer's capability to 8meg. It's important to note here that I just rattled off an extra $300. But the point I make is that the potential for added capability is there if and when you need it. I am involved with digitized speech. I do quite a bit of it, so the added memory capability is important to me.

Question: What type of printers do you recommend, and what are the price ranges on them?

Answer: I would definitely recommend the Apple Image Writer II, the printer I have for this system. It sells for just under $500 but, if you buy it within the next two weeks, I can get it for you for $250. [Laughter] Now, I know you are all saying, "He just made that up." No, this sales policy has been in force for some time, but it does expire in two weeks. The Apple endorsed policy states that, if you buy a new computer system within the period of the sales promotion, they will give you $250 cash back on the purchase of a printer. Any more questions?

Question: Do you have to worry about electrostatic discharges affecting your disks?

Answer: Yes. It has been estimated that 90% of all computer down-time is due to static electricity. It's not a problem if your system is properly grounded.

To bring these remarks to a close, let me ask you once again to remember my three questions: What can a computer do for you? Can a computer's capabilities grow as your needs grow? And finally, is it affordable? When you come to your conclusion, I believe the Apple II GS computer will be your answer. Thank you.

Moving into the off-campus business world, we find a power company executive, Rex Kelly, describing how important good speakers are to a company's communications program. His emphasis is on *the character of the speaker* as it affects the effectiveness of the speaker in communicating with an audience. Reading Mr. Kelly's presentation will "increase your understanding" of the concept of *ethos* or ethical appeal; it also provides a fine model for any talk in which the speaker first defines a concept and then explains through examples what the definition means.

Speakers and the Bottom Line: The Character of the Speaker[2]

by Rex Kelly, Director, Corporate Communications,
Mississippi Power Company

The presentation below is a slightly shorter version of the one Mr. Kelly made to the Utilities Speakers Activities Committee of the Edison Electric Institute, Denver, Colorado, August 7, 1987.

We begin, ladies and gentlemen, with a statement all of us will accept: A company that does not have a strong communication program with its employees, its customers, and the general public is courting disaster.

Because time doesn't permit touching on all the facets of a strong corporate communication program, I'll get right to the point about how effective making speeches can be.

I'd like to admit to be biased at the outset about the relative importance of the speech and the speaker. The speech itself is important, but it is the speaker that makes it happen. If you want to deliver a message, you must have a dependable messenger.

If you take nothing else away from my remarks today, I'd like you to remember this above all else: A speech is one of the most effective forms of communication, and *the character of the speaker determines whether real communication happens or not* [emphasis added].

Why do politicians go out on the campaign trail? Surely they would experience less wear and tear if they just mailed everybody 8 x 10 glossies and a copy of their platform.

Why do preachers preach? And why are television evangelists so remarkably successful. I know for a fact that the Christian and other religious messages are readily available in printed form.

And finally, with records, television, and movies, why will perfectly intelligent people pay $25 to $200 to go see an entertainer "in person"?

All of these questions have the same answer. THERE IS AN ELEMENTAL POWER IN HAVING A LIVING BREATHING HUMAN BEING--RIGHT HERE, RIGHT NOW--INTERACTING WITH OTHER HUMAN BEINGS.

And when that living, breathing human being is a skilled communicator, he or she possesses real power, the power to change the way people feel, to change the way they think, and even to change the way they act.

For a company to achieve its goals, whether they are financial or social, this power is exactly what they need. Most companies have similar goals. They provide a product or service. They seek to make money. They may advocate social changes. If they want these things to happen, they have to get people to think, feel, and act in a way that will allow the company to accomplish its goals. I maintain that there is no better way to make this happen than through communication. We must be willing to speak anywhere that three people we wish to reach are gathered together.

Once we make sure that our message is honest and correct, then the rest is up to the messenger. Getting the public to support a company's goals, creating a favorable political climate, or even meeting sales goals are helped enormously by speakers presenting the message--live.

While I want to point up the value of sending a speaker to make a live presentation to a group, I also want to present a few words of caution as well. It does make a difference who the speaker is [emphasis added].

We must insist as strongly as we are able that any speaker we send out will consistently communicate high personal credibility. The speaker must be able to create a strong positive perception of the company he or she represents.

By a few careless remarks, an arrogant or inarticulate president or CEO can destroy many years of coordinated communication effort. On the other hand, an assistant supervisor of niff-naffs can do a lot of good by being a credible and likable spokesman for his or her company.

The point is that the speaker must understand the process of communication and be eager to make the effort that makes communication happen.

This type of speaker understands that everything communicates. It may be convenient for those who spend many hours on the content of a speech to go on pretending that the content is what will get results. But that just is not the way things work out. Repeated studies suggest that well over half of what an audience remembers is nonverbal.

People respond to the quality of a voice. Is it easy to hear, comfortable and confident? Does it convey just the right level of energy and conviction?

People respond to how the speaker looks. Are the clothes appropriate, not flashy and not too casual? Is the hair neat and clean? (That may sound petty, but I've seen speakers whose hair looked as if a cat had been sucking on it for a week.) In short, a speaker owes it to the audience to look his or her best, and the audience expects this show of respect.

These elements, no matter how shallow they may seem, are the first and often strongest indications to an audience of a speaker's credibility. If you want people to respond, you not only have to know what you are talking about, but you have to look as if you know what you are talking about.

I hope that you don't misunderstand the point I am making. I am not saying that style is more important than substance. We all know that an effective speaker must be honest, well informed, and committed. This provides substance to the speech. What I am suggesting, however, is that no matter how solid the foundation, style can make or break a speech.

So, what are the characteristics we should insist on in choosing people for our speakers bureaus? What combination of traits will bring about the successful blending of substance and style? I've already touched on the visual impact of the speaker, but there are other qualities that must be apparent for a speech to really work.

An effective speaker must be committed, honest, and well informed. A speaker who is committed cares about the task at hand. He believes in the power of the spoken word and in the value of getting out in the community. She is willing to focus her intellectual and emotional resources to produce the best result possible. He will demand his best effort from himself in every situation. Doing one's best at whatever task is set is a matter of both personal and professional pride.

A speaker's honesty is intimately connected with that personal commitment. Neither one can be faked. If a speaker doesn't really believe what he is saying, the audience will sense it. With the type of audiences we face, it is foolish, even dangerous, to think we can fool very many people even some of the time. Honesty is not only the best policy, it is the only policy.

A speaker must tell the whole truth, not just part of it, even when it involves admitting a mistake. Lee Iacocca probably saved many thousands of dollars by simply stating, "Did we screw up? You bet we did!" We have to resist in every way possible being placed in the position of defending obvious mistakes.

It is next to impossible for a speaker to credibly present the truth unless he or she is truly well informed. The best of intentions do no good if speakers don't know their subjects backwards and forwards. Often it is our job to see to it that they have the best and most complete information. But we also have to insist that they take a personal interest in pursuing the best sources of information.

In short, an effective speaker must be willing to put in the time to be both an interested and interesting representative of the company. This is always what an audience hopes for, and it is what will awaken their natural willingness to respond to and agree with the speaker.

That is what an audience is most often prepared to do, by the way. At the beginning of a speech the audience is usually on the speaker's side. They want a positive experience; they want the speaker to be right. The rare audience that is spoiling for a fight calls for different strategies than those I mentioned earlier. In that case, the best outcome is likely to be little more than a grudging respect for the credibility of the speaker.

A typical audience hopes to meet an interesting person or hear a good speech. But from years of experience attending civic club lunches, they aren't too surprised if it doesn't happen. This low level of expectations creates a terrific advantage for a speaker who is well prepared and is excited about what he or she is doing.

This preparation and sense of excitement immediately raises a speaker above the prevailing mediocrity and gives an immediate boost to the credibility of that person, no matter what his or her title may be.

When an audience that is expecting to hear a standard company line, for example, is faced with someone who understands their point of view and gives it fair treatment, they open up. They pay attention. They will respond to a speaker who is concerned about responding to their feelings and values.

If we want the best possible response from our audiences, we have to give it our best shot. We cannot, in all fairness, ask more of the audience than we have been willing to give of ourselves. If we haven't given our best, if we don't mean what we say, we are engaged in deception, not communication. And the audience will know it. And the harm will be done.

Every act of communication from a company affects the environment ion which the company operates. They affect the company's ability to reach its goals, the bottom line. They affect the bottom line because the only way a company can achieve its goals is to get people to feel, think, and act in ways that contribute to those goals. And the public forum, making speeches, is one of the very best ways to influence people.

The speech gives people both what they want and what they need. It gives them a human concept to associate with a company or product. It changes the company from some abstract "thing" out there to a real, believable, likeable, person right here. Credible speakers give us one of the best ways to personify the company--

to personify it in a way that builds a positive public environment.

Through our speakers, the public will hear what we say because they can see how we look and how we talk about their concerns. The company becomes a person, and that person wins people to his or her side and thereby to the company's side.

On the theoretical level, it is not too hard to agree to the importance of the character of the speaker in every act of communication, every speech. But moving from theory to practice calls for constant watchfulness on our part. It is a demanding and sometimes frustrating responsibility, but it's one every person in this group has taken on.

I know that meeting this responsibility is not beyond your abilities. So, in closing, I simply would like to wish you and your speakers the greatest continued success.

Endnotes

1. Kelly Zmak, "Capitalize on Your Potential with a Personal Computer," *1987 Championship Debates and Speeches*, eds. John K. Boaz and James R. Brey (Annandale, VA: Speech Communication Association, 1987), Vol. 2, pp. 127-30.

2. Rex Kelly, "Speakers and the Bottom Line: The Character of the Speaker," *Vital Speeches of the Day*, 54 (November 1, 1987) 2, pp. 47-50.

Discussion Questions

1. In reference to Kelly Zmak's presentation...

When you listen to a salesperson, do you expect to hear a thorough description of important features? What does a reading of this talk reveal about this student's analysis of student likes and dislikes? Is the language appropriate? In what ways?

What is Zmak's organization? Would you have difficulty remembering the main ideas? Are there enough transitions? Are they well handled?

How well do the opening remarks fulfil the requirements of an introduction? Could you improve upon either the introduction or the conclusion?

The student presents information about the computer and then offers to answer questions. What inferences do you draw from a speaker's offering to be questioned? From a speaker's not being willing to answer questions?

Are visual aids a part of a speaker's language? What kind of language?

2. In reference to Mr. Kelly's talk on the character of the speaker...

Is he talking about the need for a speaker to have good character, that is, the need to be ethical? Or is he discussing "character" in the broader sense of ethical appeal, that is, the need for a speaker to have good sense, good character, good will, and good presence?

He seems to suggest that we should not "...go on pretending that the content [of a speech] is what will get results." Is it his position that style (i.e., the character of the speaker as opposed to content) is all that matters?

You were not among the listeners to his remarks. Nevertheless, what evidence of Kelly's "ethical appeal" do you see in the speech?

He uses the phrase "credible and likable spokesman for his company." Can you be credible without being likable? Likable without being credible? Or is being likable a part of one's "presence" which, in turn, contributes to one's credibility?

When Kelly uses the singular pronoun or possessive in reference to a speaker, it's generally he or his. Would that usage detract from his "ethical appeal" in some situations? Or even in this situation?

He says, "We must be willing to speak anywhere that three people we wish to reach are gathered together." Is that idea consistent with the view most people have of public speaking? Consistent with the view represented in this textbook?

Can you cite an instance in which a careless, arrogant, or uninformed representative of a company made a public statement which seriously damaged the company's reputation?

Application Projects

Speaking options

1. Prepare a 6-8 minute talk aimed at explaining or describing something to the members of the class. Use one or more visual aids if they will help you create or increase listener understanding.

2. Prepare a 6-8 minute presentation aimed at acquainting the members of the class with the features and advantages of some product or service. Try to choose

a product or service that lends itself to the use of one or more visual aids.

3. Prepare a 6-8 minute presentation aimed at clarifying anabstract concept. After defining the concept, clarification can take the form of examples of individuals who exemplify the concept and/or of anecdotes demonstrating it.

Listening options

1. On one page, nominate a student information-sharing speaker for above-average success in inducing the desired response from the students in the class. Explain why or how you feel this student-audience interaction worked out so well.

2. On one page, nominate a student for best choice of subject and purpose from the standpoint of class interests. Explain why that choice was especially appropriate.

3. On one page, nominate a student for his or her superior introduction. What did the speaker do to get your attention? Did you understand from the start what the talk was going to be about? Did the speaker give you a good reason for listening? Did you have confidence in the speaker's knowledge of the subject?

4. On one page, nominate a student for superiororganization. What kind of outline pattern did he or she use? Why was it easy for you to follow?

5. On one page, nominate a student for his or her "best use of one or more visual aids." Give the reasons for your choice.

Photo courtesy Rollins College, Winter Park, Florida.

12

SEEKING AGREEMENT ON ISSUES

When a nation silences criticism and dissent,
it deprives itself of the power to correct its errors.

Henry Steele Commager

In reading this chapter, your goals will be...

1. To incorporate "issue locator" questions--aimed at determining where the listeners stand on a problem or solution issue--into your speech preparation.

2. To use an issue you have "located" as the base for phrasing your specific purpose and as a guide in the search for supporting materials.

3. To "let the audience help decide" what points to make, what supporting materials to use, and in what order to present them.

4. To give credit where credit is due to the sources of the materials used.

5. To remember "to close the sale," that is, to end your presentation with a specific appeal that the listeners agree with you on the views expressed or take the action you are proposing.

The need to speak out on important issues has been recognized since the days of the first democracy in ancient Greece. In fact, the obligation "to become involved" is so deeply ingrained that a day seldom goes by without news reports of individuals speaking in support of their favorite "causes." Others are just as outspoken in opposition--so we have people taking pro or con positions on testing for drug abuse in the workplace, on abortion, on civil liberties, on the right to bear arms, on company responsibility for providing health insurance, on energy conservation, on the editorial policies of the student newspaper, on the morality of nuclear arms, on county plans to build a bypass, on environmental issues, on birth control, on food labeling, on the minimum wage, and on any problem-and/or-solution topic you can name.

Not unexpectedly, you find subjects like those above discussed by editors and commentators under the familiar headings of questions of fact, value, and policy:

Questions of Fact

Although questions of fact can be investigated simply to find out what the relevant facts are in a particular situation, those facts may also be used as the basis for arguing that a serious problem does (or does not) exist. Examples: Are we properly storing the wastes produced by nuclear plants? Are whales and other creatures of the sea threatened by pollution? So, if you feel strongly that a problem does or does not exist, you've found an speech topic; that is, you've found one unless most of your classmates already agree with you--in which case, there is no issue worth discussing...and you continue looking.

Questions of Value

When you take a position based on "a value judgment," you are choosing to argue the worth--or lack of worth--in a particular evaluative view. Examples: Was our involvement in the Persian Gulf War worth the costs in terms of human suffering, physical destruction, ecological harm, and other losses? Is medical care in this country as good as it is in Canada? Is our educational system as good as that of the Japanese? How serious is the problem of homelessness in this country? In comparison with the problems growing out of habitual drinking and smoking in this country, how serious is the drug-habit problem?

Questions of policy

A policy question asks, "What should we do about this problem?" It carries with it the assumption that a problem exists and that the problem identified has been recognized as serious. If, however, the speaker feels that the listeners do not yet recognize that the problem exists or that it is serious, she or he would first have to deal with one or both of those issues (questions of fact and value).

If you choose to speak on a policy question, you will probably be taking a position along one of these lines...

> I hope to demonstrate that this problem is serious enough to require a solution.
>
> I hope to show that this problem is serious, and I also plan to propose a solution for it.
>
> I intend to propose a solution for this problem, one we all recognize as serious.
>
> I intend to show that a particular solution to this recognized problem is better than other solutions proposed.
>
> (You could also take a stand opposite to any of the positions above.)

Since policy questions deal with *what ought to be done* in the future, you've noted that such questions usually begin with the word *should*. Examples: Should college scholarships be limited to those qualifying on the basis of academic excellence only? Should students have the right to elect one of their number to membership on a college board of trustees? Should the role of the National Security Council be restricted to counseling the President? Should the U.S. assume the role of international peace keeper? Your positive or negative answer to that kind of question, of course, becomes the position you ask the listeners to approve.

When we talk about a speaker's supporting a particular position on an issue, we're not suggesting that the speaker is doing any reasoning in the course of the presentation. The reasoning takes place before the event. The speaker plans, organizes, and rehearses the message in advance and then tries to induce the listeners to accept the evidence and the conclusions presented.

To achieve that goal, the speaker may well be emphasizing the appeal of good reasoning and good reasons. Here again, however, we have to keep reminding ourselves that rhetoric, as Weaver says, "is an art of emphasis."[1] There may be an emphasis on reasoning, but the meanings, as interpreted by the listeners, will also depend on a host of other influences. Audience acceptance of ideas, as you already know, is simultaneously influenced by how the listeners feel about the speaker, by their attitudes on the subject, by the constraints of time, place, and general atmosphere, by interfering or supporting "noises," and by streams of messages of all kinds. We do stress reason in some situations, but *reason can never be the exclusive influence or appeal.* With that understanding reaffirmed, we take up further detail on the steps a speaker follows in the effort to induce listeners to reach agreement on one or more issues.

Analyzing the Audience

At this point, the presumption is that you have a general problem in mind and, although your search for materials may still be ahead, that you have some idea of your purpose and the stands you expect to take. The next step, your analysis of the audience, requires a review of the usual questions (as outlined in Chapter 7) to decide, among other things, whether or not your subject and the approach you are considering will really benefit the student listeners and hold their interest at the same time.

In addition, you now supplement the basic audience-analysis questions with a special series aimed at helping you determine "the issues," those major positions on which the thinking of the listeners differs from yours. If, however, your listeners are not known to have taken a position on a particular issue, you will still be looking for the point at which they are waiting for you to influence their thinking.

Locating the issue or issues

The word *issue* is often misused. First of all, it is not a statement. *An issue is a question which highlights opposing points of view*. If one speaker says, "Raising the minimum wage *will* bring about a recession," and the audience (or another speaker) counters with "Raising the minimum wage *will not* bring about a recession," the issue is this question: "Will raising the minimum wage bring about a recession?"

The "issue locator" below, in use since Greek and Roman times,[2] enables a speaker to locate specific issues by working down through four stock questions:

1. *Is there really a problem?*

If your listeners can be expected to agree with you that there is a problem (e.g., acid rain, the "greenhouse" earth-warming effect), there is no issue and no point in boring them with evidence that the problem exists.

On the other hand, if your intended listeners do not agree with you that a problem exists or if they do not know that one exists, you have located an issue requiring evidence and argument that it really does exist.

Another variation--the listeners believe a problem exists and you do not; the issue arises from their answering "Yes" and your answering "No" to that first stock question.

2. *Is the problem serious?*

Differences of opinion often begin at this point. If the audience agrees with you that the answer to this second stock issue is "Yes," there is no issue here unless you intend to argue that the problem is not serious.

If you believe the audience answer to the question to be "No," you have an issue. You must then demonstrate to listener satisfaction that the problem is truly serious.

3. *Is a solution necessary?*

Here again, if listeners feel that a solution must be found, their answer to the question is "Yes." There is no issue here *unless* you take the opposite position that the problem is not serious enough to require a major change in the present system.

On the other hand, when the intended listeners oppose any marked change from the present system, and you feel that real change is the only cure, you have an issue, and you must then show that a solution is needed.

4. *Is the proposed solution practical?*[3]

a. Will it work under current circumstances?

b. Has anything like it worked in the past?

c. Is its future success likely?

d. Do the listeners consider taking action important?

Even if the listeners are thought to agree with you that a solution is necessary, their answer to this fourth stock-issue question could be that *your solution will not work.* Or their position could be that a different solution is better than the one you are proposing.

Grin & Bear It By Fred Wagner

'I intend to make it top priority to find out where I stand on that issue!'

Reprinted with special permission of North America Syndicate.

Believe it or not, using the "issue locator" can help you decide where it is that your listeners agree with you (no issues) and where they are either not known to agree with you or are likely to disagree with you (issues!). Calling attention to points of agreement does help a speaker "become one with the audience" but, beyond that point, a speaker's fire-power should be centered on discussing the issues and winning listeners over to his or her position on them. Think of it this way: your objective is to transform points of difference or issues into points of agreement or non-issues.

In other words, if your listeners are unaware that a problem exists, you will be marshalling arguments to show that it does. If they are aware of the problem but unaware that it is serious, you will want to demonstrate that it is serious. If they already know that there is a problem and that it is serious, you may or may not be proposing a solution. If a solution different in principle has already been proposed by someone else, you may be attacking it for being impractical, or you may be proposing another which you feel is better. If the main issue is a question of the relative merits of two solutions already proposed, you may decide to support one of them. Or you could decide to support a solution combining the best features of each.

Your analysis of the audience, then, including the checking of listener views on the issues, helps you decide where it is that the audience "parts company" with you and, consequently, *on what phase or phases of the overall problem you should concentrate your search for evidence and argument.*

Phrasing Your Specific Purpose

After you have decided where to take a stand, you can work out the exact phrasing of your purpose. If your listeners believe, for example, that college athletes should not be paid a salary, and you believe that they should, that is the point at which you take your stand...and you phrase your purpose accordingly: "To induce the listeners to agree that college athletes should be paid a salary."

Collecting Materials

In your earlier search for a subject, you may have already uncovered sources which will help you develop "the case" you have decided to support. You can now go back to those sources with confidence that you know exactly what you are looking for. Otherwise, as we noted in Chapter 8, the computerized catalog files in your library are remarkably efficient; feed in a topic and out comes a list of books and other references dealing with that topic! Or with a little more work, library card catalogs, indexes to magazine articles, current-event files, and helpful librarians give you essentially the same results.

Organizing the Message

Let the listeners play a part in helping you decide on the order in which you will take up your major arguments (main points) and the order of the materials supporting those points. If you have, for example, worked out a topical outline calling for two main points, consider whether or not you have enough evidence to back up those points, whether or not your evidence is of a kind the listeners will accept, and which of the two points will make the better first impression on the audience.

In your trying to induce listener acceptance of any idea, major or minor, a common practice is to state the inference or point-to-be-made and follow it with the evidence. However, where your audience analysis may have given you reason to be especially tactful, you may decide to give the evidence first ("Let's take a look at the evidence and see where it leads us") and then state what you hope is the shared inference. An initial example of that approach was cited near the end of Chapter 7.

The actual process of outlining is not too difficult, especially when you keep the audience in mind. If a step approach is possible and you want to use it, moving from step to step poses no problem; the time-to-time or chronological approach calls for a discussion of events in the order of their happening; the space-to-space or spatial approach requires movement from area to area; and the topical approach is the arrangement of main ideas of close-to-equal-importance in an order which you consider to be appropriate. Choose the kind of outline which seems to provide the best framework for the materials available to you. Take some care in phrasing the main points (always easier to remember if they are short, simple, and in similar patterns of wording), provide adequate backing for each one, and you will be well on the road to successful interaction.

For the rest of this chapter, the discussion is centered on the more flexible organization-by-topic outlines which more often than not serve as the base for positions taken on problem-solution issues.

For example, as a student in the Department of Geology, you become aware that the river supplying water to the community is being polluted by the dumping of liquid wastes from a nearby plant. Company officials discount any harmful effects, and neither the students nor the people of the area seem to be overly concerned. Use of the "Issue locator" has led you to the conclusion that, for now, you should concentrate on convincing the class that the problem is serious. In skeleton form, your initial outline could be set up as follows:

Subject sentence: The pollution in our river poses a serious problem for everyone living in this community.

I. Pollution from the plant threatens our health.

(Evidence of carcinogens and other dangerous contaminants flowing from the plant into the water.)

II. Pollution from the plant threatens the ecology of the river basin.

(Evidence of dying vegetation, fish kills, and offensive odors.)

III. Pollution from the plant threatens our economic growth.

(Evidence of reluctance on the part of new businesses or industries to locate their operations in or near the community.)

The first assumption about the planning outline above is that you have evidence leading reasonably to three different main inferences. You then consider the order in which you should arrange those inferences as points to fit your audience. If the students are ecology-conscious, perhaps main-point II should be in first position? If the students have no significant interest in the economic growth of the community, perhaps III should be discarded? Or should you concentrate only on threats to health and design main points to emphasize the direct threats to (I) the physical health of the students and (II) their mental health as well? The point is that a topical outline is one for which you do the planning in relation to the perceived concerns--or what should be the concerns--of the intended audience. Your earlier analysis of that audience helps you to decide what to include and what to exclude in the effort to reach a common goal that will benefit everyone.

In the classroom setting, of course, the time allotted to you for a presentation is often too short to permit your taking up more than one major issue. But let us assume again that everyone in the community already realizes that the problem is serious (no issue here) and also feels that something must be done before the pollution problem gets any worse (no issue here either). However, the people haven't been able to agree on a plan to solve the problem (probably as many issues here as there are solutions proposed).

If it's mainly the solution that's at issue, you know from our previous discussion of stock issues that a speaker is expected to show that a plan for solving the problem must (1) be possible, (2) have a consistently good record in the past, (3) be likely to be successful, and (4) be supported by the listeners as a necessary action. Following that sequence as a base for the statement of main points, the basic case would end up something like this:

Subject sentence: Since everyone agrees that something must be done to solve the river-pollution problem, five of us have studied the solutions proposed over the past few months. It seems to us that an *Eco-Filter System* would be the best solution to the problem.

I. That system could be readily installed.

A. It is designed to screen contaminating chemicals from plant discharge systems.

B. Its cost is somewhat lower than that of other systems, and it would be relatively easy to finance in cooperation with the company.

II. That system has a record of good performance.

A. It has a long history of successful installations in similar situations.

B. Plant managers and other experts swear by the efficiency of this system.

III. That system is likely to perform well for us.

A. Installing it will result in a cleaner river.

B. Installing it will contribute to our health.

C. Installing it will attract business and industry.

In a situation like the above, the audience already understands the importance of taking action, so it is unnecessary to make a special point of that factor.

For a complete outline on a different subject, let's see how Don Morrison, a student at Wake Forest University, supported the view that standardized tests are unfair to minority students. We assume that his audience analysis led him to believe that a student listener would either say "No" or "I don't know" in answer to this issue: Are standardized tests biased against minority students?

Specific purpose: To lead my listeners to agree that standardized tests are culturally biased against racial minorities.

Introduction

Think for a moment about the first time you took the SAT. If you were like I was, you were full of anxiety. The reason you were so nervous was that you knew the tremendous effect your scores would have on the future of your education. Standardized testing has become an institution that profoundly affects both the academic and the occupational lives of Americans.

That's why I would like to speak to you today about the cultural bias toward racial minorities that is found in the content of standardized tests.

It is a fact that racial minorities, as a group, have not performed as well as their white counterparts on standardized tests. This difference has been attributed to genetic factors, and some psychologists say that the tests measure innate ability. If "innate ability" means "ability due to heredity," that term fails to take into account the variations in innate ability that stem from long-standing economic and educational deprivation.

When I finish talking today, I hope you will agree with me that the standardized tests are culturally biased because of three major deficiencies.

Body

I. The test-making process is faulty.

A. The test-constructors have been traditionally white and middle-class.

1. According to Green and Griffore of Michigan State University, there are marked cultural differences between test-authors and minority test-takers in "style of thinking, perceiving, and reasoning."

a. (Cite their examples of early-elementary reading test vocabulary.)

b. (Cite examples of words used for second graders.)

B. Part of the test standardization process involves item tryout.

1. Items are tried out on a sample to detect inappropriate items.

a. According to Green's research, the sample group chosen led to a test biased against minority children.

2. This means that minority children may be required to answer questions that are inappropriate for them.

Transition: Now that we have discussed general differences in culture between the test-makers and the test-takers, let's look at a specific cultural difference, that of language.

II. The dialect of the individual often makes it difficult for that individual to understand the tests.

A. Again according to Green and Griffore, this form of bias was noted at the elementary reading level.

1. For example, in one study of black fourth graders, Gray's Oral Reading Test was used.

a. When a test was scored to a regular key, 46% of the errors made by the entire group could be attributed to dialect differences.

2. In the case of reading readiness, the problem is even more serious.

a. On the basis of a single test alone, most minority children are placed in "slow groups" or are not allowed to begin formal reading instruction.

Transition: The final issue I would like to deal with goes back once again to the people who construct these standardized tests.

III. Certain test items of common knowledge in middle-class white circles are not common knowledge in minority circles.

A. Green and Griffore state that reading comprehension tests contain two types of items biased against minority children.

1. Some items, common knowledge to middle-class whites, can be answered by those whites without their even reading the relevant passage.

a. For example, items dealing with food recipes or with a night at the theater.

2. Other items requiring both information from the passage and middle-class common knowledge are also easier to answer for the whites.

Conclusion

From our discussion today, I hope you are as concerned as I am about the unfairness of a testing system that is subject to cultural bias.

That bias is due, in part, to the fact that the test-making process is faulty, that individuals with dialects have trouble understanding test items, and that test items based on so-called common knowledge are more difficult for minorities to answer.

You will be interested in this question, one which appeared in the Winter 1983 edition of the education journal, *Adolescence*: "Are tests to be used to adapt people individually and collectively to the presently dominant model of western industrial society, or are they to uncover human potentialities to which cultures can be adapted?"

Let's hope that the tests are indeed intended to "uncover human potentialities" and that the tests of the future will help rather than hinder the aspirations of minorities for a their fair share of that future.

Finally, you know now that the problem of culturally biased testing is serious. As students who also know how important an education is, I ask you to use whatever influence you have now or in the future to help correct a system of testing that so obviously discriminates against so many of our citizens. Thank you.

Bibliography

Green, Robert L., and Robert J. Griffore., "The Impact of Standardized Testing on Minority Students," *Journal of Negro Education*, 49 (1980), pp. 238-262.

Roberts, Eileen, and Richard DeBlassie, "Test Bias and the Culturally Different Early Adolescent," *Adolescence* (Winter, 1983), pp. 837-844.

Looking at the outline above, a critic (one is usually lurking nearby) might observe that subject and purpose are well phrased, that the general argument is reasonably well designed, that it has in it evidence that is still current but also too narrowly based and quite dated (one 1980 study and one 1983 article), and that introduction and conclusion meet overall requirements for a speaker's opening and closing remarks. With or without the prior observations of a critic, this student's supporting ethical appeal was operating at high velocity throughout the actual presentation in November, 1990. Perceiving him to be a speaker of good sense, good character, good will, and good presence, his listeners roundly applauded him at the finish.

We don't have the complete text of the test-bias-against-minorities presentation, but we do have the full transcript of a model effort by a University of Northern Iowa student, Shelley Schnathorst. Once you've read it, a discussion of her organizational plan will follow.

We Need Better Protection Against Dangerous Medical Devices[4]

by Shelley Schnathorst, University of Northern Iowa

In Roman times the Latin phrase "Caveat emptor" or "let the buyer beware" was an appropriate warning to the citizens of that time. In the United States today, we pride ourselves on a system which protects consumers from dangerous products. And while we understand that we still have responsibilities for our own protection, we have come to trust the safety of the products we must use. But for thousands of people each year that trust is misplaced. They are the ones who use medical devices ranging from x-rays to incubators and pacemakers to prostheses.

There are over 1,000 different types of medical devices in use today by virtually every patient who enters a doctor's office for tests or a hospital for an operation. Although the range of medical devices may seem broad, they are all subject to the medical regulatory system.

The Food and Drug Administration or FDA for short has been given responsibility to approve medical devices. Yet Representative Henry Waxman of California stated on May 4, 1987, that "only a handful have actually been so approved." Because most devices have not gone through rigorous approval processes, they present enormous hazards to us. In testifying before a committee of the House of Representatives in May of last year, Stephen Ferguson, President of one of the world's largest manufacturers of medical devices, stated, "Everyone in this room will someday want one of the devices we have under development as the best available choice for yourself or someone you know." So that we can improve the safety of those choices, we need to look, first, at the importance of regulating medical devices, secondly, at flaws in current regulations and, finally, at workable solutions to insure that we are adequately protected.

Adequate regulation is essential for two reasons. First and foremost, medical devices are often critical to the health and survival of individuals. By definition, a medical device is any instrument or apparatus intended to prevent, diagnose, or treat a human illness or disorder. And of course, when we seek the help of a doctor or a hospital, we hope that the devices they use will make us better, and we trust that they will not make us worse. Yet sometimes devices that are considered life-supporting become life threatening.

John Villforth, an FDA administrator, reported in the May, 1986, FDA Consumer that a heart resuscitation unit failed when the machine, like many of its type, had no warning device to indicate that the batteries powering the unit were defective. In addition, a July 2, 1987 segment of "20/20" reported that investigators discovered a flaw in the Therac 25, a radiation machine used in the treatment of cancer. Each of three persons interviewed on that program complained of being burned by the machine. After the loss of two lives, investigations led to the discovery of a computer error which had given some patients forty-five times the amount of radiation prescribed. As amateurs in health care, we cannot be expected to have a clear understanding of every medical device and its hazards. Yet, it's our lives that are at stake.

A second reason for better regulation was described by Representative Waxman, chairman of the House Subcommittee on Medical Devices, whose interests in this area I've already mentioned. He stated that, unlike a consumer product like a child's toy or even a Toyota which can be recalled, it is more difficult to deal with medical devices for oftentimes they have been implanted in the human body. Consider the case of Constance Walters, who testified via videotape in the House hearings. To correct a curvature in her spine, she had an operation in which a medical device called a Weiss Spring was implanted in her back in February of last year. By April she was experiencing tremendous pain. The Weiss Spring, which had never been submitted for testing, had snapped inside her back. As Walters said, "It is worse now. I can't be anybody. Do something so that someone else's life is not totally ruined like this."

According to Waxman, the best solution is to have a system that provides reasonable assurance that devices are both safe and effective. Well, there is a law intended to provide such an assurance. However, that law, the Medical Device Amendment of 1976, is flawed itself.

In testimony before the Subcommittee in May, 1987, Dr. Sidney Wolf, Director of the Public Citizen Health Research Group, outlined three specific flaws in current regulations. First, current legislation requires that most devices meet FDA standards. The catch is that the FDA has never devised any standards, and thus cannot regulate the devices.

In the absence of standards, the FDA relies upon Article 510K of the Medical Device Amendment. 510K allows a manufacturer to introduce a new device on the market simply by claiming it is substantially equivalent to devices on the market in 1976. There is no need to claim that the devices are any better than the devices in 1976, and the claims that are made go uncontested. Dr. Wolf testified that this second flaw is perhaps the biggest loophole in the law. In fact, Representative Waxman noted that well over 98% of the new medical devices that enter the market each year do so by claiming substantial equivalence rather than by going through pre-market safety tests and reviews. What this means is that Americans continue to serve as guinea pigs for new medical devices. Constance Walters was a guinea pig, for the Weiss Spring had never been submitted for testing.

Now the question that some of you may be asking is how common is such a problem. The third flaw in this system insures that we will never know the answer, for complete, systematic reporting of defects is not required. At the present time, the law requires that manufacturers report defects directly to the FDA. But those who actually work with the devices, namely hospitals, doctors, and distributors, are not mandated to report the defects to anyone. And for the information that is reported, a General Accounting Office study published in December, 1986, found that there is as funneling effect at work. They examined what happened to nearly 1,200 reports of medical device problems, and found that, because of the informality of the process and lack of required reporting, less than 1% of those problems ever reached FDA files.

Failure to develop standards, reliance on an equivalent standard instead and, finally, incomplete reporting--all combine to create inadequate protection. It is protection which Tama and James Jackson wish they had had when their firstborn baby, a baby boy, developed jaundice. The baby was placed in an illuminated hospital incubator which rid the child's body of the yellow coloration. The next day the incubator was empty. They baby was found in intensive care with a fever of 106 degrees. The next morning, the Jackson's firstborn died. The cause of death, the incubator. With a broken thermostat and alarm and a defective on-off switch, the incubator literally became an oven. To prevent such horrors, immediate action needs to be taken. As is evident, current regulation must be modified.

First, the FDA should be required to develop the standards called for twelve years ago, so that the design of the device will be safe to begin with. For none of the examples that I have provided is an isolated malfunction but rather a flaw in the design itself.

Second, establishing design standards will close the 510K loophole, and products won't be approved only because they are equivalent to devices in 1976. For as you well know, since 1976, improvements in medical technologies have occurred. Therefore, we should demand that such technologies be incorporated in new medical devices.

Third, reporting of defects should be mandated, not just by manufacturers but, of course, by doctors, hospitals, and distributors. This again should be standardized format of reporting. This proposal will work, for when reports of problems do reach the FDA, they have been proven to be quite effective in protecting our interests. For example, when the FDS received reports of faulty sleep apnea monitors which help children prone to sudden infant death syndrome, they were able to respond quite quickly. The FDA received reports that faulty monitors had electrocuted one child and burned several others. With this information, the FDA was able to issue safety alerts to health care professionals, home users, sleep apnea support groups and, of course, to those manufacturers who could improve the device.

Currently, there is a bill before the House Subcommittee on Health, Environment, and Energy. Although not yet in its final form, this bill will insure that necessary alterations be made in FDA regulations. It is this bill, HR 2595, which you should encourage your legislators to support.

Again, although we cannot be expected to know everything about every medical device, there are times that we or someone we know will be using one. There, we need to trust the proverb, "let the buyer beware," and become more informed about such devices.

The 1976 bill was well-intentioned. However, after a decade of talk and no action, it is time that Congress with our assistance takes serious steps in regulating this multibillion dollar medical device industry. With timely action we can discover and correct what otherwise might be a fatal flaw. But we must act. For as Helen Keller once wrote, "Science may have found a cure for most evils, but it has found no remedy for the worst of them all, the apathy of human beings."

As we look at the talk above, the essential elements of Shelley's organization are these:

Specific purpose: To induce the listeners to agree that we need better protection against dangerous medical devices.

Subject sentence: So that we can improve the safety of those choices [of medical devices], we need to look at the importance of regulating medical devices, flaws in current regulations, and finally workable solutions to insure that we are adequately protected.

I. Adequate regulation is essential for two reasons.

  A. Medical devices are often critical to the health and survival of individuals.

  B. It is difficult to recall medical devices for often they are implanted within the body.

II. Current regulations are flawed.

  A. Although a 1976 law is in place, the FDA has set up no standards which medical devices must meet.

  B. Manufacturers can put a device on the market by simply claiming it is equivalent to devices on the market in 1976.

  C. Complete, systematic reporting of defects is not required.

III. Current regulation must be modified.

  A. The FDA should be required to develop standards for medical devices.

  B. Devices should not be approved unless they meet those standards.

  C. Reporting of defects should be mandated.

Note that this student's subject sentence includes, first, a statement of the overall goal, namely, to "improve the safety of those choices [of medical devices]" and, secondly, a listing of the three points she intends to cover in describing how to reach that goal. The main points are not always worded in exactly the same way throughout the speech but, whatever the terminology, there is never any doubt that Shelley is (1) discussing the problem: a need for adequate regulation, (2) attacking the present "solution": ineffective regulation, and (3) proposing a new solution: effective regulation. Our critic would also comment favorably on the neat parallelism existing between her criticism of current regulations on three grounds and her outlining of three modifications designed to cure them. Another nice touch is her repetition of the "Let the buyer beware" warning in the first sentence of the introduction and again near the end of the conclusion.

In class or outside it, no one can say everything that should or could be said in support of a problem-solution speech like that above. Audience impatience with overly long presentations, the complexity of some issues, and other constraints often force us to back an idea with less than all available means.

Not only are we unable to say everything we'd like to say but, to an educated audience, the speaker may seem to be unfair or uninformed if she or he doesn't take the time to recognize whatever legitimate arguments there may be "on the other side." Especially when you are talking with listeners who are opposed to your point of view, they expect you to acknowledge that opposing arguments do exist. That "bow to the opposition" gives your listeners confidence that you have looked at both sides of the issue. There is also some evidence that mentioning opposing arguments helps to weaken or diffuse them.[5]

For their part, listeners are generally willing to accept limited arguments and data for what they are--examples typical of other materials which the speaker can supply. And when there is time, a post-event question-and-answer session adds to listener interest and also offers the well prepared speaker a final opportunity to answer objections and reinforce "the case" with additional evidence and argument.

We conclude this chapter with the full transcript of a problem-solution address as it was presented to a Pittsburgh audience by the director of a foreign investment agency.

The Perils of Protectionism[6]

by Pierre F. Dobbelmann, Executive Director,
U.S. and Canada, Netherlands Foreign Investment Agency

This presentation (May 19, 1987) to the World Affairs Council of Pittsburgh, PA, appears here in slightly edited and shortened form. Original content and basic structure remain the same.

Good morning, everyone. It is a distinct pleasure to be here today. I arrived only yesterday, but already it's quite clear to me why Pittsburgh was recently rated the most livable city in America. This is a city on the move. You can feel it just walking down the street!

The World Affairs Council of Pittsburgh regularly tackles the important issues affecting our lives. There is nothing more important in a free society than this open airing of ideas-regardless of how revolutionary they may be. Pennsylvania has a long and proud tradition of this. After all, it was in this state that the United States Constitution was created two hundred years ago.

Like the United States, the Netherlands has a proud tradition of free thinking and open discussion. Holland also has a longstanding tradition of free trade--the subject of my talk today. We had no choice but to make it a Dutch tradition if we were to compete on the world stage. Our small size and relative lack of natural resources demanded it. Today, nearly sixty percent of the Dutch economy is devoted to foreign trade.

Our two countries have long enjoyed a mutually beneficial trading relationship with each other. How beneficial? Well, from the U.S. point of view, the Netherlands provides it with its highest trade surplus in the world, currently about three-and-a-half billion dollars.

Likewise, Pittsburgh and my country can point to a high level of economic cooperation. The list of Pittsburgh-based companies with Dutch operations reads like a "Who's Who" of American industry: Alcoa, Dravo, Rockwell International, United Technologies, to name just a few.

For America, too, trade has been steadily growing as a key component of the economy and now stands at more than twenty percent.

But a cloud has begun to darken this otherwise sunny trade horizon. That cloud does not bode well for those who believe that free flow of goods is nothing less than the foundation on which global prosperity is built. As you may have guessed, the ominous dark cloud I am referring to is trade protectionism.

The title of my talk today, "The Perils of Protectionism," best sums up my position on this crucial matter. For I see serious perils in the chilly winds of protectionism that have been blowing with increasing strength and frequency. I speak both as a Dutchman and a European whose strong opinion is that free trade works--and that protectionist barriers ultimately do more harm than good.

First, I'll describe the roots of the growing protectionism trend. Secondly, I'll cite some recent examples of protectionism. Next, I'll describe the specific perils that are caused by protectionism. Finally, I'll explain why protectionism represents a dangerous palliative--the wrong cure that may only worsen the economic maladies for which it has been prescribed.

Now, let's consider some of the roots of the growing protectionism trend in the U.S.

Once such root is the intense lobbying for import barriers by both business and labor. They apparently believe that this is the only way to deal with heavy competition from foreign producers. But the benefits of such measures are short-lived at best. In actuality, the barriers that are intended to protect domestic markets simply beget retaliation by trading partners. This is just as true for the U.S. as it is for Europe and Japan.

Another major--and well publicized--root cause of the recent move toward protectionism is the soaring U.S. trade deficit. As this has ballooned to over one hundred and seventy billion dollars, an increasing number of policymakers and business leaders have called for protectionism. It's a deceptively simply way out of a problem that defies easy solution.

An example of how complex the problem really is can be seen in the recent unprecedented free-fall in the value of the dollar. Conventional wisdom says a lower dollar makes American-made products more competitive in world markets. In other words, U.S. exports should rise and the trade deficit should fall. But instead, the deficit has continued to worsen. The conventional wisdom no longer applies. Many observers explain this by saying the dollar had long been overvalued, so its correction ended up not affecting either exports or imports. And America's massive trade deficit remains as daunting as ever, casting a pall over the entire economy.

Everyone agrees that something needs to be done, but there is significant disagreement as to exactly what. Increasingly, the popular--and political--answer seems to be protectionism. At least that's what we're hearing from many in the Congress and from a growing number in the business community. The talk focuses on "level playing fields," dumping, and loss of competitiveness: America has gotten the short end of the world-trade stick for too long, and American jobs are paying for it.

And to a certain extent, they have a valid point. We are all aware of certain countries that still restrict--or even prohibit--foreign goods. These countries discourage domestic growth and rely on exports to drive their economies. That's protectionism--and it's wrong.

So I can understand why many are seduced by a "reciprocity" amendment to the trade bill currently before the House. Supporters talk about rebuilding U.S.

industries, generating jobs, and making America great again. They also talk about getting tough with America's trading partners. But they never mention the word protectionism. And that's a slippery slope that inevitably leads you to a worse position than where you started.

Now, let's look at some recent examples of what I call the "perils of protectionism."

The first example is the U.S. government's imposition of one hundred percent duties on selected Japanese products. Washington's action highlighted the growing tensions in the lopsided U.S.-Japan trading relationship. The U.S. is running a deficit of nearly sixty billion dollars with the Japanese--and it's not alone. Worldwide, as of 1987, Japan has a total trade surplus of over eighty-five billion dollars.

The U.S. cast its action as a temporary reprisal: the Japanese had reneged on an agreement not to dump semiconductors. Meanwhile, the Japanese denied that they had ever violated the agreement, claiming their U.S. partners had again misunderstood them. In the long run, such actions do little to benefit the industries supporting them. It's better to let the free market and free trade determine the relative competitiveness of a particular industry or company.

Another example of protectionism: Last year, the U.S. and the European Community played a game of brinkmanship in what came to be known as the "Yuppie Products" trade dispute. This was triggered when Spain and Portugal joined the EC. American farmers were faced with significant losses of corn and sorghum exports to those countries due to heavy EC duties.

The U.S. threatened to retaliate by slapping two hundred percent duties on such luxury items as white wine, brandy, and cheese from all the EC countries. Thus the "Yuppie" moniker! In fact, Holland's famed gouda cheese would have tripled in price had the tariffs been levied here. After much eleventh-hour negotiating, the battle was avoided. But not without considerable bad blood between the U.S. and the EC.

By the way, the twelve-member European Community is America's largest export market--taking some thirty-five billion dollars of U.S. goods in 1986. That's more than either Japan or Canada. There is certainly a great deal for both sides to lose if this critical trading relationship deteriorates.

Another example of trade protectionism is the European steel cartel. Working together, EC member governments have used trade barriers and massive public subsidies to gently ease the Community's steel industry onto the path of necessary restructuring and cutbacks.

By contrast, other European heavy industries have had to "face the music" of market forces all at once and benefited from the experience. Take, for example, Europe's chemical industry. Some years ago, evolving global markets dictated that European chemical producers move away from traditional activities into specialty chemicals and pharmaceuticals. All in all, it was a positive move for a maturing industry that now is strongly competitive worldwide.

The contrasting examples of the European steel and chemical industries clearly demonstrate the value of free trade versus protectionism. Protectionism and other government interference have caused the European steel companies to go slow in make the important structural changes. That will only further delay the day when they are truly competitive. On the other hand, the chemical industry let the free market--and free trade--dictate its direction with very positive results.

Another recent example of protectionism occurred when the Americans and Europeans went to the mat again over fruits and pasta. Parochial concerns such as domestic market share took precedence over the larger economic interests shared by both sides. Threats and counter-threats were the order of the day.

Then there was the textile bill introduced in Congress earlier this year. That would have imposed a global quota on U.S. imports of clothing and textiles. The European Community's reaction was fast and furious. Retaliation was threatened but, fortunately, the legislation was vetoed. Two major trading partners had gone to the brink once more.

There is a very real danger in this international game of brinkmanship. It necessitates going closer to the brink the next time. And the next battle may be the final one that pushes us into the bottomless void of a trade war.

Let me list, then, the specific perils of protectionism.

Peril Number 1: A global trade war. It's difficult to imagine a worse peril than a global trade war. It could spark the dissolution of the Western trading alliance. As your President put it:

"High tariffs inevitably lead to retaliation by foreign countries and the triggering of fierce trade wars. The result is more and more tariffs, higher and higher trade barriers, and less and less competition. Markets shrink and collapse, businesses and industries shut down, and millions of people lose their jobs."

What a depressing scenario but, in the past twelve months, we have come dangerously close to realizing such a scenario.

Peril Number 2: Shrinking markets and subsequent job losses. When the retaliatory spiral of protectionism escalates, key export markets shrink, and some even dry up.

America has much to lose in this regard: Last year, it exported $220.2 billion dollars worth of goods. And according to the Commerce Department, five-and-a-half million jobs depend on these exports. Protectionism and the resulting retaliation of trading partners would force businesses to cut back because of diminished market demand. Jobs would be lost, a very serious peril.

Peril Number 3: Prices will increase. According to the Organization for Economic Cooperation and Development, protectionism has increased the average price of protected goods by as much as 10%. On specific items, the rise has been much more. The people most affected by such increases are low-income households that can least afford it. They depend on the low-cost goods from developing countries.

Peril Number 4: Disruption in global financial markets. When the House passed the protectionist trade bill last month, financial markets reacted with alarm. Stock prices plummeted. There was no joy on Wall Street.

An even more serious peril concerns Treasury Bonds. The U.S. government borrows from foreign as well as domestic investors to finance its huge budget deficit. And the Japanese are some of the biggest buyers of these debt securities. When the U.S. took the semiconductor action against Japan, there was talk in Tokyo of pulling out of the next T-Bond auction as retaliation. Panic ensued in U.S. capital markets, and bond prices nose-dived. This is a telling example of just how interdependent the global economy has become--and why protectionism can oftentimes backfire in unforeseen ways.

Peril Number 5: Damage to developing nations. Trade barriers would be a big blow to developing countries, which depend on exports to pay their debts. If those countries were unable to export, they just might choose to carry out their threats of walking away from their loans. The effect on U.S. moneycenter banks would be disastrous.

Up to now, I've examined the roots of the current protectionism trend, provided some recent examples of protectionism, and described perils that are caused by such policies. I hope I have made the point that the risks are high and the slope dangerously steep on the path to protectionism. Now I'd like to explain why protectionism will never be the right answer because it ignores the serious economic problems plaguing our world today.

Here's a brief rundown of some of those economic problems:

1. The U.S. budget deficit in the billions of dollars.
2. The mounting debt burdens of developing countries.
3. Under-consumption and high levels of excess savings in Japan.
4. Over-consumption and inadequate savings by U.S. consumers.
5. Agricultural production that has become divorced from markets.
6. Structural problems and weak growth in Europe's internal markets.
7. Lack of competitiveness of U.S. industry.

Instead of solving these problems, protectionism allows governments and industries to sidestep and delay the hard choices that would effect viable solutions. Making the hard choices--and implementing the tough measures that will begin to bring about real progress--will not be easy. It never is. But we can derive some solace from the fact that this is the ONLY alternative if we are serious about preserving and improving global prosperity.

There are international mechanisms intended to help keep members of the Western Alliance from choosing the protectionist option. For one, the General Agreement on Trade and Tariffs, GATT for short, was specifically set up after World War II to bring order to global trade.

I contend that we need to strengthen the international mechanisms--in particular, GATT--that are so crucial in mediating trade disputes and enforcing fairness in international economic relations. That is easier said than done, but the belief here is that a GATT with more teeth--and with more support from member nations--would go a lot further toward solving current economic problems than protectionism. As I come to the end of my talk, I'd like to illustrate how the specific Dutch experience has, in my view, validated the argument that protectionism is not the answer.

In Holland, we believe that free and open trade is the best policy for economic growth and vitality. My organization, the Netherlands Foreign Investment Agency, is a good example of this. Our mission is to help companies in North America exploit free trade by tapping into the three trillion dollar European marketplace. In fact, the reputation of the Netherlands as the consummate free trading nation has made my job comparatively easy.

Such major U.S.-based companies as Hewlett-Packard, Honeywell, Pet, and Abbott Laboratories have chosen to invest in Holland largely because of its free-trade advantages. From their Dutch bases, they manufacture, assemble, and distribute goods throughout Europe and to major markets worldwide.

The more than one thousand U.S. companies doing business in my country would probably have been less interested in investing there had it not been for our free-trade practices. Those companies are a significant boost to our economy. They employ more than one hundred and twenty thousand Dutch workers. Then there are the thousands of job created by the twenty-five hundred companies from other foreign countries. In fact, the recent revitalization of the Dutch economy could not have been achieved without the stimulus provided by the foreign companies operating in the Netherlands.

Finally, I'd like to return to a point I made earlier about the key role of people like you in helping shape trade policy. We can't just let the politicians decide our fates on such vital matters. Why? Because we are not just innocent onlookers. We're all in this together--individuals and nations. Once business leaders and academicians start playing a greater role in worldwide trade negotiations, I believe we will see a diminishing of the negative rhetoric-and possibly a lowering of the U.S. trade deficit.

If I leave you with only one thought today, I hope it is this: Although it sometimes get lost in the swirling debate, there really are considerable friendship and common interest between the U.S. and its trading partners. And in the final analysis, that friendship and common interest--not protectionism--will be the answer to the economic and traderelated problems affecting us today. Thank you.

Now, I'd be delighted to take your questions.

In the address above, Mr. Dobbelmann tells his audience that he will be taking up four points. The first three constitute his analysis of the problem. The fourth point, beginning with a prediction that protectionism could only make things worse, covers the details of his solution to the problem. If he had asked you to work out the organization of his argument, it might have looked like this:

Subject sentence: We should encourage free trade. It is our only hope for world prosperity.

[Problem]

I. Protectionism discourages economic growth.

A. Its past is a record of failure

B. Its present is no more promising.

C. These perils would cloud its future:
1. A global trade war
2. Shrinking markets and jobs
3. Rising prices
4. Disruptions in global financial markets
5. Damage to developing nations
6. Damage to the Western Defensive Alliance

[Solution]

II. Free trade encourages economic growth.

A. Protectionism is the wrong solution.

B. Strengthening free trade agreements is the right solution.

C. More support from individuals would also help.

Although you may not recognize the organization above as Mr. Dobbelmann's, it's *essentially the same as his*. The subpoints A, B, and C under the first main point are Dobbelmann's original first three main points. Main point II above is the same as the speaker's original fourth point.

Why, then, are we taking the time to redesign the talk under two main points, each having three subpoints? Because audiences sometimes find it easier to follow a carefully phrased and balanced two-point (or three-point) organization than one with four loosely phrased points. It would be hard to improve on Mr. Dobbelmann's speech as presented; still, it is just possible that the organization above would have been easier for his listeners to grasp and remember.

You have been organizing as strong a presentation as possible with the idea of inducing listeners to feel the same way you do about a problem-solution issue or issues. As you work on the conclusion of the talk, *you* know what you'd like the listeners to do; be sure that the conclusion has in it a line or two to let *them* know what you'd like them to do. Examples: The complete outline in this chapter and both of the full-text speeches end with a call for personal commitment on the part of the listeners. The student writer of the outline asks his listeners "to use whatever influence you have now or in the future to help correct" an unfair testing system. The student speaking about unsafe medical devices urges writing to legislators in support of a bill to solve that problem. The investment agency executive asks his trade oriented listeners to help shape trade policy. For your part, after working hard to induce listeners to agree with you on one or more issues, you will want to follow through by directly asking for whatever kind of cooperation or action is appropriate: "Call this number and complain to the mayor." "Be sure to attend the tax meeting at the county assessor's office." "Join us in our campaign to improve the teaching in our local schools." When listeners see or sense that the speaker has their interests at heart, they are generally more than willing to join forces with the speaker in whatever response or action is required to reach a common goal. One thing is certain: if you don't "ask your prospects for the order," you're unlikely to get it.

So much for organization and outlining. You already know the importance of moving on through the sixth step, "rehearsing the message to present it in a way you consider best suited to your audience." All you have to do now is finish the message, rehearse it, and win your audience over to agreement with you. Not too easy but not too difficult either...and certainly worth the effort in terms of learning and experience.

Endnotes

1. Richard M. Weaver, Language is Sermonic: [Essays of]*Richard M. Weaver on the Nature of Rhetoric*, eds. Richard L. Johannesen, Rennard Strickland, and Ralph T. Eubanks (Baton Rouge, LA: Louisiana State UP, 1970), p. 217.

2. For a sketch of the early history of systems for finding the issues, see Ray Nadeau, "Classical Systems of Stases [Issues] in Greek: Hermagoras to Hermogenes," *Greek, Roman, and Byzantine Studies*, 2 (January, 1959), pp. 51-71. For detail on Hermogenes, see Ray Nadeau, "Hermogenes' On Stases [On Issues]: A Translation with an Introduction and Notes," *Speech Monographs*, 31 (November, 1964), pp. 361-424.

3. For a similar passage in Aristotle, see section 1392a in any translation of his *Rhetoric*.

4. Shelley Schnathorst, "We Need Better Protection Against Dangerous Medical Devices," *1988 Championship Debates and Speeches*, eds. John K. Boaz and James R. Brey (Annandale, VA: Speech Communication Association, 1988), Vol. 3, pp. 112-14.

5. Carl I. Hovland, Irving L. Janis, and Harold H. Kelley, *Communication and Persuasion* (New Haven, CT: Yale UP, 1963), pp. 99-122.

6. Pierre F. Dobbelmann, "The Perils of Protectionism," *Vital Speeches of the Day*, 53 (July 15, 1987) 5, pp. 590-594.

Discussion Questions

1. On Shelley Schnathorst's "We Need Better Protection...."

Does she establish herself in the introduction as being sufficiently knowledgeable on the subject of medical devices? Does she give her listeners good reason to listen?

Do the issues she discusses (need for regulation, failure of current regulation, proposals for solution of the regulation problem) arise from listener opposition to her points of view or from listener ignorance of the problem and possible ways to solve it?

Is the talk organized in such a way that you can readily understand and follow it? Could she have done a better job of phrasing the main points? How would you have stated them? Does she have enough evidence to back up each one?

Are her sources adequate for the case as presented? Are they current? Does she depend too much on any one source?

Were you satisfied with her handling of transitions? She efficiently uses numbers as signals (e.g., "First and foremost," "A second reason"). Does she use any other kind of transition? Where?

Closing a problem and/or solution talk with a call for a change in thinking or with a call for action is characteristic of such presentations. Which approach does she use? Is her suggestion practical?

2. On Pierre Dobbelmann's "Perils of Protectionism"...

According to Chapter 8 in this text, a speaker's introductory remarks should get the attention of the listeners, tell them the purpose of the talk, give them a reason to listen and, if necessary, include comment on the speaker's personal competence to speak on the subject. Does Dobbelmann omit any of those requirements? If so, why?

A good speaker tries to become one with his or her audience and see things from "the listeners' point of view." Does Dobbelmann try to establish that relationship?

Find a definition or a classification in the talk. Is it clear? Necessary? Appropriate?

Find an inference or generalization based on evidence. Is the evidence from a reputable source? Is the generalization justified?

Does Dobbelmann quote anyone as an authority? Do you recognize the authority as an expert?

Take any one point advanced by Dobbelmann in support of his general purpose. How is it supported? Is the support adequate? Are you convinced that he is right on that point? Why? If not, why not?

How would you rate his personal image? Does he say anything to increase his "ethical appeal"? Does he say anything that would seem to reduce it?

Was Dobbelmann talking with people who already agreed with him? Or was he facing a group needing to be convinced? Does he recognize and take up any opposing arguments?

Dobbelmann closes by saying, "Now, I'd be delighted to take your questions." What question or questions would you ask?

Application Projects

Speaking options

1. Prepare an 8-10 minute presentation aimed at inducing listeners to recognize that a serious problem exists, or that the causes of some condition (e.g., urban decay) are now apparent, or that a certain situation did indeed occur (e.g., bribery of officials to cover up a financial scandal).

2. Prepare an 8-10 minute presentation in support of or in opposition to a value judgment. Instead of simply asking what conclusions may be drawn from the facts (as in the first speaking option above), you arrive at an evaluation of the situation (e.g., "This problem is serious enough to require a solution") and ask the listeners to accept both your account of the facts and your evaluation of their significance.

3. Prepare an 8-10 minute presentation in support of or in opposition to a question of policy. Example: "The public schools in this county should be in session the year round." A policy question, as you know, looks to what *should* be done about a problem. (If your audience analysis has led you to believe that the listeners do not yet recognize that the problem exists or that it is serious enough to require solution, you would have to begin with one or both of those earlier steps.)

4. Find another student whose position is opposite to yours on an issue. Arrange with your instructor to have a 16-20 minute debate. The "pro" speaker could speak for up to eight minutes, the "con" for up to ten, and the "pro" again for a final 2 minutes. At the end of the debate, time not used by the speakers could be opened to the listeners for questioning.

Listening options

1. Which of the student speakers in this series seemed to you to offer listeners the best inducement for agreeing with the speaker on an issue or issues? Now that you have heard that "case," did it or will it have any influence on the way you think or act? (Write a one-page review to answer those questions.)

2. Choice of subject aside, which of the student speakers was most effective in identifying herself or himself with the members of the audience? What did this particular student do to make this a we-are-all-in-this-together occasion? (Write a one-page review to answer those questions.)

Additional Activities

1. Early attention should be given to key elements of any talk and especially to one in which the student faces the challenge of seeking agreement on one or more issues.

Well in advance of the date scheduled for your presentation on an issue or issues, fill out and turn in to the instructor a Proposal for a Presentation. Either use a form provided by the instructor or simply make one up for this purpose.

2. If time permits, the forms submitted above could be redistributed to "committees" of no more than five students each. The forms should be allocated in such a way that the students in a given committee would not be checking their own proposals. Objective of the in-class committee discussions would be to get student reactions on choices of subject, statements of purpose, etc. Committee observations could be entered on a separate sheet, attached to the original proposal by the instructor, and returned to the student making the proposal.

13

EVOKING EMOTION AND MOTIVATING CHANGE

Emotion is that form of appeal in which a speaker enlists the feelings of the audience in support of his cause.

Aristotle

The noblest motive is the common good.

Virgil

When you finish this chapter, you will be aware that...

1. A speaker motivates listeners by enlisting their basic emotions or feelings in support of his or her purpose.

2. A speaker also motivates listeners by stressing their shared needs, wants, desires, and values as well as the feelings associated with those motives.

3. Self-interest and "the common good" are key incentives in modern motivational theory.

4. The attitudes and beliefs of listeners have a direct bearing on how those listeners respond to emotional and motivational appeal.

Of the three components of appeal to an audience (ethical, logical, and emotional), that of emotional appeal is the one remaining to be discussed. The degree of reliance on that particular appeal may be relatively light in talks having an informational emphasis and not much heavier in those dealing with practical problems and their solutions. However, the emotional appeal to an audience can be quite intense when a speaker is concentrating, for example, on proposing a very unpopular solution to an emotion-laden problem, or on arousing enthusiasm for some worthwhile goal or ideal, or on trying to change or modify a deeply-seated attitude or prejudice.

In this chapter, then, we first discuss the role played by "Emotion and Emotional Appeal" in the motivating of listeners.

Secondly, we continue the discussion of listener motivation under the heading of "Motives and Motivation," a topic closely related to and intertwined with emotion and emotional appeal.

Third, we take up "Attitudes and Beliefs," states of mind to which people are emotionally committed and which, for that reason, are among the more difficult targets for change.

Finally, the remainder of the chapter is centered on practical examples of "motivating change."

Emotion and Emotional Appeal

You have already encountered degrees of emotional appeal in speeches you've heard as well as in the outlines and reprints of speeches in this text. Could you read Bonnie Richardson's outline on illiterates without feeling sympathy for those unfortunates? Were you enough motivated by Julie Smith's outline to file away for future reference her comments on extended-wear contact lenses? Did Don Morrison's outline bring to mind your own anxieties about taking standardized tests? As you read Shelley Schnathorst's description of the broken spring in a patient's back, were you at all concerned and angry that things like that could happen? Does reading a speech like Rex Kelly's help inspire you to be honest and well informed when you're the speaker? In the instances above and in presentations generally, we see that speakers do depend on emotion to help win a favorable response from their listeners.

Appealing to the feelings of listeners is not new; rabble rousers and propagandists have been doing that since the beginning of time. For the responsible speaker, however, emotional appeal is not a matter of cleverly playing on the emotions of listeners. It is a matter of using one's knowledge of the human emotions in an ethical way and for a legitimate purpose, either to spur listeners to make a decision or to act, or to keep them from deciding or acting. In more ways than one, emotional appeal is the speaker's "people mover."

For one example of emotional appeal, this is the opening to a 1987 speech on "Belief in Fairness Makes Democracy"[1] by Vernon Jordan, Jr.:

> On a recent newscast, an elderly farmer from my home state of Georgia came on the TV screen. He had just lost his farm, and he said: "It don't seem fair. You work all your life, then lose it in the end."
>
> A couple weeks later, another newscast had an interview with a laid-off steelworker. "I spent my whole life in that mill," he said. "Now I've got nothing to show for it but a mortgage I can't pay and kids I can't feed."
>
> There are more people like that farmer and that steelworker today --young Americans who can't find work, middle aged Americans who have lost their jobs, older Americans who are forced into an early retirement they don't want and can't afford.
>
> They are white and black, old and young, low income and middle income. They're bitter, they're angry. They, too, say, "It don't seem fair."
>
> Standing on the unemployment lines, they read the papers. They read about public officials sent to jail in New York, in Washington, and elsewhere, and about federal officials who take the Fifth Amendment. They read about freelance Rambos turned loose to run a foreign policy in defiance of Congress and of the Administration's own anti-terrorist rhetoric.
>
> They read about top Wall Street figures sentenced to jail or under investigation for illegal activities.
>
> And as they wonder how to pay the grocery bill, they read about corporate CEOs getting huge pay raises and stock bonuses.
>
> Fairness is not something we can take for granted any more. It is the glue that binds our system together. The belief that the system is fair makes democracy and the free enterprise system work.

> Take away that faith in fairness, and the system loses legitimacy. And today, that faith is being eroded by public and private actions.

You have heard many speakers whose messages were similarly supported by the weaving of feeling into the fabric of a presentation. Note that Jordan takes advantage of common knowledge and *recent audience experience* in order to set the stage for a resounding plea for fairness in our free enterprise system. A businessman himself, Jordan speaks with authority to his audience of business people in Chicago. His own feelings are revealed as he describes the bitterness, despair, and anger of the poor and unfortunate. We weren't there to hear him, but the listeners could not have been anything but emotionally affected by Jordan's appeal to their sense of fair play.

For another instance of emotion at work in support of the speaker's purpose, this passage appears in John Jacob's address[2] on the 75th anniversary of the founding of the National Urban League:

> If those founders of our Movement [The National Urban League] were to return to us today, they would tell *us*--their successors--to keep on fighting, to keep on struggling to overcome poverty and discrimination, to keep on carrying our battle to a nation that tolerates hungry children and homeless families. And that is what we are here in Washington to do.
>
> We come to the seat of national power to plead our righteous cause.
>
> We come to the capital of the free world to remind our nation that we are far from achieving a just society--still far from realizing the American Dream.
>
> And we come to the capitol of our nation to protest the policies that have driven more and more black people deeper and deeper into poverty.
>
> That is a certified non-partisan statement of fact.
>
> In today's America, if you are a white male, there's employment. If you're black, there's Depression.
>
> If you're rich, the government cut your taxes. If you're poor, the government raised your taxes and took away desperately needed programs.

> If you're a yuppie couple, life is all roses and Easy Street. If you're a single mother trying to feed your hungry children, life is all thorns and heartbreak.
>
> In recent years, a philosophy of selfishness and meanness has taken hold instead of the philosophy of caring and sharing that our nation needs. A mean society says, "I've got mine," but a good society says, "All for one, and one for all."

Can you read those lines without feeling the anger and frustrations of the disadvantaged? Jacob feels strongly about the battle for social justice, and the depth of his feeling is both touching and demanding.

It is safe to say that neither Jordan nor Jacob decided in advance that they were going to arouse this emotion here and that emotion there. Emotional appeal is not a faucet that you turn on and off at will. Yet, if you are genuinely concerned about the interests and welfare of the audience, if you feel strongly about the issues at hand, and if you really believe that you and your listeners must arrive at a common decision or take some kind of action, the problem of becoming one emotionally with the audience will generally take care of itself.

Motives and Motivation

As we said in the introduction to this chapter, emotion and emotional appeal are closely associated and intertwined with the concept of motives and motivation. For example, an instructor promises good grades if you work hard to succeed in a course--that's motivation. When she or he comments on the feeling of satisfaction you'll get from good grades in contrast to the emotional low resulting from the other kind--that's emotional appeal. Emotions are not only closely associated with motives; they sometimes serve as motives themselves. Your incentive (motive) for not skipping classes, for example, could be fear (emotion) of the consequences.

By definition, a motive is a need, urge, desire, drive, impulse, incentive, or "carrot" that is held out to entice a person to think or to act in a certain way. Sales managers try to motivate their sales staffs. Coaches try to motivate their teams. Instructors try to motivate their students. Candidates try to motivate the voters. Whenever you try to win over an audience, one or more personal motives are pushing or pulling you take that action. And as the audience listens to you, it has its own motives for doing or not doing whatever it is you are asking of it. Since you are going to have to deal with listener motives as they are, or try to change them, or try to substitute new ones, it is in your interests to know more about the key motives common to our society, namely, the motive of self-interest and, an encouraging trend, the higher motive of "the common good."

The motive of self-interest

Everyone is concerned about food, drink, sleep, sex, and shelter (not necessarily in that order). But with our physical needs more or less taken care of, our psychological needs come to the fore.[3] We then do the things we do because there is a pay-off of some kind for us. We see or sense that our actions will somehow benefit us or, at least, keep us out of harm's way.

Speaking of the role played by self-interest in our decision making, S. Guernsey Jones looks back on a long career in the business world and says:

> Every day of our lives we make decisions, both important and unimportant. But in every one the conclusion is that I do what, at that time, I think is the best thing for me to do. It is in my self-interest.[4]

Or to quote a Confederate foot soldier in *The Barefoot Brigade*, "Nobody looks out for nobody, 'cept his own self."[5] In discussing speech introductions, Aristotle puts it less bluntly but cites "matters that concern their own interests" as one of the things listeners pay most attention to.[6]

In general, the average listener is concerned with "I" or "me" questions like these: What does this speaker's message mean to me? Personal gain? A boost to my ego? Satisfaction of some need or desire? Avoidance of pain or discomfort? Why should I go along with the idea or action suggested? As Robert White[7] and others say, an audience of typical listeners will do whatever it must to defend, maintain, or enhance its collective self-interest.

The motive of "the common good"

When Virgil says, "The noblest motive is the common good," he echoes a moral theme held high from long before his days in Rome (70-19 B.C.). "Becoming one with your listeners" is not too hard when you are offering employees benefit-without-pain (e.g., a better health insurance plan for which the company will cover the higher costs). The more difficult task would be the earlier selling of that idea to company executives on the "common good" grounds that everyone in the company will benefit from its clear concern for the welfare of its employees (higher employee morale, less absenteeism, etc.).

Amitai Etzioni is among the moderns who say that we place too much emphasis on the self-interest motive, and that we should recognize the validity of the more general umbrella concept, one which recognizes both the need we feel to look out for ourselves *and* the age-old view that we should also look out for the welfare of others.[8] In some instances, as he points out, self-interest does determine what we do; in others, however, values and feelings win out. You see this conflict in action when a water shortage exists and, as a result, the local water board asks people not to water lawns or wash cars. Those governed primarily by self-interest may ignore that request; others, considering "the common good" to be more compelling, choose to cooperate. For another example, some people go into relief organizations like the Peace Corps for self-interest reasons (e.g., get away from home, learn another language, become acquainted with another culture, travel at government expense). Others go into it for reasons having little or nothing to do with self-concern; to them, a main purpose in life is to improve the lot of those less fortunate than themselves. Peace Corps members have the same needs and desires as the rest of us but, for some of them at least, the "comforts of home" lose out to higher values. (Read James Michener's *Journey* for a fine novel about explorers sticking to higher values at great personal risk.) We conclude that you cannot identify with any audience without some knowledge of the motives of the listeners in it and without an understanding of the emotions and motives to which you may reasonably appeal in trying to induce a favorable response.

Attitudes and Beliefs

To the extent that any future goals of your speaking may be to motivate change in listener attitudes and beliefs, we turn now to a discussion of those concepts. Again by definition, an attitude is a learned and strongly-held overall belief to which a person feels emotionally committed and which determines how that person may react to specific people, ideas, and things.[9] If you have the attitude that "No one should ever pass up the chance to vote!," you are likely to be upset when you learn of someone's never bothering to vote.

In other words, you have a strongly-held belief, you feel committed to it, and you tend to react in a predictable way. Any attitude normally has a number of underlying beliefs supporting it; in this particular instance, the beliefs supporting your attitude could be that failing to vote (1) is bad citizenship, (2) runs the risk of losing that right, (3) lets unqualified candidates into office, (4) leads to abuses in office, (5) sets a bad example for others, and so on.

You are also familiar with the kind of attitude-belief we call *prejudice*. It is an overall attitude or belief resting on a scaffolding of mistaken beliefs. A religious or racial bigot may be totally honest; the problem is that she or he believes too many myths and fictions about other religious or racial groups. Unfortunately, all those untruths come together in an attitude like "I don't have any use for those people."

Below the level of strongly-held attitude-beliefs (and below the beliefs supporting them) are your incidental beliefs, opinions, tastes, preferences, views, etc. Maybe you prefer a certain brand of soft drink; you like it and, in your opinion, it is as good as any such drink on the market. However, you don't feel so strongly about your brand preference that someone couldn't rather easily talk you into trying another brand.

At the opposite or top end of the belief scale is that special class of beliefs which we call *basic values* (e.g., a world at peace, family security, freedom of speech, happiness, justice, etc.).[10] When all or practically all the members of a society or organization are very strongly committed to the same overall belief, that *broadly accepted view* is commonly called a basic value or value-belief. Although people cling tightly to their basic values, they hang on somewhat less firmly to their attitudes; that is why speakers generally concentrate on trying to effect changes in that secondary level of belief.

As always in communication, the meaning of a word depends heavily on the listener's interpretation of it. When you hear someone begin a statement with "I believe," it is up to you to decide whether or not the speaker is stating a broadly accepted basic value, or is revealing an attitude, or is just expressing an opinion. Assuming, for the sake of example, that someone is expressing an attitude when she tells you that she believes the government of your state to be behind others in needed social legislation, you may be able to change or weaken that belief (attitude) by listing the growing numbers of social-progress bills being passed by your legislature each year. If someone says he is against large corporate farms (attitude), you may ask him for his reasons (beliefs) and, after pointing out some weaknesses in them, you may try to sell him on your reasons (beliefs) for holding a different view (attitude).

It goes without saying that an understanding of beliefs in general and attitudes in particular can help us discover the reasons *why* a particular group of listeners holds a certain attitude. And you need to know something about the beliefs behind an attitude before you can go about changing it. For example, freedom is one of the basic American values. Yet, some of our citizens have the attitude that an organization like the American Civil Liberties Union is "Un-American." A speaker planning to try changing that attitude would quickly discover that opposition to the ACLU is based on that organization's support of unpopular causes like the rights of "fascist-type" groups to hold rallies, the rights of "racist-type" groups to march, the rights of high school students to resist search of their lockers, the rights of citizens to prevent use of public property for religious displays, etc., etc. In any attempt to convince an audience that the ACLU protects everyone's freedom, a speaker would have to begin by pointing out that the "rights" to which some people object are all protected by the Constitution. The message would be, "If you want your own rights protected, you will in justice [basic value] recognize the need to protect the rights of others, even when they're doing something that offends you." And the speaker would not want to miss the opportunity to encourage attitude-change by showing in some way that he or she considered the listeners to be "responsible" and "open-minded" (personal standards which everyone is known to admire).

As the present time, for a second example, everyone is concerned about solving "the drug problem." The great majority of our people currently favor stronger laws and stronger enforcement programs in the "war" against drug addiction and abuse; very few publicly favor legalizing or even decriminalizing drugs. If the situation has not changed by the time you read this (and assuming that the students in the class reflect the national view), you could conceivably argue for some form of drug legalization. The point of all this: the drug problem exists, it is presently very serious, and it cries out for solutions. You would be wasting everyone's time if you did more than offer a quick summary of those non-issues in your introductory remarks. The real drug issues lie in the fundamental disagreements we have about solutions. To make sense to most audiences, your statement of purpose would have to be a proposal for trying some new approach to the drug problem.

Understanding what an attitude is, its place in one's belief system in relation to other beliefs, and its susceptibility to change, we turn now to a brief review of the pressures and tensions within all of us as they affect a speaker's trying to effect that change.

Typical listener reactions to pressure for change[11]

When you ask listeners to modify or change an attitude, you are working "against the grain." The attitude in question has already passed through their "selective perception gates" and is now a part of their nicely ordered belief systems. The listeners feel one way about a person, thing, or situation, and you are suggesting that they feel another way--the proposed change makes them tense or, at the very least, uneasy. In the face of the discomfort created by someone's trying to talk them into a change in attitude, listeners will (1) change or modify the attitude to relieve the tension created by the new idea, or (2) try to shunt the tension aside by justifying the old attitude and by blocking out what the speaker has to say, or (3) become angry and try to dodge, distort, and attack the incoming message.

As a speaker, you hope that your listeners will be in Group 1, and that they will adjust or change the attitude in question or join with you in following whatever proposal you are making. If the listeners fall into Group 2, "breaking through the shell" of their resistance to new thinking is more difficult. Their answer to tension is, "Ignore it and it will go away." Your answer is to plan an approach that is flexible enough to provide still more justification for the change in attitude or, if that angle seems to be unwise, to modify your approach in order to make it more acceptable to the audience. Finally, if you have any reason to believe that the majority of the audience will be in Group 3, plan from the start to adopt the approach which will be least threatening to that audience. For instance, people who smoke know that smoking is hazardous to their health. You may be able to badger a few into quitting, but a better strategy would be to talk about the negative impact that one's smoking has on the health of non-smoking members of the household. In short, listeners have to "sense the possibility of personal rewards as well as the approval of those persons closest to them."[12] Listeners to any presentation at any level must not only recognize that "the motivational carrot" is within reach but that it is also of enough value to them to make a change worth the effort.

Some Conclusions

It would be nice to be able to say that the experts on emotions, motives, and motivation have worked out some sure-fire formulas for motivating change in an audience attitude or for enlisting audience endorsement of any other proposal for listener thinking or action. Unfortunately, about all the experts really agree on is that *knowing your listeners is fundamental to success.* But even if your adaptation to the listeners has been close to perfect and even if they do what you want them to do, you can't jump to the conclusion that your interacting with them was the cause. They may have been planning the action long before you appeared on the scene, and you may have irritated them almost to the point of their not doing it. Or they may be doing it only because they like you personally and don't want to let you down. Or they may be doing it because they "owe you one" or have a matching favor to ask of you in the near future. Or someone else had already convinced them to do it. Or they may have been wavering between doing and not doing, and you just happened along when they were on the "doing" wave length. In other words, when the desired response follows a presentation you make, be happy but modest--other factors may have contributed mightily to that result. The problem here as elsewhere is that it is difficult to pin down the causes of success or failure when no two speaking situations are alike, no two audiences are alike (even in the classroom), no two speakers are alike, no two messages are alike...and no two audience responses are alike. But enough of theory, supportive or otherwise--let's try to put some of what we've learned into practice.

Motivating Change

Choosing subject and purpose

We take it for granted that, if you are planning a talk in the "motivating change" area, you already have in mind a project calling for your motivating the class (l) to accept a problem-solution to which it is strongly opposed, or (2) to weaken an attitude or belief, or (3) to strengthen an attitude or belief, or (4) to become enthusiastic about some idea or organization. The subject you choose to discuss doesn't have to be national or even regional in scope. Newspaper and magazine articles and editorials often reflect views held by almost everyone in the community. And if you choose to attack a prejudice, it should be one to which a majority of your immediate audience is thought to be addicted.

Analyzing the audience

In your analysis at this level, you will want to augment the approaches outlined in Chapters 7 and 12 with an especially careful look into the *reasons why* your audience holds a particular position or attitude. This slightly expanded list of analytical questions will remind you to search for those reasons (if appropriate to your subject and purpose) and will also help you meet the greater demands of audience-analysis at this level:

Who will be in the audience? What reason or reasons will the listeners have for putting in an appearance at this meeting?
Why should they listen to me on this subject?

What do they know about the subject:

Very much___Much___Some___Little___Practically nothing___

What is likely to be their view of my purpose:

Very favorable___Favorable___Neutral___Hostile___Very hostile___

If feelings of hostility toward my purpose are known or thought to exist, what can I do to overcome or neutralize them? What do the listeners stand to gain from hearing me out?
How can I best phrase that advantage to the listeners?
If my purpose is to oppose a position held by the listeners or to weaken an attitude they have, what are the main beliefs or "points" backing their position or attitude?

Can those listener "points" provide some or all of the framework for the organization of my case? Can their tone be softened by phrasing them more neutrally or as questions?

Can I find evidence and reasons which could serve to weaken or refute the beliefs supporting their position or attitude?

Or what evidence and reasons are available to support my position or the new attitude I hope they will accept?

What precisely is the common ground which we all share and from which we could move into a discussion of "disputed ground."

To what specific listener needs and desires can I appeal? Can the motive of "the common good" be introduced?

What group pressures may be at work among the listeners? To what extent can I neutralize them? Or take advantage of them?

Is there anyone from whom I can get an account of her or his experiences with these listeners? Or with listeners like them?

Finally, do I know what the physical setting will be? Is there anything I can do about occasion or setting which could increase my chances for successfully motivating change?

Will there be time for a post-presentation question-and-answer session? (If so, consider asking for it.)

We all know, of course, that you will be making this presentation to members of the class. Still, the day will come when you will doing your best to change another group's attitudes and beliefs, so the questions are phrased to help you meet that broader challenge in the class or outside it.

Although the questions themselves are obviously an extension of those you have become accustomed to in analyzing listeners, your special focus, if the circumstances call for it, must be on the reasons why listeners hold a particular attitude toward your purpose. What are the beliefs underlying the attitude? And what does holding that attitude do for the self-concept and self-esteem of the individuals in that audience?

The beliefs underlying an attitude are usually apparent through statements made by those holding the attitude and, sometimes, through pamphlets or books written to support or justify that belief. For example, the intended listeners may have the attitude that handgun control would be an infringement on their rights. Your investigation would reveal one or more supporting beliefs like these: "The Constitution guarantees each of us the right to bear arms." "In a time of rising crime rates, we need arms to protect ourselves." "Guns don't kill people; people do." "Personal ownership of arms is an American tradition." "Banning one kind of gun would be the first step in banning all personal guns." For that subject and for almost any other, a check of library subject-files or a few phone calls will ordinarily obtain for you the "supporting beliefs" information you need.

Phrasing your specific purpose

Attitudes are hard to change because those holding them feel strongly about them. Even when your personal standing with a particular audience is very high, the weakening of an attitude, rather than the reversing of it, is the only reasonable goal for a single speaking event. Continuing with the handgun example, you would want to state your purpose in a tactful way; for example: "Let's look at the facts surrounding the problem of handgun control in this country."

Collecting materials

With the handgun project still in mind, the next step is looking for "the means" to appeal to your listeners. As usual, you begin by collecting facts, figures, examples, illustrations, quotations, etc. Then, from the available evidence (as well as from any ready-made arguments you find), you draw inferences and conclusions in the ways described in Chapter 3. A primary problem, of course, is assembling the materials needed to counter the audience's view of the matter, either as it exists in printed materials or as it is reconstructed by you.

If you do the reconstructing, the audience attitude serves as its specific purpose, and the major beliefs supporting the attitude are, for the time being, the audience's "main points." Much of your search for materials will be aimed at putting yourself in a position (l) to discount the evidence behind the beliefs supporting the attitude and (2) to find arguments opposing those beliefs.

In your earlier analysis of the audience, you will also have reached some conclusions about the audience's motives for holding the attitude. You now decide how best to motivate the audience to make the change you're proposing. As a part of that motivational plan, you need to select the kind and size of the "carrot" incentive that will make it worthwhile for the listeners to make the change. You'll also want to note information about yourself that may add to "ethical appeal" in the eyes of the listeners. Even if you're not an expert on a subject, you can still make yourself believable by satisfying the listeners that your research is thorough, your conclusions are fair, and that you're looking out for the interests of all.

Organizing the message

Newspaper caption:

> 5-year-old killed by bullet from gun shown him by friend.

Unless present trends are reversed by the time you read this, almost every woman and man (to say nothing about teenagers and some children) will possess a handgun. Some already have automatic assault weapons. It is unlikely that solutions to gun-ownership controversies will be found soon...but even if they are, we can still use the handgun question to continue our illustration of steps in bringing about attitude change.

The beliefs supporting one version of the overall audience attitude ("Whether or not to own a handgun must be left to the individual citizen") could seem to you to be these:

I. Possessing a handgun enhances personal safety.

II. Possessing a handgun is a constitutional right.

Those two "main points" in the listeners' position could be used by you in countering them. All you need do in this instance is soften the phrasing to question form:

I. Does possessing a handgun enhance personal safety?

II. Is possessing a handgun a constitutional right?

Your reconstruction of beliefs supporting the attitude of the listeners may have led you to main points different from those above. In any event, a possible plan for the structure of your outline is ordinarily sitting there waiting for you.

In planning the subordinate arrangement of your ideas, you have the option of presenting one side or both sides of the case. Speaking to a student audience or to an equally well-educated off-campus group, your decision could be to discuss both sides:

I. Does possessing a handgun enhance our personal safety?

A. Some say we need handguns to be safe.

[Statistics and other factual information on the rise in armed burglaries, inability of law enforcement agencies to cope with the problem, numbers of handgun owners who have successfully protected themselves from attack, etc.]

B. Others say handguns endanger our safety.

[Views of law enforcement heads who oppose the possession of handguns by individual citizens. Statistics on the numbers of handgun owners who are maimed or killed in the process of protecting themselves, or who use handguns to kill others by accident or by design, whose handguns fall into the hands of children who suffer accidents, etc. Comparison of the numbers of handgun related deaths in the U.S. with the numbers in other industrial democracies.]

II. Is possessing a handgun a constitutional right?

A. Some say handgun possession is a right.

[Materials on the constitutional right to bear arms as guaranteed in Article II of the Bill of Rights: "A well-regulated militia being necessary to the security of a free state, the right of the people to keep and bear arms shall not be infringed." If we give up any part of that right, we shall have opened the door to the gradual losing of it, etc.]

B. Others say handgun possession is not a right.

[Materials based on the original meaning and intent of Article II. In the days before mobile military forces and National Guards, a *militia* was a force of citizens called up as needed to maintain, defend, or restore state security.

Strictly interpreted, Article II protects the right "to keep and bear arms" only for those trained and capable of taking their places in a "well-regulated militia" (e.g., law-enforcement agencies, members of the National Guard, and the military). In any event, sensible gun-control procedures could be no infringement on the rights of those who are not members of any such force or "militia."]

After you've planned the necessary sign-post transitions and made any other adjustments that occur to you, the next order of business is preparing your introductory and closing remarks.

Introduction

> [Attention-getter]: The other day, an Ohio woman's car broke down and she accepted a ride home from a passing motorist. When he stopped short of her home and tried to assault her, she pulled a handgun, fired, and escaped. She was lucky--and some would say she was in more danger with the gun than without it. And then there are the accidents--a few days ago, for example, a two-year old in our neighborhood shot himself with the handgun he found under a pillow on his grandmother's bed.
>
> [Reason to listen and personal competence]: No matter what our views on handguns may be, we all place a very high value on personal safety and freedom. My research on the subject doesn't make me an expert, but I have studied it carefully and, at the close of my remarks, I'll distribute a list of my sources.
>
> [Statement of purpose]: So let's examine some of the *pros* and *cons* on the subject of handguns and handgun control.

Having established an order of ideas for your introduction, you do the same for the conclusion.

Conclusion

> In summary, having a personal handgun is dangerous at best. You could be lucky like the stranded Ohio woman. However, owning a handgun, as we've seen, brings with it more risk than it does safety.
>
> Very few of us really contest the possession of guns, especially those in collections or those designed for hunting or target-shooting. Many do oppose the availability of the cheap handguns and automatic spray-guns which are useful only as weapons for killing people, either accidentally or on purpose.
>
> The next time you have a chance to vote or express an opinion on handgun control, I hope you will support it--for the sake of greater safety and continued freedom for all of us. Thank you.

In the short-form example above, you are aiming at weakening the attitude of opposition to handgun controls. The situation could readily be reversed. Addressing an audience favoring handgun controls, a speaker could attempt to weaken support for such controls. In any event, the responsible speaker always takes the position which she or he believes to be in the best interests of the listeners.

Whatever position you take or whatever your goal, you are by now well aware that gaining control over the message is just as essential and vital as organizing it. Finally, able speakers don't just happen; they get that way by plan. If your presentation is well adapted to the listeners, and if you are effective in interacting with them, you can be sure you will be favored with some degree of "the desired response."

So far in this chapter, the topic choices and examples cited have been highly controversial in nature; they call upon the speaker to motivate change in audience positions or attitudes of the hard-shell variety. For contrasting examples of the soft-shell inspirational variety, we turn to two transcripts of "occasional speeches," the first a sensitive commencement address aimed at stemming the materialistic attitude of the times, and the second a typical after-dinner award-acceptance talk in which the speaker focuses entertainingly on the attitudes and attributes required of business leaders. Both speakers give us a fine and final demonstration of the importance of "becoming one with the audience."

Pursue Not Just the Material[13]

by Alexander M. Schindler, Rabbi,
Union of American Hebrew Congregations

A commencement address at the University of South Carolina, Aiken, South Carolina, May 7, 1987.

It is a privilege which I greatly appreciate to be here and to participate in the joyous ceremonies of this commencement hour, joyous because it is in the nature of a release. Some of you may even think of this moment as a release from a kind of prison.

George Bernard Shaw called college even "more cruel than a prison" for, as he put it, "In a prison, at least, you are not forced to read books written by the guards."

The passing years will mellow your judgment, as it did mine, once you begin to reap the abundant harvest planted in your minds and hearts within these hallowed halls. In any event, I take great pride in the fact that by granting me an honorary degree, the President and Faculty of this school have made me your fellow alumnus.

In musing about what I was to say to you, it occurred to me that for all the fine words that attend our most significant life ceremonies, there is nearly always a hand gesture that marks the actual moment of transformation and passage.

At a wedding it is the exchange of rings. At a funeral it is the first handful of dirt thrown upon the casket; mourning truly begins with that gesture of finality. At birth it is the slap on the behind that brings forth the newborn's first, gasping cry.

And at a college graduation? Only when the sheepskin is handed to you, followed by a handshake--only then will you all sigh and cheer and no longer secretly fear that some computer somewhere has made a mistake that will force you to repeat your English composition course. Commencement has genuinely occurred when you walk the aisle back to your seat clutching that diploma in your hand.

My musings about hand gestures led me to remember an ancient rabbinical saying which sharpens a paradox of life that merits being brought to your awareness at this hour. I speak of life's self-contradictory demand which enjoins us to cling to its many gifts even while it ordains their eventual relinquishment. The rabbis of old put it this way: "A man comes into this world with his fist clenched, but when he dies, his hand is open."

We begin by grasping, ultimately we must renounce, and the art of living is to know when to hold fast and when to let go. Surely we ought to hold fast to life, for it is wondrous, full of a grandeur and a worth, full of a beauty that breaks through every pore of God's own earth.

We know that this is so, that life is passing wonderful, but all too often we recognize this truth only in our backward glance when we remember what was and then suddenly realize that it is no more. We remember a beauty that faded, a love that waned. But we remember with far great pain that we did not see that beauty when it flowered, that we failed to respond with love to love when it was tendered.

A recent experience re-taught me this truth. It happened a week or so after I was hospitalized following a rather severe heart-attack. I had been in the intensive care unit for long days and nights. It was not a pleasant place. My own pains and fears aside, its noises were not restful to the ear: the running feet of doctors and nurses, the creaking of machines wheeled in for some emergency, and moans and groans and cries of pain, and on two occasions during those days the dances and the rattling of death, and then the weeping of the suddenly bereaved.

About a week after I arrived, I had to have some tests, but the required machines were located in a building at the opposite end of the hospital campus, and so I had to be wheeled across the courtyard on a gurney. And as we emerged from our unit, the sunlight hit me. That's all there was to my experience. Just the light of the sun. And yet how beautiful it was, how warming, how sparkling, how brilliant!

And then I looked about me to see whether anyone else relished the sun's golden glow, but men and women and children were hurrying to and fro most of them with their eyes fixed on the ground, seemingly heedless of all the glory about them. And then I remembered how often I too had been indifferent to the grandeur of each day, too preoccupied with petty and sometimes even mean concerns to respond to the splendor of it all. The insight gleaned from that experience is really as commonplace as was the experience itself; life's gifts are precious--but we are too heedless of them.

Thornton Wilder makes this point in one of his magnificent creations, his immortal *Our Town*. In this play, as many of you will recall, a young woman who died in childbirth is allowed to return to earth for just one day. She chooses her sixteenth birthday as the day she would like to re-live. But as she comes upon the scene so familiar to her, she finds that everyone is far too busy to relish the day's wonder.

And so she cries out: "Momma, Papa, let's look at one another while yet we may." But nobody looks and nobody listens and all of the business of life goes on. Saddened by it all, she begs to be taken back and these are her words of farewell:

> Goodbye Momma, goodbye Papa, goodbye Grovers Corners.
>
> Goodbye to clocks ticking, and hot coffee, and newly ironed dresses...
>
> and lying down and getting up again.
>
> Oh earth, you are far too wonderful for anyone to realize you.

She turns to the stage manager and asks:

"Tell me, does anyone on earth ever realize life while he lives it...every, every minute?"

"No," replies he, "maybe the poets and the saints, maybe they do some."

And then she speaks her final words: "That's all human beings are, blind people...."

Is not this the malady that afflicts us?

We are blind, blind to so much of the beauty which abounds in our world. We walk about in a cloud of ignorance. We trample on the feelings of those who love us. We spend and waste time as though we had a million years to live always at the mercy of one self-centered passion after another.

How heedless we often are of our good until it is too late. Like birds whose beauty is concealed until their plumes are spread against the sky, our blessings brighten only as they take their flight.

Here, then, is the first pole of life's paradoxical demands on us:

> Life is precious, it is ineffably dear.
>
> Never be too busy for the wonder and the awe of it.
>
> Be reverent before each dawning day.
>
> Embrace each hour.
>
> Seize each golden minute.
>
> Cling to life with all your soul and might while yet may.
>
> Hold fast to life while yet you may.
>
> Hold fast to life...but not so fast that you cannot let go.

This is the second side of life's coin, the opposite pole of its paradox: we must accept our losses, we must learn how to renounce, how to let go. This is not as easy a lesson to learn and to internalize, especially when we are young, for when we are young, we think that the world is ours to command, that whatever we desire with full force of our passionate being can, nay will be ours.

Ah, but then life moves along to confront us with its grim realities and slowly but surely this second truth dawns upon us: Life not only offers us gifts. It also makes us suffer losses and we must learn to accept them. In a sense, I suppose, this very moment in your lives involves a loss. A contemporary humorist once described college as a place "that keeps you warm between high school and an early marriage."

Well, you must leave the warmth of this place and its security to go out into a colder world and embark on a life of your own. Nor will this be the first loss you suffered or will suffer. At every stage of our life we sustain losses--and grow in the process.

Why, we begin our independent lives only once we emerge from the womb and lose its protective shelter. Then we leave our mothers and fathers and our childhood homes. We enter a progression of schools and leave them. We get married and have children and then have to let them go, even as, in a sense, your parents are losing you today. We confront the death of our parents and our spouses. We must renounce our childhood dreams and accept the fact that live will not allow us to realize them. We must face the gradual or not so gradual waning of our own strength. And ultimately we must confront the inevitability of our own demise, losing ourselves as it were, all that we were or dreamed to be.

Life is never just a being. It is always a becoming, a relentless flowing on. We move through the various stages of life, as Shakespeare had it, each with its entrances and it exits, the infant becomes the boy, the boy the man, and there simply is no turning back.

Life is the great teacher in the art of renunciation. To heed this truth is not only just and right. It is the very gate of wisdom. Our parable of the open and closed hand confronts us with life's contrary demands. First we were enjoined to cling to life, to appreciate its every gift. Then we are told: Learn how to renounce these gifts, yea each and every one of them. How can we do both, and at the very same time? More important, why should we do it? Why fashion things of beauty when beauty is evanescent? Why give our hearts in love when those we love will ultimately be torn from our grasp?

In order to resolve this paradox, we must gain a wider perspective, reaching beyond ourselves in time both past and future, viewing our lives as through windows that open on eternity. Once we do that we realize that though our lives are finite, our deeds on earth to weave a pattern that is timeless. Our parents live on through us, and we will live on through our children. The institutions we build endure, and we will endure through them...

Shakespeare was wrong.

The good is not interred with our bones.

The beauty that we fashion cannot be dimmed by death.

The love we give in life lives on, long after we are gone, to bless the lives of others... Our flesh may perish, our hands will wither, but that which they create in beauty and goodness and truth, lives on for all time to come.

If my baccalaureate address must have its message, then let it be this: Don't spend and waste your lives accumulating objects that will only turn to dust and ashes. Pursue not so much the material but rather the ideal, for ideals along invest life with meaning and are of enduring worth.

Look about you and see these truths:

Add love to a house and you have a home.

Add righteousness to a city and you have a community.

Add truth to a pile of red brick and you have a school.

Add religion to the humblest of edifices and you have a sanctuary.

Add art and imagination to a series of spires and arches and you have a cathedral.

Add justice to the far flung round of human endeavor and you have civilization.

Put them all together, exalt them above their present imperfections, add to them the vision of humankind redeemed, forever free of need and strife, and you have the Temple of the Future, the kind of future we dream you to have--a future lighted with the radiant colors of hope.

A Personal Primer on Leadership[14]

by Edward L. Flom,
Chairman of the Board and Chief Executive Officer,
Florida Steel Corporation

A presentation made to the Harvard Business School Club of Florida West Coast, Tampa, Florida, May 6, 1987. It appears below in slightly edited and shortened form.

First and foremost, my family and I thank the Harvard Business School Club of Florida West Coast for this great honor [recognition as Business Citizen of the Year]. I particularly appreciate it, being a graduate of Cornell University--a sometimes competitor of Harvard. If you sit back and rationalize what talent of mine made this award possible, I can only think of my ability to select well. I made a great selection of wife, kids, parents, in-laws, friends, and particularly associates of Florida Steel. And I thank them all for this award.

When Howard Bradley informed me of this honor, he also told me of the responsibility of giving a talk. And so, appropriately I hope, I have chosen to give a short talk on my perception of the attributes and attitudes required of someone placed in a leadership role, or more important and surprising sometimes, where to obtain these attributes and attitudes.

To me, the single most important function of a chief executive officer is to surround himself with individuals who are more astute and knowledgeable in their positions than he is. Florida Steel has had only five presidents in its history, and I had a hand in the selection of three. Our company is presently run with a core of only six people and, excluding myself, you couldn't find five better qualified people anywhere. I've heard two sports figures exemplify this attribute. Several years back, I heard Leo Durocher say that if he could find a baseball player with the five abilities of hitting to all fields, hitting with power, running bases, throwing, and fielding, then he, Durocher, would be a great coach. Along came Willie Mays.

The head football coach at the University of Miami [for the other example] was expounding on his teaching his players to be innovative in critical situations. Miami had the ball on their opponent's five yard line and called an option play to the left. Their quarterback, George Mira, Sr., took the ball to the left and spotted an open receiver to his left. The only problem was Mira was right-handed and a six-foot seven inch, 275 pound tackle was hanging on his right shoulder. Without hesitation Mira switched the ball to his left hand and threw his only left-handed pass in his life for a touchdown. The coach exclaimed, "Now, that's coaching!"

If you are surrounded by excellent core management and they in turn surround themselves with excellence and so forth, the only task left is to be sure to allow full employee participation throughout a company. This is probably the most vital area to success. Corporate excellence has been defined as "many incidents of unusual effort on the part of many ordinary employees." In order for a company to excel, the vast majority of its employees must be motivated to the achievement of corporate goals. Of course, these goals must assume our responsibility to shareholders, customers, employees, suppliers, and the communities in which we operate.

A leader not only has to know who he is, he also has to always know where he is. A balloonist friend of mine was lost one day. He spied a farmer walking along a road, lowered the balloon and yelled to the farmer, "Where am I?" The farmer replied, "You're in a balloon." True, but no help at all, so my friend yelled again, "Where are you?" The truthful straight reply came back, "I'm on the road!"

Every company needs to know where it is or rather what it is actually trying to achieve. To illustrate this: I took my daughter at age five to the State Fair on a rainy day. She wanted some cotton candy and since there wasn't a single person in the cotton candy line, I said, "O.K." She received for one quarter a cotton candy ball approximately two feet in diameter. Since usually cotton candy is so much smaller, I asked the vendor how he could afford to provide this much cotton candy for only a quarter. He replied, "I don't sell cotton candy, I collect quarters. No one is in line behind you. Come here on a sunny day and wait in a long line, and I'll provide you with cotton candy only four inches in diameter. I don't miss many quarters." This man understood his niche in the marketplace and how to accomplish that task.

These niches change and you must be ever alert. You remember the former sales manager at General Motors when he said, "Don't worry, boss; nobody's going to buy those little Japanese cars!" Or the record company president who said, "Oh come on, don't tell me that they can put music on scotch tape." The best statement probably made was, "Now who would want to buy six bottles of the same thing in a package with a handle?"

In business one requires innovative solutions to critical situations. A high school friend of mine was working in a small town grocery store. He had a date after the store closed when the owner told him he'd have to finish up by himself, lock up, and then he'd be free to leave. As luck would have it, just as he was about finished, a little old lady came into the store and asked for a four-pound chicken. My friend, on checking in the cooler, saw there was only one chicken left looking about four pounds, and brought the chicken out for the lady's inspection. The lady said the chicken looked a little small and did he have one larger. My buddy went back into the cooler, fluffed up the only chicken there and again presented it to the lady. The lady said, "Oh, that's better. I'll take both of them."

One of the hardest tasks of leadership is understanding that you are not what you are, but what you're perceived to be by others. A perfect example of this is what happened in New York City when I was about ten or eleven. Preferring not to be delayed, my father made a U-turn in the middle of 5th Avenue and was promptly stopped by one of New York's finest. For those of you who knew my father, he was very intelligent, very articulate, very calm, and also was a transplanted Yankee. When the policeman asked if he had any idea of what he had done, my father said--in a slow Southern drawl, "Man, back home we always whip around to go the other direction." Then the officer shook his head and said, "Just please proceed on home."

A Chief Executive Officer is usually well compensated because that individual is expected to make decisions, be they right or wrong. One should not worry about criticism because usually there is someone somewhere that agrees with you. My training in this field was extensive; for five years I coached Little League and in this endeavor I received more advice from more sources than anyone could believe.

If I had to choose the one talent that is most beneficial in a leadership role, my first choice would be insight. But then insight is a given rather than a learned talent. Probably the second best talent to have is patience. Lord Chesterfield explained it perfectly when he said, "Patience is a most necessary quality for business; many a man would rather you hear his story than grant his request." Our company has always had an open policy. Most people refer to policies like this as open door policy. We go one step further. Not only can anyone make an appointment to see anyone in Florida Steel, but anyone can telephone any person without having to identify himself. Whenever possible, which is most of the time, we all answer our telephones. No one is allowed to ask, "May I say who's calling?" And the caller can decide whether or not to interrupt a meeting. Lord Chesterfield was right; most people would rather talk to you than get their way.

The companies we recently purchased, Knoxville Iron and Steel Service, were a lesson in patience. I was involved in acquisition discussions with these companies while under four different owners over a period exceeding twenty years. Now that's patience--even though my wife may tell you I drove her batty. Florida Steel is continuing its acquisition program under the theory stated by Caesar: "Hasten slowly."

Which reminds me--if any of you are timing this talk, I should begin to wind down. To be included in the same group as the past ten recipients of Business

Citizens of the Year really begins to humble a person. I could expound on this and still not be able to express my thoughts. So to the Harvard Business School Club I say, "Thank you and good night."

Endnotes

1. Vernon E. Jordan, Jr., "Belief in Fairness Makes Democracy," *Vital Speeches of the Day*, 53 (May 15, 1987) 15, p. 466.

2. John E. Jacob, "A Human Society Is Based on Values," *Vital Speeches of the Day*, 51 (September 1, 1985) 22, p. 687.

3. Frederick Williams, *The New Communications* (Belmont, CA: Wadsworth, 1984), p. 72.

4. S. Guernsey Jones, "Human Conduct," *Vital Speeches of the Day*, 53 (June 1, 1987), p. 493.

5. Douglas C. Jones, *The Barefoot Brigade* (New York: Holt, Rinehart and Winston, 1982), p. 178.

6. Aristotle's *Rhetoric*, 1415b.

7. Robert W. White, "Motivation Reconsidered: The Concept of Competence," *Studies in Educational Psychology*, ed. Raymond G. Kuhlen (Waltham, MA: Blaisdell, 1968), p. 81.

8. Amitai Etzioni, *The Moral Dimension: Toward a New Economics* (New York: The Free Press, 1988). See p. 8 f. for an outline of "the responsive community," the theme treated variously throughout the book.

9. Patricia Niles Middlebrook, *Social Psychology & Modern Life*, 2nd ed. (New York: Alfred A. Knopf, 1980), p. 157.

10. Milton Rokeach, *The Nature of Human Values* (New York: The Free Press, 1973), p. 57 f.

11. For a review of theories on tension-release and strains toward consistency, see Martin F. Hunt, Jr., and Gary B. Wilson, "Attitude Change and Consistency Theories," in *Communication and Behavior*, eds. Gerhard J. Hanneman and William J. McEwen (Reading, MA: Addison-Wesley, 1975), pp. 167-174.

12. Williams, pp. 118-20.

13. Alexander M. Schindler, "Pursue Not Just the Material," *Vital Speeches of the Day*, 53 (August 15, 1987) 21, p. 659 f.

14. Edward R. Flom, "A Personal Primer on Leadership," *Vital Speeches of the Day*, 53 (August 15, 1987) 19, pp. 594-96.

Discussion Questions

1. In our culture, we are somewhat wary of emotion but less self-conscious about feeling. Why is that? Are the two words the same in meaning? Similar? If there is a difference, what is it?

2. The motive or emotion of fear may be used to influence behavior. Can you recall a public speaking situation in which the speaker aroused fear in order to win a "desired response" from the listeners? Or tried to reduce fear?

3. Robert White says we do everything with the idea of defending, maintaining, or enhancing our self-image. Can you give an example of somebody's taking an action without that in mind?

4. We sometimes keep from doing things which we want to do and could do. Can you remember such an instance in your past experience? What kept you from following through? Would you call the want a motive? What would you call the restraining factor? An attitude? Or just some form of group pressure?

5. Cite an attitude which you "inherited" from your parents. How, in your opinion, did that attitude become a part of their belief systems? Have you ever questioned that attitude? Or the beliefs behind it? What was the result of the questioning?

6. What is the difference between a basic value and an attitude?

7. Becoming one with the audience is crucial to success in communicating with it. Excluding classroom speakers, can you cite a situation in which the speaker succeeded in convincing you that she or he had your interests at heart?

8. On the commencement address by Rabbi Schindler...

How do you believe he made his choice of subject?

If you were planning to address a graduating class, what would you need to know about the graduates?

Did he meet the requirements for a good introduction? Would you have changed that introduction in any way?

Is the speaker intentionally or unintentionally enlisting the feelings of the audience in support of his purpose? Does he tell you clearly what his purpose is?

Is the speaker concerned about "benefits to the audience"? In what ways does he try to identify himself with his listeners?

What instances of emotional appeal do you find in the Schindler address?

What is the speaker's personal motive or motives in urging a less materialistic outlook? What does the address do for him?

What motivation does the speaker offer his listeners in asking them to be less materialistic? Do you consider the "carrots" provided to be substantial enough to motivate the listeners?

How does he ally himself with his audience? Do members of the clergy have ethical appeal simply by virtue of their calling?

9. On the after-dinner talk by Edward Flom...

Flom's talk is really a string of stories which he uses to elaborate on his theme. Does he tell stories effectively? Why are stories particularly appropriate for an after-dinner talk? In contrast to Mr. Flom's talk, if you have someone just telling a series of funny stories, the sole purpose of which is to entertain, do you have a speech there? Or do you have a stand-up comic or semi-theatrical event?

What emotions does he try to evoke? Is humor an emotion? Some of his stories are self-deprecating. Is that a good technique?

What evidence is there that he was identifying with his listeners and thinking about their interests? From reading the speech, what do you believe the members of the Harvard Club learned from it? What did you learn from it?

Flom brings the talk to an end by referring to the timing of it and the fact that he should be winding down. Is this a good way to conclude? Is it acceptable in this instance?

Application Projects

Speaking options

1. Prepare an 8-10 minute talk designed to weaken a position, attitude, or belief thought to be strongly held by a majority of the students in the class.

2. Prepare an 8-10 minute talk designed to strengthen a position, attitude, or belief which seems to you to be losing ground. For example, "What happened to the idea of a day's work for a day's pay?"

3. Prepare an 8-10 minute inspirational talk designed to generate enthusiasm for some concept, moral principle, idea, organization, or team enterprise.

Listening options

1. In this series of student presentations, what speaker seemed to be superior in enlisting the feelings of the audience in support of her or his purpose in speaking? Write a one-page explanation of your choice.

2. What speaker seemed to you to be superior in his or her effort to motivate a change in a hard-shell position or attitude held by the students. Write a one-page explanation of your choice.

3. What student seemed to you to be superior in his or her overall effort to evoke emotion and motivate change? Write a one-page explanation of your choice.

4. Of those who attempted an inspirational talk, what student seemed to you to have been most successful in interacting with the student audience? Write a one-page explanation of your choice.

Additional Activity

Analyzing emotional/motivational appeal in action.

Read or view the videotape of a strongly emotional address like Jesse Jackson's "Common Ground and Common Sense" at the 1988 Democratic Party Convention. Oral reports, written reports, or class discussion could center your attention and that of the other students on the ways in which intensity of feeling supports a speaker's plea for change and strikes a responsive chord in listeners at the same time.

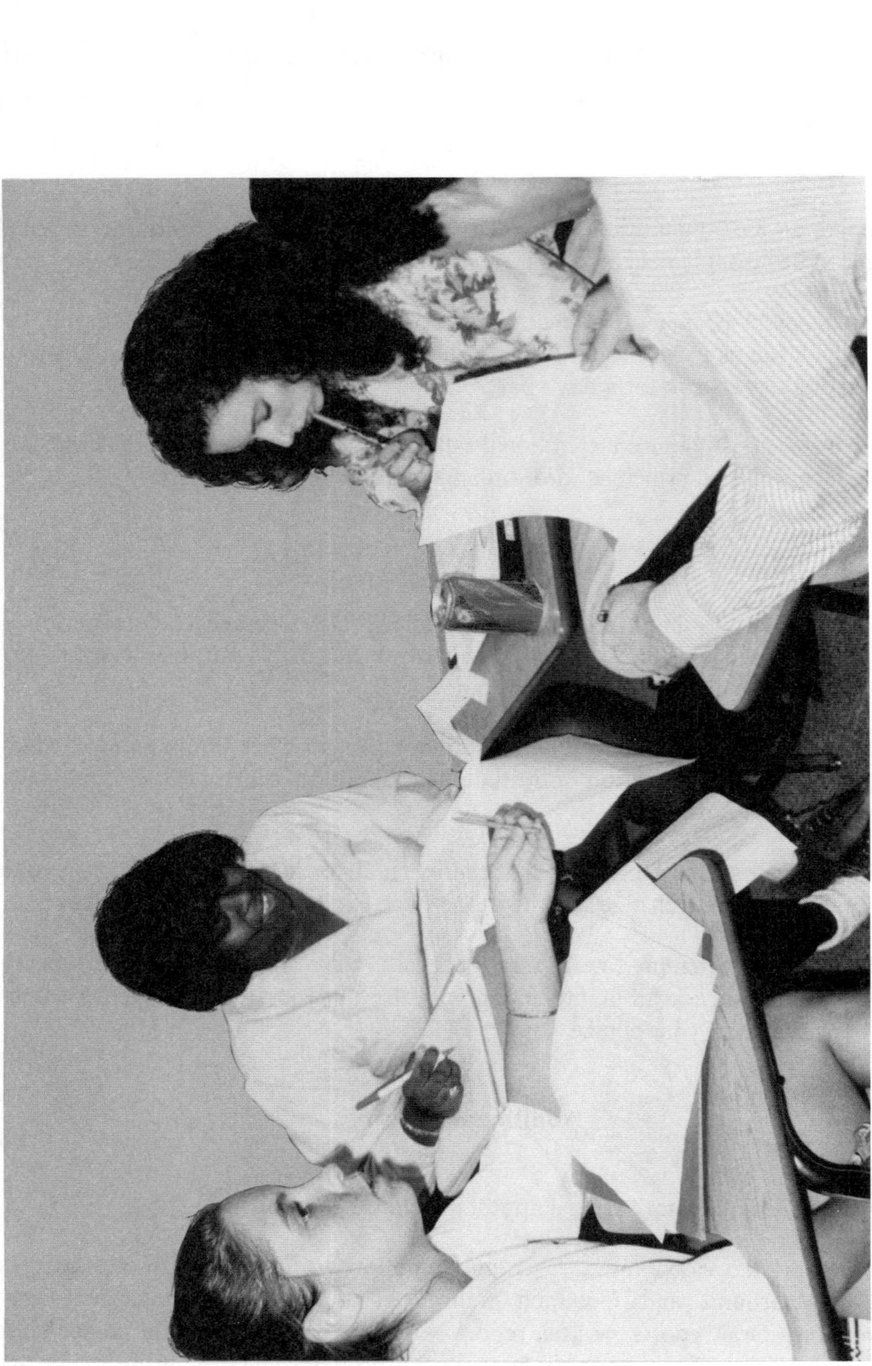

A

APPENDIX

Speaking in Small-Group Discussion

When commenting in earlier chapters on a speaker's "recognizing the need to communicate," we said that a topic or subject will find you more often than the other way around. The same is true of discussions; unless you are personally calling for a discussion which you see as necessary, you will more often be asked (or directed) to participate in one.

For example, an office manager or department store supervisor who notices a steady increase in the number of employees arriving late for work won't make any points by opening a conference on the problem with "What do I have to do to get you people here on time?" She or he could do much better with "What can we do to get off to a better start in the morning?" A pleasant word or compliment is the way to set the stage for a productive conference. When people receive encouragement to discuss a common problem, they are usually willing "to give it a try."

Just how useful is it to know something about the speaking and listening we do as members of a small group? Listen to the experts: "To anyone familiar with business and industry, it hardly seems necessary to point out the amazing amounts of time that are spent in meetings."[1] "No educated person in a responsible position can avoid participation [in discussion]; for this reason, understanding of the small group is essential."[2] In both quotations, the writers are referring to an individual's speaking and listening to reach a common goal in the course of meetings of all kinds during working or business hours, at lunch, in the evening, or on weekends. In other words, much of our information-sharing, problem-solving, and decision-making occurs in direct communication with a few individuals assembled "in conference."

Since we are going to be involved in purposeful discussion, we should know as much as we can about it. In many ways, it is a kind of mini-scale public speaking. The "audience" with which a member of the group interacts is usually very small (preferably no fewer than five individuals and no more than seven)[3] but, for the person speaking at any one time, it poses many of the same problems as "public speaking." While no one member of the discussion group has responsibility for being the speaker, all members are, by turns, both speakers and listeners. Discussion provides a unique opportunity to work with others in finding materials, using them as a base for reasoning to solve a problem and, later, as a base for inducing listeners to accept the solution worked out. Discussion also increases your sensitivity to listeners--to their ways of speaking, to their ideas, to their feelings, to their needs for recognition as human beings. More importantly for the individual student, taking part in discussion is a relatively pressure-free way to sharpen one's reasoning and communication skills at the same time. Your interacting with the other "members of the committee" is close and direct, and feedback is continuously seen, heard, and felt. There is, in fact, no better practice in becoming one with the audience, be it large or small. As President Lyndon Johnson used to say, "Come let us reason together."

The best discussion questions, of course, are those on which you and others can profitably share your experience and judgment. For instance, if a group of students is working to find out what professional educators are recommending to improve public school education, each student is likely to learn more about that subject by working with others than if she or he were working alone.

The wording of a discussion question should be *open ended*, that is, it should not restrict the number of choices to two. A question like "Should billboards along interstate highways be abolished?" is too narrow for discussion--it offers only two choices and would only end in argument. At the other extreme, "How can the administration of justice be improved?" is a question so open-ended that no real discussion is possible. "What can be done to improve the administration of justice in the traffic courts of our city?" is both specific enough to provide focus and open enough to permit a number of different approaches.

However it may be worded, the specific phrasing of a discussion question determines its classification as well as the goal which members of a group hope to reach in discussing it. Some groups come together to share information on questions of fact; some go a step farther to evaluate people, movements, situations, etc., that is, to discuss questions of value; and others try to solve the problems involved in questions of policy.

The Information-Sharing Group

...answers questions of fact

When a discussion group is trying to find out and describe what has happened or what is happening, the first question is "What are the facts?" What is a fact to one member of a committee, however, may not be a fact to another. We should think of facts in the context of personal or reported *observations* subject to error in both the observing and the reporting. Just as we have to be wary of "facts," we have to be just as wary of the inferences we draw from them. One individual looks at the police shooting of an innocent bystander during a bank robbery and decides that "accidents will happen" and the officers acted properly; another looks at the same facts and concludes that there is too little restraint on the actions of the police in that kind of situation. In any event, the interpretation of facts and the inferences drawn from them often depends on who's doing the interpreting. Above all, we have to be careful not to confuse facts with inferences and inferences with facts.

A few examples of discussions centered on facts and the meanings of facts: A financial institution may be losing money; someone establishes a committee to investigate and report on what is going on. Airline mechanics and inspectors may be reporting an unusual number of landing-gear problems in a certain model of airliner; a group of experienced aircraft engineers tries to track down the source or sources of the problem. Sales are down in only one supermarket of a chain of twenty; the president of the company asks a group of managers to find out why. At a time when the number of enrollments in a college is climbing, the number of majors in a particular department is going down; a student-faculty committee looks into the reason or reasons. In these kinds of small groups, in other words, the members are looking for and exchanging information for the purpose of drawing some useful conclusions from the available facts. They are concerned with coming to grips with three main questions:

1. *What are the relevant facts*? Statistics? Opinions of experts?

2. *What do we make of these facts*? How do we interpret them? How do we rank them in order of importance?

3. *What conclusions can we safely draw from them*? Do the facts seem to point to any specific causes? Can we agree on a description of the situation based on the facts and our interpretation of them?

Here are some questions typical of those requiring looking into facts, into their meanings, and into the conclusions to be drawn from them:

How does a poor and unemployed mother of three children go about qualifying for "welfare" in this state?

What are the trends in religious beliefs and ideas in this country?

What are the causes of urban decay in this city?

What is the extent of the problem of the homeless in our state?

The Value-Determining Group

...answers questions of value or worth

A discussion group looking into the facts on sex education in the public schools (as in the question of fact cited above) could be asked to include in its report an evaluation of the current situation. Using their investigation of the facts as a base, the committee could list its reasons for believing the status of sex education to be satisfactory, or unsatisfactory, or unsatisfactory but improving, or totally inadequate, or....

In other words, the group members try to answer essentially the same questions as for a question of fact. They, too, are interested in information-sharing, but the emphasis of the inquiry (third question below) shifts from simply drawing conclusions from the facts to making evaluations based on them. In business and industry, as you well know, it is common for a company to ask a small group of employees to act as a committee to evaluate new equipment being considered for purchase. Or in an advertising agency, a promotion planned by two or three people is presented to an in-house evaluation group before being proposed to a client. For another example, if you should ever be on a committee charged with choosing and hiring the best candidate for a post of any kind, your group would be seeking the answers to questions like these:

1. *What are the relevant facts*? What do we know and what do we need to find out about each candidate: education, performance in similar jobs, references from people who know him personally and on the job, special accomplishments, awards, etc.? Personality, attitudes, potential for growth, etc., etc.?

2. *What do we make of the facts*? How do we rank the qualities of degrees earned? The conditions under which the needed experience was gained? The sources of the references provided? Other factors?

3. *What evaluation can we now reasonably make of each candidate*? Whom should we recommend as the best qualified candidate? What reasons should we advance in support of our choice?

A few examples of value questions:

Is a college education worth the time, trouble, and expense?

Of what value to the student is the study of Latin?

Which is the best of the available lap-top computers?

Of the candidates for the presidency of this organization, who is the best qualified?

Is it moral for a rich country to ignore human rights to food, shelter, jobs, and medical care?

The Problem-Solving Group

...answers questions of policy

At this level, you will also note the regular use of the word *should* in the phrasing of the question. When you see that word--or any equivalent of it--in a discussion question, you know that you and the other members of the group are talking about a problem in order to make a suggestion about policy-what ought to be done about it.

Therefore, when asked or required to go beyond sharing information or offering an evaluation, conference or committee members ask themselves "*What should be done about the problem or situation* under study?" The related questions[4] which the group must answer are, of course, more detailed than for the earlier investigations:

1. *Is the problem clearly stated* in the form of an openended question that is neither too narrow nor too broad? Do we agree on the meanings of the terms in the question? Should we rephrase it?

2. *What is the nature and extent of the problem*?

   a. *What are the facts*? Available statistics? Opinions of experts? Similar situations elsewhere? How are they being handled? What exactly is wrong? How serious is the problem?

   b. *Can we pinpoint the cause(s)* of the problem? Are there other contributing or related causes? What is the relative importance of each cause?

   c. *What standards must a solution meet* in order to solve the problem?

3. *What should be done about the problem*? What are some possible solutions? Should we improve the present system? Or aim at something entirely new?

4. *How does each solution, old or new, meet the solution standards* we agreed upon? What are the advantages and disadvantages of each approach? Costs for each? Chances for success? Possible effects of failure?

5. *Does one solution now stand out as best*? Or should we construct a new one by combining the best features of those available? Or by making a few changes in the one we consider best?

You have already taken part in many an informal or formal discussion, and you know that few attempts to solve problems by "group process" follow the orderly series of steps outlined above. However, the topics represented by those steps are normally covered at one time or another. In other words, a group seldom moves toward its goal in rigid lockstep.[5] Instead, it "spirals" or circles its way upward in trying to arrive at agreement at any one level.

> An idea is introduced spontaneously by one of the participants. Another in the group suggests an extension, a different emphasis, an example, a substitution, et cetera, or perhaps merely expresses affirmation or rejection of the point. Others volunteer similarly. Thus there is an idea-in-the-making...[which continues] until it represents more or less well their cumulative, developing, mutual point of view.[6]

The problem-solution questions below are typical of those on which you and other members of a group would be doing your "spiraling":

What day-care responsibilities should companies assume for the children of their employees?

What measures should we take to bring about an increase in the numbers of minority faculty? Or minority students?

What courses should be required of all students at this college or university?

What should college and university students do about drugabuse on campus?

What changes should be made in the laws governing the financing of political campaigns at the national level?

What measures should we undertake to overcome indifference toward voting [or toward any other political, economic, or social problem]?

What should the U.S. do to improve relations with Latin American countries?

Suggestions for Group Leaders[7]

The members of the group do most of the work, but somebody has to take on primary responsibility for getting the discussion off to a good start and for keeping it moving toward its goal. The leader (elected, appointed, or otherwise designated) tries to do his or her part in establishing a good discussion atmosphere by a friendly approach to the others in the group, by consideration for the feelings of others, by actively listening to them, and by linking the ideas of one member to those of another in order to call attention to the relationships existing between them.

Leading the discussion, however, should not be left to the leader only. Leading is a function resting with the members of the group as much as with a designated leader or chairperson.[8] Assuming that the chairperson exercises leadership only to the extent necessary, and assuming that each member of the group takes on a fair share of responsibility for progress in the discussion, the suggestions below are intended not only for the "official leader" but also for each member as well:

1. ***Decide on the goals to be reached.*** If the focus of the group is on fact-finding and the conclusions to be drawn from that activity, the goals are answers to the three questions posed on page 239. If the purpose of the group is to solve a problem, the goals are answers to the five question-areas on pages 241-2. The chairperson for a given day should make it his or her business to assess what needs to be done or what remains to be done to make progress toward completion of "the committee's charge."

2. ***Keep the discussion on track.*** Once the discussion begins, try to maintain the step-by-step procedure suggested by the general questions governing it. Comments, ideas, quips, and incidental questions are not always on target. Some skipping, circling, jumping ahead, and backtracking is to be expected and, in fact, is necessary. Unless a "contribution" is totally beside the point (e.g., proposing a solution in the first five minutes), there is no reason to take remedial action. In a discussion, all that is really necessary is to keep making progress in a general way through the steps required to reach the goals decided upon.

These are some of the things a leader (or any member) can say to help maintain that progress:

Are we all satisfied that we have a good basic statement of our goal or problem?

We've agreed on the choice of an interesting question and on a possible wording of it. Let's define the terms in it, so that we can all agree on what they mean.

Let's move on now to review what we already know about the problem.

Does anyone have anything to add to our collection of facts?

Do we have enough information? Or should each of us report additional information when next we meet?

Should each of us take on a specific topic to avoid duplicating our search effort?

Is the fact just stated actually a fact? Or is it an opinion?

How important to us do you think fact A should be? Fact B?

Do you feel that fact C may be one of the causes of our problem?

At this point, *let's summarize the facts* as we see them.

Do you feel that we now have enough information to evaluate the facts and draw some conclusions from them?

We now seem to have the factual situation under control. Are we ready to look into the underlying cause(s) of the problem?

Do you think we've talked about this topic long enough? If so, let's move on to another one.

Is this line of thought related directly enough to our discussion?

That sounds something like a solution. Are we ready for solutions at this point?

Let's summarize what we have accomplished so far in our attempt to pin down the causes of the problem.

Are you ready now to move on to a discussion of possible solutions?

Is it possible that the solution just suggested would cost too much?

Has this other idea for a solution been tried anywhere? Is it practical?

Are we ready to write up our recommendation of one of the solutions proposed? Or our recommendation of a solution made up of the best features we can find in the other solutions?

3. ***Encourage everyone to participate.*** Keeping a discussion on track assumes that the members of the group are actively cooperating to make it a success. As a chairperson, you can also use general questions and comments to (a) keep the contributions flowing, (b) set aside any misinformation, and (c) modify suggestions:[9]

Would anyone like to comment on that last statement? Do any of you have anything further to add?

And?

Let me reword the question this way.

Let's approach the topic from this angle.

Could you explain that more fully?

What has been your experience" (Especially useful to draw out someone who has not been actively participating.) Most of what you say is correct, but I wonder about...? Do all of you agree with that statement?

Could you tell us the source of your information?

Where can we find that information?

Do you mean that...?

Would it be better to...?

Your suggestion may work, but....

4. ***Summarize at regular intervals.*** As a discussion moves along, the leader (or anyone else willing to do the recording) jots down notes on the information contributed, on the interpretations discussed, and on the conclusions reached. At various stages of the discussion, the individual doing the recording should be ready to summarize what has been said. (Examples of the kinds of comments

leading into a summary appear in suggestion #2 above.) As a group moves from one major step to another, a summary helps set the stage for the move and it also serves as a transition, a notice to all that the focus of the discussion is now on the next step in the process. When the meeting nears its close, the usual procedure is for the leader to handle the final summary.

The emphasis throughout any discussion should be on cooperation and compromise. The chairperson acts as "tour guide" but also participates as one of the members. (In the classroom scene, chairing responsibility can be rotated so that, in successive sessions, more than one student in each group gains this kind of experience.) As we have seen, the leader's function is to ask leading questions, to make suggestions offering encouragement and reinforcement, and to help guide the group through appropriate steps of the problem solving sequence. The leader provides direction but does not attempt to "tell the others what to do or what to think...."[10]

Similarly, the members are not restricted to dealing only with subject-related contributions; any one of them should feel free to call attention to omissions or errors in reasoning or in procedure. Just as the chairperson should take an active part in discussion of the question itself, so also should the members assume a share of the "collective leadership" implicit in the idea of *group* process. Ideally, the leader leads and follows, and the followers follow and lead.

Suggestions for Members of the Group

There is more to worry about in discussion than just drawing conclusions from assembled facts or solving problems...and that "more" is people problems. "It is inevitable that when people engage in discussion they will respond not only to each other's *ideas*, but also to each other as *people*."[11] The fact that a group is engaged in studying a problem does not suspend the "rules" of the relationships between you and the other members of the group. Instead of having listener attention focused on a single speaker, as in public address, the focus in group process is constantly shifting from one person to another.

If you visualize discussion groups, for example, in which the numbers of participants range from three to seven, you readily see that there are three possible lines of two-person communication in a group of three, 10 possible lines in a group of five, and 21 in a group of seven! In that last instance, in other words, each of the seven individuals sitting around the table has the option of talking with any one of the other six while the discussion as a whole is supposed to be proceeding under the combined leadership of the chairperson and the other members of the group. With that many lines available in a larger group, there's always the unfortunate possibility that two or three separate conversations may be going on at the same time.[12]

And even when everyone in a group gets along well, things can and do happen. Somebody takes offense at an imagined or real slight; somebody goes into a "silence strike" because of not getting a chance to speak; somebody feels that the chairperson is "running" the meeting and decides not to cooperate; somebody is trying to make a good impression on someone else in the group and pays little attention to the question being discussed; or someone contests with someone else to see who can make the greatest number of "contributions." There is often a great deal going on in a conference that has little to do with the subject at hand.

So each of us comes to the group with a kind of double personality. One side of us works on the problem, and the other side of us works on the people. We try to cooperate with them most of the time but, for a variety of personal reasons, we sometimes hold back or may not cooperate at all. How well we succeed in our people relationships depends on how much we know about getting along with and understanding others; it also depends on how much we want to get along with them in the interests of solving a common problem.

How to relate *personally* to others in order to set up a supportive "people atmosphere" is the primary focus of the suggestions that follow:

1. ***Be willing to cooperate***. When you agree with someone, indicate your support in some way (comment, smile, etc.). If you disagree, make clear that you are in disagreement with the idea, not with the person involved. (Make an enemy of that person, and he or she will disagree with you from that point on.) If tension arises over some hotly contested point, do what you can to keep the emphasis on the point at issue and not on the people. Here again, a smile, a good-humored remark, and a quick move to another topic serves to help the group over the occasional rough spot. Your cooperation should extend to encouraging a shy person by making it easy for him or her to take an active part in the proceedings.

2. ***Be ready to compromise***. The whole idea behind a conference is to apply "collective brain power" to a problem. The assumption is that the more heads involved, the better the final result or decision. Each of us, because of different experiences and background, has something special to offer to the group. At the same time, none of us knows everything. Don't be timid about saying something, but be prepared to accept reasonable changes and "amendments."

3. ***Respect the views of others***. People say things because they believe them. If you are not ready to accept someone's statement of fact or opinion, your chiming in with "That's not true!" won't help the situation or change any views. A more

friendly approach: "Could you tell us where those figures came from?" or "What are your reasons for taking that position?" As a member of the group, a part of your job is to help establish an all-ideas-are-welcome atmosphere, one in which everyone feels free to make a contribution without worrying about being directly contradicted or criticized. It is possible to have healthy differences of opinion and a good discussion atmosphere at the same time; the only requirement is that the members of the group have an honest regard for each other as co-workers and human beings.

4. ***Listen actively***. The point has been made in Chapters 2 and 5 (and elsewhere in this text) that you can communicate with a speaker by really listening to her or him. On the other hand, if you're looking at the ceiling while someone is trying to make a point, the one doing the speaking will also be inspecting the ceiling when you are doing the talking. Listening, always important, is especially so in groups, where there are at least as many distractions as there are people.

A Typical Discussion Outline

Students often prefer to look for and deal with on-campus issues, but there are also other problems affecting students at the community, state, national, and international levels. We bring this section of the chapter to a close with the following outline of the kind one could write as a guide for the discussion of a specific concern:

Problem-solution question: How should we cope with the problem of racial tension in this state?

1. Is the question, as worded, a clear statement of the problem?

   What do we mean by "cope with"? By "racial tension"? Should we rephrase the question to focus on racial tension in a city of the state? Can we agree that, for purposes of discussion, racial tension and racial unrest mean the same thing?

   Should we consider only incidents of racial unrest which grow out of housing discrimination? Out of activities by agencies of law enforcement? Out of inner-city economic problems? Out of some other situation?

2. What is the nature and extent of the problem?

What are the facts? What is the history of racial tension in this state? What incidents of unrest have occurred recently? Where did they occur? Why are we discussing the problem now? What recent, official reports are available to us? What conclusions have been reached by commissions studying the problem? Is racial tension typical of major cities only? What statistics do we have on the problem? What other studies?

What seem to be the major causes of racial unrest? Lack of minority opportunity? Inability of the poor to break out of poverty? Political refugees coming in from other countries? Distrust of government and police? Do those who engage in riots feel that violence is the only way to get something done about their problems? Do the newspapers and other new media play a part in creating racial tension?

What standards should be met by any solution we propose? Do we know enough about the facts and about the possible causes to be thinking about standards for a solution? Should a solution be aimed at improving living conditions in the so-called ghetto areas? Should it be aimed at job-training and job-guarantees? Should it be aimed at more attention to race relations in the classrooms of the public schools? Could the churches play a greater role in fostering good racial relations?

3. What should be done about racial tension in the state?

Should some plan for coordinated federal, state, and city action be adopted to lessen racial tensions? Should a part of any plan include improved educational opportunities? Improved job opportunities? Improved housing? Reform of the welfare program? Provision for child-care centers? Better policing? More listening on the part of officials and more action in response to complaints of prejudice and discrimination?

What can be done by institutions and organizations other than those associated with government?

What can be done by the news media to foster racial understanding? To publicize the legal and other services designed to help victims of racial tensions and unrest?

Are there commission reports and recommendations which have merit but which have never been implemented? Could they provide the base or bases for new plans or programs?

What other solutions could be considered?

4. How does each solution meet the solution-standards we agreed upon?

What are the comparative advantages and disadvantages of the solutions being considered?

What costs are involved for each plan? Where would the money come from? What are the chances for success of each plan?

5. Does one solution stand out as best?

Can we now agree on one solution as it stands? Or as we may amend it? Or on a combination of the solutions proposed?

Is there some practical way to test the final solution we choose in a limited setting? What steps do we need to take to have some agency or agencies undertake that testing procedure?

If the test is successful, how do we go about getting the backing required to put the proposed plan into effect?

Endnotes

1. Dean C. Barnlund and Franklyn S. Haiman, *The Dynamics of Discussion* (Boston: Houghton Mifflin, 1960), p. 3.

2. Gerald M. Phillips, *Communication and the Small Group* (New York: Bobbs Merrill, 1966), p. 5.

3. Bernard Berelson and Gary A. Steiner, *Human Behavior: An Inventory of Scientific Findings* (New York: Harcourt, Brace and World, 1964), p. 360.

4. For a discussion of these steps, traditional since ancient times, see John Dewey, *How We Think* (Boston: D.C. Heath, 1933), p. 107, and Gerald Phillips and Eugene C. Erickson, *Interpersonal Dynamics in the Small Group* (New York: Random House, 1970), p. 22 f.

5. Thomas M. Scheidel and Laura Crowell, "Idea Development in Small Discussion Groups," *Quarterly Journal of Speech*, 50 (April, 1964), pp. 140-145.

6.______, p. 141.

7. For a comprehensive treatment of discussion leadership, see John F. Cragan and David W. Wright, *Communication in Small Group Discussions: An Integrated Approach*, 2nd ed. (St. Paul, MN: West Publishing, 1986), pp. 125-154.

8. Thomas Gordon, "Group-Centered Leadership and Administration" in Carl R. Rogers et al., *Client-Centered Therapy* (Boston: Houghton Mifflin, 1951), pp. 320-383.

9. Thora Kron, *The Management of Patient Care*, 4th ed. (Philadelphia: Saunders, 1976), pp. 141-143.

10. Irving J. Lee, *How to Talk with People* (New York: Harper and Row, 1952), p. 7.

11. Barnlund and Haiman, p. 186. For more detail on the management of interpersonal relationships in discussion as well as in making presentations to small groups, see George David Kieffer, *The Strategy of Meetings* (New York: Simon and Schuster, 1988).

12. See Robert D. Breth, *Dynamic Management Communications* (Reading, MA: Addison-Wesley, 1969), p. 86.

Application Projects

Discussion options

1. Take part in a fact-finding discussion which has as its goal the pooling of basic information about a situation or problem, the interpretation of that information, and the drawing of conclusions from it.

2. Take part in a value-determining discussion which, following examples of questions of value in the text, calls for a final evaluation of the ideas, persons, or things under consideration.

3. Take part in the discussion of any open-ended problem-solution question aimed at finding out as much as possible about a problem and recommending a solution for it.

Listening options

1. Write a short report (no more than two pages) on the efficiency of your group in following through on the steps required for the discussion of a particular question. In what ways, for example, was the group systematic in working on the problem? Was any important step hurried or left out?

2. Write a short report on the "people problems" which seemed to you to ease or hinder the progress of the discussion in a particular session. In what ways, for instance, was a friendly and cooperative atmosphere sustained or promoted?

3. Write a short "looking-back-on-my-day report" on how well you participated in the discussion in any one session. Did your comments help to advance the discussion toward its goal? How would you describe your personal relationships with other members in the group? Did those relationships help or hinder the discussion?

B

APPENDIX

Select Day-by-Day Course Outlines

Outline 1

10-week, 30-hour course with two major presentations

This term or trimester outline requires you, the student, to participate in two major presentations, the first an effort to induce in your classroom audience an acceptance of a body of knowledge or information and the second an effort to bring your audience to agreement on an issue or to evoke emotion and motivate change.

For the first project, for example, you may choose to describe the steps in a process or make known the facts related to a problem or define and clarify an abstract concept.

For the second project, you may choose to support a position on a question of fact, value, or policy, or try to effect a change in audience feeling or attitude.

Class meeting	Topic/Activity	Reading assignment
1	Course overview, objectives	
2	Communication as process	Ch 1
3	Rhetoric as communication	Ch 2
	Student exchanges of information in preparation for student introductions.	
4	Reasoning logically	Ch 3
5	Student introductions of fellow students	

6	Student introductions (continued)	
7	Using language resourcefully	Ch 4
8	Listening responsibly	Ch 5
9	Choosing subject and purpose	Ch 6
	(From this day forward, the student should be working on one or both of the required speaking projects.)	
10	Analyzing the audience	Ch 7
	Need for and steps in analysis. Focus on the part played by analysis in shaping the content and form of any well-planned rhetorical effort.	
11	Planning the message	Ch 8
	Discussion of visual aids	
12	Organizing the message	Ch 9
	Emphasis on trial or skeleton outlines.	
13	Organizing the message (continued)	Ch 9
	Emphasis on complete outlines.	
14	Mastering the message	Ch 10
15	Open date or mid-term exam	
16	Inducing acceptance of information	Ch 11
17	Student presentations having an informational emphasis	
18	Student presentations (continued)	
19	Student presentations...	
20	Student presentations...	
21	Seeking agreement on issues	Ch 12
22	Seeking agreement on issues (continued)	Ch 12
23	Discussion of problems which students may encounter in working on this final project.	
24	Evoking emotion and motivating change	Ch 13
25	Evoking emotion, etc. (continued)	Ch 13
26	Student presentations seeking agreement on issues or motivating change.	

27 Student presentations (continued)
28 Student presentations...
29 Student presentations...
Note: If time allows, a short question and answer period could follow each presentation.

30 Summary and review for finals.

Notes

Notes

Outline 2

15-week, 45-hour course with two major presentations

This is a longer, semester version of Outline 1. The increase of 15 hours is allocated to more in-class discussion and to related speaking-listening activities. (Suggested activities appear near the ends of selected chapters in the textbook.)

This outline calls for your participation in two major presentations, the first an effort to induce acceptance of a body of knowledge or information and the second an effort to reach agreement on an issue or to evoke emotion or motivate change. For the first project, for example, you may choose to describe the steps in a process or make known the facts related to a problem or define and clarify an abstract concept.

For the second project, you may choose to take a position on a question of fact, value, or policy, or try to effect a change in audience feeling or attitude.

Class meeting	Topic/Activity	Reading assignment
1	Course overview, objectives	
2	Communication as process	Ch 1
3	Communication as process (continued)	Ch 1
	Student exchanges of information in preparation for student introductions.	
4	Rhetoric as communication	Ch 2
5	Student introductions of fellow students, either as individuals or as "speakers."	
6	Student introductions (continued)	
7	Reasoning logically	Ch 3
8	Reasoning logically (continued)	Ch 3
9	Using language resourcefully	Ch 4
10	Using language resourcefully (continued)	Ch 4
11	Application projects from end of Chapter 2 and/or from end of Chapter 4.	

12	Application projects (continued)	
13	Listening efficiently	Ch 5
14	Listening efficiently (continued) Oral reports by students reporting on their experiences in listening actively, analytically, or defensively to one or more speakers in a public setting.	Ch 5
15	Choosing subject and purpose Emphasis on choice of subject and purpose for the student's *first* presentation. From this day forward, the student should be working on the speaking project(s) required by the course.	Ch 6
16	Choosing subject and purpose (continued) Emphasis on early choice of subject and purpose for the student's *second* presentation.	Ch 6
17	Analyzing the audience Need for and steps in analysis. Focus on the part played by analysis in shaping the content and form of any well-planned rhetorical effort.	Ch 7
18	Analyzing the audience (continued) Oral reports by those students who chose to or were asked to report on an outside speaker's success or failure in analyzing the audience.	Ch 7
19	Planning the message	Ch 8
20	Planning the message Discussion of visual aids.	Ch 8
21	Organizing the message Emphasis on the trial or skeleton outline.	Ch 9
22	Organizing the message (continued) Emphasis on the complete outline.	Ch 9
23	Mastering the message	Ch 10
24	Open date or mid-semester exam	
25	Mastering the message (continued)	Ch 10
26	Inducing acceptance of information	Ch 11
27	Student presentations having an informational emphasis	
28	Student presentations (continued)	

29	Student presentations...	
30	Student presentations...	
31	Overall evaluative discussion of the speaking series just ended. Answering of questions students may have on any phase of preparation for the second speaking project.	
32	Seeking agreement on issues	Ch 12
33	Seeking agreement on issues (continued)	Ch 12
34	Seeking agreement on issues (continued)	Ch 12
35	Discussion of problems students may be encountering in working on the final project.	
36	Evoking emotion and motivating change	Ch 13
37	Evoking emotion and motivating change	Ch 13
38	Evoking emotion and motivating change	Ch 13
39	Student presentations based on seeking agreement on issues or on evoking emotion and motivating change. To provide additional opportunity for experience, a student could chair the program for a given day; after each presentation, the student chair could also act as monitor for a short question-and-answer period.	
40	Student presentations (continued)	
41	Student presentations...	
42	Student presentations...	
43	Student presentations...	
44	Evaluative discussion of the series just ended.	
45	Summary and review for finals.	

Notes

Notes

Outline 3

15-week, 45-hour course with two presentations and participation in a group discussion

For your first solo presentation, in which the emphasis is informational, you may be asked to make known the facts associated with a problem. Depending on how the course is structured, other options may be to describe the steps in a process or to clarify an abstract concept.

For the discussion project, you will become one of a small group working to reach whatever discussion goal has been decided upon by the group. (The problem-solving discussion process--and suggestions for participating in it--is outlined in Appendix A of this text.)

For your second solo presentation, you may seek agreement on one or more of the issues associated with an earlier discussion question. In other words, you may seek agreement on a position taken by one of the classroom discussion groups on a question of fact, value, or policy. Again depending on how the course is structured, you may have the option of speaking on a subject having an inspirational/motivational emphasis (as described in Chapter 13).

Class meeting	**Topic/Activity**	**Reading assignment**
1	Course overview, objectives	
2	Communication as process	Ch 1
3	Communication as process (continued)	Ch 1
	Student exchanges of information in preparation for student introductions.	
4	Rhetoric as communication	Ch 2
5	Student introductions of fellow students, either as individuals or as "speakers."	
6	Student introductions (continued)	
7	Reasoning logically	Ch 3
8	Reasoning logically (continued)	Ch 3
9	Using language resourcefully	Ch 4

10	Application projects from end of Chapter 2 and/or from end of Chapter 4.	
11	Listening responsibly	Ch 5
12	Listening responsibly (continued) Oral reports by students reporting on their experiences in listening actively, analytically, or defensively to one or more speakers in a public setting.	Ch 5
13	Choosing subject and purpose Emphasis on choice of subject and purpose for the student's *first* presentation and, if time permits, for the *second* as well. From this day forward, the student should be working on one or both of the speaking projects required by the course.	Ch 6
14	Analyzing the audience Focus on the analytical process and on the part played by analysis in shaping the content and form of any well-planned rhetorical effort.	Ch 7
15	Planning the message Discussion of visual aids.	Ch 8
16	Organizing the message Emphasis on the trial or skeleton outline.	Ch 9
17	Organizing the message (continued) Emphasis on the complete outline.	Ch 9
18	Mastering the message	Ch 10
19	Inducing acceptance of information	Ch 11
20	Student presentations having an informational emphasis	
21	Student presentations (continued)	
22	Student presentations...	
23	Student presentations...	
24	Open date or mid-semester exam	
25	Evaluative discussion of the series of informational-emphasis presentations. Preview of the work to be done in the second half of the semester.	
26	Seeking agreement on issues	Ch 12
27	Seeking agreement on issues (continued)	Ch 12

28	Speaking in small-group discussion	Appendix A
29	Organization of the class into small discussion groups; selection by each group of a discussion question and a chairperson; initial work on phrasing of the question, etc.	
30	Speaking in discussion (continued) Focus on interpersonal aspects of the discussion process.	Appendix A
31	Beginning of discussion series, each group to proceed independently toward its agreed upon goal or goals.	
32	Discussion series (continued)	
33	Discussion series...	
34	Discussion series...	
35	Final day of series or discussion/listening options or overall evaluation of the series.	
36	Evoking emotion or motivating change	Ch 13
37	...motivating change (continued)	Ch 13
38	Student presentations based on seeking agreement on issues or on any other approved option	
39	Student presentations (continued)	
40	Student presentations...	
41	Student presentations...	
42	Student presentations... To provide additional opportunity for experience, a student could chair the program for a given day; after each presentation, the student chair could also act as monitor for a short question-and-answer period.	
43	Listening-option reports based on application projects at end of Chapter 12 and/or, if appropriate, from end of Chapter 13.	
44	Over all evaluative discussion of the speaking-listening series just ended.	
45	Summary and review for finals.	

Notes

Outline 4

15-week, 45-hour course with three major presentations

This semester outline calls for your participation in three major presentations, the first with an informational emphasis, the second seeking agreement on one or more issues, and the third on any approved option, including a presentation with an inspirational or motivational emphasis.

Class meeting	Topic/Activity	Reading assignment
1	Course overview, objectives	
2	Communication as process	Ch 1
3	Communication as process (continued) Student exchanges of information in preparation for student introductions.	Ch 1
4	Rhetoric as communication	Ch 2
5	Student introductions of fellow students, either as individuals or as "speakers."	
6	Student introductions (continued)	
7	Reasoning logically	Ch 3
8	Reasoning logically (continued)	Ch 3
9	Using language resourcefully	Ch 4
10	Listening responsibly	Ch 5
11	Listening-option reports as described at the end of Chapter 5 and/or at the ends of any designated earlier chapters.	
12	Choosing subject and purpose Focus on choice of subject and purpose for the student's first presentation and, if time permits, for the second and the third as well. Emphasis on choosing worthwhile subjects that can be made interesting to the student audience. No "pretend" situations acceptable.	Ch 6

13	Analyzing the audience Focus on the analytical process and on the part played by analysis in shaping the content and form of any well-planned rhetorical effort.	Ch 7
14	Planning the message Discussion of visual aids.	Ch 8
15	Organizing the message Emphasis on initial "trial outlines."	Ch 9
16	Organizing the message (continued) Emphasis on the complete outline.	Ch 9
17	Mastering the message	Ch 10
18	Inducing acceptance of information	Ch 11
19	Student presentations having an informational emphasis	
20	Student presentations (continued)	
21	Student presentations...	
22	Student presentations...	
23	Open date or mid-semester exam	
24	Evaluative discussion of information-emphasis series just ended.	
25	Renewed discussion of the two speaking projects still to come, kinds of subjects appropriate for them, etc. Opportunity for students to ask questions about any problems they may have encountered in preliminary thinking about or work already done on those projects.	
26	Seeking agreement on issues	Ch 12
27	Seeking agreement on issues (continued)	Ch 12
28	In-class session on details students are still trying to work out for the second speaking project.	
29	Student presentations based on positions taken on questions of fact, value, or policy	
30	Student presentations (continued)	
31	Student presentations...	
32	Student presentations...	

33 Student presentations...

To provide additional opportunity for experience, a student could chair the program for a given day; after each presentation, the student chair could also act as monitor for a short question-and answer period.

34 Listening-option reports from those listed at the end of Chapter 12.

35 Evaluative discussion of the series just ended and/or further review of the final speaking project still to come.

36 Evoking emotion or motivating change Ch 13

37 ...motivating change (continued) Ch 13

38 In-class session on details students are still trying to work out for the third speaking project.

39 Student presentations based on any option approved for the third speaking project

40 Student presentations (continued)
41 Student presentations...
42 Student presentations...
43 Student presentations...

Again, to provide additional opportunity for experience, a student could chair the program for a given day; after each presentation, the student chair could also act as monitor for a short question-and-answer period.

44 Open day or listening-option reports based on application projects from end of Chapter 13 and/or overall evaluative discussion of the series just ended.

45 Summary and review for finals.

BIBLIOGRAPHY

Adler, Ronald B. *Communicating at Work*. 2nd ed. New York: Random House, 1986.

Adler, Ronald B., and Neil Towne. *Looking out, Looking in*. 5th ed. New York: Holt, Rinehart and Winston, 1987.

Alexander, Hubert G. *Language and Thinking*. Princeton, NJ: D. Van Nostrand, 1967.

Anderson, Kenneth, and Theodore Clevenger, Jr. "A Summary of Experimental Research on Ethos." *Speech Monographs*, 30 (June, 1963), 59-78.

Aristotle. *The "Art" of Rhetoric*. Trans. John Henry Freese. In Vol. 3 of Aristotle [23 vols.], Loeb Classical Library Series. Cambridge, MA: Harvard UP, 1982 rpt.

_______. *The Rhetoric of Aristotle*. Ed. Lane Cooper. New York: Appleton-Century-Crofts, 1960 rpt.

Arnhart, Larry. *Aristotle on Political Reasoning*. DeKalb, IL: Northern Illinois UP, 1981.

Barnlund, Dean C., and Franklyn S. Haiman. *The Dynamics of Discussion*. Boston: Houghton Mifflin, 1960.

Barker, Larry L., et al. *Groups in Process: An Introduction to Small Group Communication*. 3rd ed. Englewood Cliffs, NJ: Prentice-Hall, 1987.

Beardsley, Monroe C. *Thinking Straight*. Englewood Cliffs, NJ: Prentice-Hall, 1956.

Benson, Thomas W., and Michael H. Prosser, eds. *Readings in Classical Rhetoric*. Boston: Allyn and Bacon, 1969.

Benson, Thomas W., ed. *Speech Communication in the 20th Century*. Carbondale, IL: Southern Illinois UP, 1985.

Berelson, Bernard, and Gary A. Steiner. *Human Behavior: An Inventory of Scientific Findings*. New York: Harcourt, Brace and World, 1964.

Billig, Michael. *Arguing and Thinking: A Rhetorical Approach to Social Psychology*. New York: Cambridge UP, 1987.

Birdwhistell, Ray L. *Kinesics and Context: Essays on Body Motion Communication*. Philadelphia, PA: U. of Pennsylvania Press, 1970.

Bitzter, Lloyd F. "The Rhetorical Situation." *In Rhetoric: A Tradition in Transition.* Ed. Walter R. Fisher. East Lansing, MI: Michigan State UP, 1974. Also in *The Rhetoric of Western Thought.* Eds. James L. Golden, Goodwin F. Berquist, and William E. Coleman. 3rd ed. Dubuque, IA: Kendall/Hunt, 1983. Also in *Philosophy & Rhetoric*, 1 (Winter, 1968), 1-15.

Borden, George A., Richard B. Gregg, and Theodore G. Grove. *Speech Behavior and Human Interaction*. Englewood Cliffs, NJ: Prentice-Hall, 1969.

Breth, Robert D. *Dynamic Management Communications.* Reading, MA: Addison-Wesley, 1969.

Brilhart, John K. *Effective Group Discussion.* 5th ed. Dubuque, IA: Wm. C. Brown, 1986.

Burke, Kenneth. *A Rhetoric of Motives.* New York: George Braziller, 1955.

Burns, David D., M.D. *Feeling Good: The New Mood Therapy.* New York: Penguin, 1980.

Burt, Forest D., and E. Cleve Want. *Invention & Design: A Rhetorical Reader.* 4th ed. New York: Random House, 1985.

Cicero. *De inventione*. Trans. H. M. Hubbell. In Vol. 2 of Cicero [28 vols.], Loeb Classical Library Series. Cambridge, MA: Harvard UP, 1976 rpt.

_____. *De Oratore*. Trans. E. W. Sutton and H. Rackham. In Vol. 3 of Cicero, Loeb Classical Library Series. Cambridge, MA: Harvard UP, l979 rpt.

Cherry, Colin. *On Human Communication.* 2nd ed. Cambridge, MA: MIT Press, 1966.

Clark, Donald Lemen. *Rhetoric in Greco-Roman Education.* New York: Columbia UP, 1957.

Cohen, Arthur R. *Attitude Change and Social Influence*. New York: Basic Books, 1964.

Cohen, Morris R., and Ernest Nagel. *An Introduction to Logic and Scientific Method.* 3rd printing. London: George Routledge & Sons, 1947.

Connors, Robert J., Lisa S. Ede, and Andrea A. Lunsford, eds. *Essays on Classical Rhetoric and Modern Discourse.* Carbondale, IL: Southern Illinois UP, 1984.

Cooper, Lane. See Aristotle.

Corbett, Edward P. J. *Classical Rhetoric for the Modern Student*. 2nd ed. New York: Oxford U P, 1971.

Cragan, John F., and David W. Wright. *Communication in Small Group Discussions: An Integrated Approach*. 2nd ed. St. Paul, MN: West Publishing, 1986.

Dewey, John. *How We Think.* Boston: D.C. Heath, 1910.

Downs, Cal W., et al. *Professional Interviewing*. New York: Harper & Row, 1980.

Etzioni, Amitai. *The Moral Dimension: Toward a New Economics.* New York: The Free Press, 1988.

______. "The 'Me First' Model in the Social Sciences Is Too Narrow." In *The Chronicle of Higher Education* (February 1, 1989), p. A44.

Fisher, Walter R., ed. *Rhetoric: A Tradition in Transition* [in honor of Donald C. Bryant]. East Lansing, MI: Michigan State UP, 1974.

Goffman, Erving. *Behavior in Public Places*. New York: Free Press, 1963.

Golden, James L., Goodwin F. Berquist, and William E. Coleman. "Rhetoric as Value: Ethos and Image." In *The Rhetoric of Western Thought.* Golden et al., eds. 4th ed. Dubuque, IA: Kendall/Hunt, 1989.

Gordon, Thomas. "Group-Centered Leadership and Administration. In Carl R. Rogers et al., *Client Centered Therapy*. Boston: Houghton-Mifflin, 1951.

Gottlieb, Marvin. *Interview*. New York: Longman, 1986.

Hennig, Margaret, and Ann Jardim. *The Managerial Woman.* Garden City, NY: Anchor/Doubleday, 1977.

Holtzman, Paul D. *The Psychology of Speakers' Audiences.* Glenview, IL: Scott, Foresman, 1970.

Hovland, Carl I., Irving L. Janis, and Harold H. Kelley. *Communication and Persuasion.* New Haven, CT: Yale UP, 1963.

Hunt, Martin F., Jr., and Gary B. Wilson. "Attitude Change and Consistency Theories." In *Communication and Behavior*. Eds. Gerhard J. Hanneman and William J. McEwen. Reading, MA: Addison-Wesley, 1975.

Karlins, Marvin, and Herbert I. Abelson. *Persuasion: How Opinions and Attitudes Are Changed.* New York: Springer, 1970.

Katz, Elihu. "The Diffusion of New Ideas and Practices." In *The Science of Human Communication.* Ed. Wilbur Schramm. New York: Basic Books, 1963.

Kennedy, George Alexander. *The Art of Rhetoric in the Roman World,* 300 B.C.-300 A.D. Princeton, NJ: Princeton UP, 1972.

______. *Classical Rhetoric and its Christian and Secular Tradition from Ancient to Modern Times*. Chapel Hill, NC: U of North Carolina Press, 1980.

Kieffer, George David. *The Strategy of Meetings.* New York: Simon and Schuster, 1988.

Kinneavy, James L. *A Theory of Discourse*. New York: W. W. Norton & Co., 1971.

Kowitz, Albert C., and Thomas J. Knutson. *Decision Making in Small Groups: The Search for Alternatives*. Boston: Allyn and Bacon, 1980.

LaBenne, Wallace D., and Bert I. Greene. *Educational Implications of Self-Concept Theory.* Pacific Palisades, CA: Goodyear, 1969.

Lee, Irving J. *How to Talk with People*. New York: Harper and Row, 1952.

Matsen, Patricia P., Philip Rollinson, and Marion Sousa, eds. *Readings from Classical Rhetoric*. Carbondale, IL: Southern Illinois UP, 1990.

Meyrowitz, Joshua. *No Sense of Place: The Impact of Electronic Media on Social Behavior*. New York: Oxford UP, 1985.

Middlebrook, Patricia Niles, et al. *Social Psychology & Modern Life*. 2nd ed. New York: Alfred A. Knopf, 1980.

Miller, George A. *Language and Communication.* New York: McGraw-Hill, 1951.

Murphy, James J. *Rhetoric in the Middle Ages: A History of Rhetorical Theory from Saint Augustine to the Renaissance.* Berkeley, CA: U of California Press, 1974.

Nadeau, Ray. "Hermogenes' On Stases [On Issues]: A Translation with an Introduction and Notes." *Speech Monographs*, 31 (November, 1964) 4, 361-424.

Nichols, Ralph G., and Leonard A. Stevens. *Are You Listening?* New York: McGraw-Hill, 1957.

Perelman, Ch., and L. Olbrechts-Tyteca. *The New Rhetoric: A Treatise on Argumentation.* Trans. John Wilkinson and Purcell Weaver. 2nd printing. Notre Dame, IN: U of Notre Dame Press, 1971.

Pfeiffer, J. William, and John E. Jones, eds. *A Handbook of Structured Experiences for Human Relations Training.* La Jolla, CA: University Associates, 1974.

Phillips, Gerald M. *Communication and the Small Group.* New York: Bobbs Merrill, 1966.

Phillips, Gerald M., and Eugene C. Erickson. *Interpersonal Dynamics in the Small Group.* New York: Random House, 1970.

Quine, W. V., and J. S. Ullian. *The Web of Belief.* 2nd ed. New York: Random House, 1978.

Quintilian. *Institutio Oratoria*. 4 vols. Trans. H. E. Butler. In Loeb Classical Library Series. Cambridge, MA: Harvard UP, 1980 rpt.

Quitman, Lynn. "The Basic Writer." In *Essays on Classical Rhetoric and Modern Discourse*. Robert J. Connors, Lisa S. Ede, and Andrea A. Lunsford, eds. Carbondale, IL: Southern Illinois UP, 1984.

Richards, I. A. *The Philosophy of Rhetoric.* New York: Oxford UP, 1936.

Rokeach, Milton. *The Nature of Human Values*. New York: The Free Press, 1973.

Rokeach, Milton, et al. *The Open and Closed Mind.* New York: Basic Books, 1960.

Scarr, Sandra, and James Vander Zanden. *Understanding Psychology.* 4th ed. New York: Random House, 1984.

Scheidel, Thomas M., and Laura Crowell. "Idea Development in Small Discussion Groups." *Quarterly Journal of Speech*, 50 (April, 1964), 140-145.

Sorells, Bobbye D. *The Nonsexist Communicator.* Englewood Hills, NJ: Prentice-Hall, 1983.

Steil, Lyman K., Larry L. Barker, and Kittie W. Watson. *Effective Listening: Key to Your Success*. Reading, MA: Addison-Wesley, 1983.

Stewart, Charles J., and William B Cash. *Interviewing: Principles and Practices.* 5th ed. Dubuque, IA: William C. Brown, 1988.

Tedford, Thomas L. *Freedom of Speech in the United States.* New York: Random House, 1985.

Toulmin, Stephen. *The Uses of Argument.* Cambridge, UK: Cambridge U P, 1958.

Vander Zanden, James W. *Social Psychology.* 4th ed. New York: Random House, 1987.

Verderber, Rudolph F. *Working Together: Fundamentals of Group Decision Making.* Belmont, CA: Wadsworth, 1984.

Weaver, Richard M. *Language is Sermonic: [Essays of] Richard M. Weaver on the Nature of Rhetoric.* Eds. Richard L. Johannesen, Rennard Strickland, and Ralph T. Eubanks. Baton Rouge, LA: Louisiana State UP, 1970.

White, Robert W. "Motivation Reconsidered: The Concept of Competence." In *Studies in Educational Psychology.* Ed. Raymond G. Kuhlen. Waltham, MA: Blaisdell, 1968.

Winterowd, W. Ross. *Rhetoric: A Synthesis.* New York: Holt, Rinehart and Winston, 1968.

Williams, Frederick. *The New Communications.* Belmont, CA: Wadsworth, 1984.

Wilson, Gerald L., and Michael S. Hanna. *Groups in Context.* New York: Random House, 1986.

Wolvin, Andrew D., and Carolyn Gwynn Coakley. *Listening.* 2nd ed. Dubuque, IA: Wm. C. Brown, 1985.

Wood, Julia T., Gerald M. Phillips, and Douglas J. Pedersen. *Group Discussion: A Practical Guide to Participation and Leadership.* 2nd ed. Cambridge, MA: Harper & Row, 1986.

Wortman, Camille B., Elizabeth F. Loftus, and Mary E. Marshall. *Psychology.* 2nd ed. New York: Alfred A. Knopf, 1985.

Young, Paul Thomas. *Emotion in Man and Animal.* 2nd ed. Huntington, NY: Robert E. Krieger, 1973.

Zimbardo, Philip G., Ebbe B. Ebbesen, and Christina Maslach. *Influencing Attitudes and Changing Behavior.* 2nd ed. New York: Random House, 1977.

Index

D

E

F

P

Q

R

S

About the authors...

Ray Nadeau, professor emeritus and former head of the Purdue University Department of Communication, has published many journal articles, a monograph, and three earlier Addison-Wesley textbooks in communication. A University of Michigan Ph.D., his career in teaching and research was followed by several years as head of an Indiana advertising agency. Since moving to Florida, he has continued to write.

Carol Jablonski is an associate professor in the Department of Communication, University of South Florida (Tampa). A Purdue University Ph.D., she has earned many honors--e.g., the Karl Wallace Speech Communication Association Award, three teaching awards--for teaching, research, and scholarly writing. She has directed the basic course at USF, has chaired the Public Address Division of the Speech Communication Association, and serves on journal editorial boards.

Greg Gardner, a Bowling Green University Ph.D., is a professor of Speech Communication at Rollins College, Winter Park, Florida, where he heads the Department of Organizational Communication. He also directs the program of the Rollins College Hamilton Holt School in that field. Active on convention programs, his writing appears in a number of conference proceedings and in articles on debate and trial diplomacy.